T0318821

Portfolio Optimization with Different Information Flow

Optimization in Insurance and Finance Set

coordinated by
Nikolaos Limnios and Yuliya Mishura

Portfolio Optimization with Different Information Flow

Caroline Hillairet
Ying Jiao

First published 2017 in Great Britain and the United States by ISTE Press Ltd and Elsevier Ltd

ISTE Press Ltd
27-37 St George's Road
London SW19 4EU
UK

www.iste.co.uk

Elsevier Ltd
The Boulevard, Langford Lane
Kidlington, Oxford, OX5 1GB
UK

www.elsevier.com

Notices
Knowledge and best practice in this field are constantly changing. As new research and experience broaden our understanding, changes in research methods, professional practices, or medical treatment may become necessary.

Practitioners and researchers must always rely on their own experience and knowledge in evaluating and using any information, methods, compounds, or experiments described herein. In using such information or methods they should be mindful of their own safety and the safety of others, including parties for whom they have a professional responsibility.

To the fullest extent of the law, neither the Publisher nor the authors, contributors, or editors, assume any liability for any injury and/or damage to persons or property as a matter of products liability, negligence or otherwise, or from any use or operation of any methods, products, instructions, or ideas contained in the material herein.

For information on all our publications visit our website at http://store.elsevier.com/

British Library Cataloguing-in-Publication Data
A CIP record for this book is available from the British Library
Library of Congress Cataloging in Publication Data
A catalog record for this book is available from the Library of Congress
ISBN 978-1-78548-084-3

Printed and bound in the UK and US

Contents

Introduction

The utility maximization problem has been largely studied in the literature. In the framework of a continuous-time financial model, the problem was studied for the first time by Merton [MER 71] in 1971. Using the methods of stochastic optimal control, the author derives a nonlinear partial equation for the value function of the optimization problem. There exist mainly two methodologies in the literature. One methodology is to use the convex duality theory, as it is done in the book of Karatzas and Shreve [KAR 98]. We can quote, for instance, Karatzas, Lehoczky and Shreve [KAR 87] for the case of complete financial models, and Karatzas *et al.* [KAR 91a] and Kramkov and Schachermayer [KRA 99] for the case of incomplete financial models. The convex duality theory is exploited to prove the existence of an optimal strategy. However, this approach does not provide a characterization of either the optimal strategy nor the value function in the incomplete market case. Another methodology, using the dynamic programming principle (see El Karoui [ELK 81]) consists of reducing the analysis of a stochastic control problem to the one of a Backward Stochastic Differential Equation (BSDE) (see El Karoui *et al.* [ELK 97]). We can quote Jeanblanc and Pontier [JEA 90] for a complete model with discontinuous prices, Bellamy [BEL 01] in the case of a filtration generated by a Brownian motion and a Poisson measure, Hu, Imkeller and Muller [HU 05] for an incomplete model in the case of a Brownian filtration. We refer the readers to Pham's book [PHA 09] for a survey on continuous-time stochastic optimization with financial applications and to Øksendal and Sulem's book [ØKS 05] for stochastic control of jump-diffusions. See also the books of Jacod and Shiryaev [JAC 03], Protter [PRO 05], Revuz and Yor [REV 91] for the related results of stochastic analysis.

Some papers add uncertainty on the time horizon of the optimization problem, modeling the situation of an investor who may not be allowed to trade on the market after the realization of some random event arriving at a random time τ. Using convex duality theory, Karatzas et al. treat in [KAR 00] the case of a stopping time, and Blanchet-Scalliet et al. [BLA 08] and Bouchard et al. [BOU 04] treat the case of a general random time. Using dynamic programming principle and BSDE technics, Kharroubi et al. [KHA 13] study the context of mean-variance hedging, and this was extended to a general utility maximization with random horizon in Jeanblanc et al. [JEA 15] in the case of a random time whose distribution support is assumed to be bounded (and thus having unbounded intensity). Combining these two approaches, Jiao and Pham [JIA 11] study the impact of a default event on the optimal wealth and strategy of investment.

More recently, some works question the relevance of fixing a deterministic utility criterion for cash flows that will take place in the future. Instead, they propose that the utility criterion must be adaptive and adjusted to the information flow. Indeed, in a dynamic and stochastic environment, the standard notion of utility function is not flexible enough to help us to make good choices in the long run. Musiela and Zariphopoulou [MUS 10b, MUS 10a] were the first to suggest to use the concept of progressive dynamic utility instead of the classic criterion. Progressive dynamic utility gives an adaptive way to model possible changes over the time of individual preferences of an agent. Obviously, the dynamic utility must be consistent with respect to a given investment universe. In the general setting, the questions of the existence and the characterization of consistent dynamic utility have been studied from a PDE point of view in El Karoui and Mrad [ELK 13]. Although this framework is very meaningful and full of potential, we keep the standard setting of utility function in this book, and focus on the information asymmetry issue.

All the literature listed above is indeed written in the classic setting of financial markets where the agents share the same information flow, which is conveyed by the prices. But, it seems clear that financial markets inherently have asymmetry information.

Asymmetry information concerns either partial information, using filtering techniques (see, for instance, Frey and Schmidt [FRE 11] or Runggaldier and coauthors [RUN 91, FUJ 13]), or insider information, using enlargement of filtration tools. Papers with partial information are essentially studied in the literature in a complete market framework. Gennotte [GEN 86] uses dynamic programming methods in a linear Gaussian filtering, while Lakner [LAK 95,

LAK 98] solves the optimization problem via a martingale approach and works out the special case of linear Gaussian model. Pham and Quenez [PHA 01] treat the case of an incomplete stochastic volatility model. Callegaro *et al.* [CAL 06] study the case of a market model with jumps, extended in [CAL 15] to a jump-diffusion model for stock prices, which takes into account over and underreaction of the market to incoming news. BSDE and filtering techniques are used by Lim and Quenez' study in [LIM 15] in the case of an incomplete market.

This book only deals with private information by enlargement of filtrations. It does not consider the case of weak information (see Baudoin [BAU 02, BAU 01]). Weak information relies on the law of a random variable that will be realized on a future date, and not on the realization ω-wise of this random variable. It is modeled through a change of probability measure and not an enlargement of filtration. This book focuses on the framework of insider strong information, which is private information modeled through an enlargement of filtrations.

The theory of initial enlargement of filtration by a random variable was developed by the French in the 1970s–1980s, through works such as those of Jacod [JAC 79, JAC 85], Jeulin [JEU 80], Jeulin and Yor [JEU 78, JEU 85]. The main question studied is which martingales in the small filtration remain semimartingales in the enlarged filtration, and what are their semimartingale decompositions. In particular, if the filtration is enlarged by a random variable L, Jacod has shown that semimartingales are preserved if the conditional law of L is absolutely continuous with respect to the law of L. This assumption, also called Jacod's condition (or Jacod's absolute continuity condition), is often used in the literature of enlargement of filtration. If the absolute continuity is in fact an equivalence, it is called density hypothesis or Jacod's equivalence condition. The theory of enlargement of filtration receives a new focus in the 1990s for its application in finance in the study of problems occurring in insider modeling, such as the existence of arbitrages or the value of private information. This theory relies on the resolution of an insider optimization problem, in which the crucial question of arbitrage opportunities arises.

The first paper that used enlargement of filtration techniques to compute insider optimal trading strategies was Karatzas-Pikovsky [PIK 96], in a setting of logarithmic utility, and where the additional information consists of the terminal value of prices, either exactly or with some uncertainty. Other papers with logarithmic utility have followed, with a focus on the value of private information (see, e.g. Amendinger *et al.* [AME 98, AME 03]). A useful result in the resolution of the insider optimization problem is the transfer of a martingale representation theorem from a given filtration to the initially enlarged filtration. This has been done by Amendinger [AME 99, AME 00] under the density hypothesis and recently by Fontana [FON 15a] under the Jacod's absolute continuity hypothesis. Following Föllmer and Imkeller [FOL 93], Grorud and Pontier [GRO 98] constructed an equivalent martingale measure under which the reference filtration is independent to the random variable L, and proposed a statistical test to detect insider trading.

Some papers are devoted to insider trading in the case where the prices are discontinuous semimartingales. For instance, in a mixed diffusive-jump market model, Elliott and Jeanblanc [ELL 99] and Grorud [GRO 00] studied the case where L is the number of jumps over the interval. In a framework of jumps in the price processes, Hillairet [HIL 05] compares theoretically and numerically the insider optimal strategies depending on the type of side information. Gasbarra [GAS 06] *et al.* apply a dynamical Bayesian approach to some problems concerning initial enlargement of filtration theory, in a context of a Lévy market. They propose a Bayesian interpretation of utility gain related to asymmetric information. Kohatsu and Yamazoto [KOH 08] propose a reformulation of Jacod's theorem to deal with perturbed random times in the framework of jump processes. In those papers, it appears that the presence of jumps in the dynamics of price processes tends to mitigate the value of the private information.

Another approach dealing with initial enlargement consists of applying Malliavin's calculus: the integration by part formula of Malliavin calculus provides an explicit description of the information drift – that is, the drift to eliminate in order to preserve the martingale property in the enlarged filtration. A financial application is given by Imkeller in [IMK 02, IMK 03], focusing on the computation of the additional utility of the insider and a study of her free lunch possibilities. The information drift turns out to be the crucial quantity needed to answer these issues. It is most elegantly described by the logarithmic Malliavin trace of the conditional laws of the insider information with respect to the filtration of the regular trader. It allows us to derive criteria for non-existence of an equivalent martingale measure for the insider and this provides tools to access the existence of free lunches and arbitrages in simple examples. The study of the information drift in a mixed diffusive-jump market model is presented in details in the thesis of Ankirchner [ANK 05] and in related papers by Ankirchner *et al.* [ANK 08, ANK 06]. Using forward anticipative calculus Øksendal *et al.* [BIA 05] compute the information drift and Di Nunno-Øksendal compute in [DIN 06] the optimal portfolio in a market driven by a compound Poisson process.

In the above references, all traders are just acting as price takers. But insiders may have some influence on the dynamics of prices. Kohatsu-Higa and Sulem [KOH 06] consider market models where the insider is also a large trader, that is her financial behavior influences the prices of the underlying assets. More precisely, it influences the drift of the underlying price asset process. Using anticipating calculus, the paper provides a characterization of the optimal logarithmic portfolio of an investor with a different information flow from the one of the insider. Explicit results in the partial information case are given and extended in order to incorporate the enlargement of filtration techniques for markets with insiders. Similarly, in Grorud and Pontier [GRO 06], the informed investor's strategies affect the risky asset trends and the interest rate. The informed influential investor's optimization problem is solved. The main result is the construction of statistical tests to detect if, from observing asset prices and agent's strategies, there exists an influential investor optimizing her strategy on the market and if this investor is informed.

In a setting in which the insider influences the long- or medium-term evolution of prices of the Black-Scholes type model through the drift of the model, Hata and Kohatsu-Higa [KOH 08] give sufficient conditions for the existence of a partial equilibrium and study some explicit models. In a forthcoming paper by Rheinländer et al. [BLÜ 16], the insider strategy may impact both the drift and the volatility of the asset. Under the assumptions that there are no arbitrage opportunities for the small trader in periods where the large investor does not change her position, the authors exhibit two different scenarios: a stable regime, in which an optimal strategy can be found, and an unstable regime, in which the presence of the large trader completely destabilises the market. This is caused by the fact that in an unstable regime it is optimal for the large trader to buy or sell as many shares as possible to maximize her expected utility from terminal wealth.

Another kind of enlargement of filtration that has been widely studied in the literature is the progressive enlargement of filtration. It consists of the smallest enlargement of a filtration that makes a given random time a stopping time. Brémaud and Yor [BRÉ 78], Jacod [JAC 79], Jeulin and Yor [JEU 78], Mansuy and Yor [MAN 06] are some first and important papers on the topic. The specific case of honest times has been studied in full generality in Barlow [BAR 78], in Jeulin [JEU 80] and in papers of Nikeghbali et al. [NIK 13, NIK 06] (τ is an $\mathbb{F}$-honest time if for all $t > 0$ it coincides with an $\mathcal{F}_t$-measurable random variable on $\{\tau < t\}$). The applications in finance and credit risk are studied, among others, in Bielecki *et al.* [BIE 02, BIE 04] and Elliott *et al.* [ELL 00]. Kchia *et al.* [KCH 13] have studied the link between progressive and initial enlargement to obtain semimartingale decompositions.

Initial enlargement of filtration, such as the modeling of a piece of private information received at time 0 that does not evolve or get more accurate through time, seems to be a bit too strong, at least for its financial application. Several papers have studied this issue, from different point of view. Corcuera *et al.* [COR 04] study situations in which the private information is affected by an independent noise process vanishing as the revelation time approaches. The authors prove that the semimartingale decomposition of the driving Wiener process is a projection of the semimartingale decomposition in Jacod's theorem. Finally, they apply it to the study of the logarithmic utility of the insider. It is proved that if the rate at which the independent noise disappears is slow enough, then the market does not allow arbitrage and the logarithmic utility of the insider is finite. This is related to the fact that the Wiener process becomes an integrable semimartingale with a bounded variation part whose Radon–Nikodym derivative (with respect to the Lebesgue measure) is square integrable in the enlarged filtration. Kchia and Protter [KCH 15] study a progressive filtration expansion with a càdlàg process. Song [SON 87, SON 13] uses the local solution method to study the semimartingales properties in a filtration enlarged by another filtration of countably generated sub-Borel σ-algebras, with very weak assumptions.

A central question arising in insider information setting is the question of arbitrage opportunities. In the literature, there are several notions of arbitrage. Roughly speaking, an arbitrage opportunity is the possibility of "making money out of nothing". Since the seminal paper of Delbaen and Schachermayer [DEL 94], the No Free Lunch with Vanishing Risk (NFLVR) condition (a condition slightly stronger than the classical No Arbitrage condition) is standard and the vast majority of models proposed in quantitative finance satisfy it. [DEL 94] proves the equivalence between the NFLVR condition and the existence of an Equivalent Local Martingale Measure (ELMM) i.e. a new probability measure equivalent to the original one such that the discounted asset price process is a local martingale under the new measure. A weaker condition of no arbitrage is the No Unbounded Profit with Bounded Risk (NUPBR), see, for example, the paper of Takaoka and Schweizer [TAK 14]. Fontana in [FON 15b] proposes a unified analysis of a whole spectrum of no-arbitrage conditions for financial market models based on continuous semimartingales. Chau and Tankov define and study in [CHA 15] optimal arbitrages. Choulli and Deng give in [CHO 14] results concerning arbitrage in a discrete time filtration.

The study of arbitrage in progressively enlarged filtration is more recent. The first papers dealing with arbitrages related to honest times are Imkeller [IMK 02] and Zwierz [ZWI 07], by considering the cases of arbitrages occurring after the random time τ. For the case of arbitrages occurring before τ, we refer to Fontana *et al.* [FON 14] and Aksamit *et al.* [AKS 14a, AKS 14b].

The purpose of this book is to present recent progresses on stochastic portfolio optimization with exotic filtrations. In particular, we explain how to apply the tools of the enlargement of filtrations to solve the optimization problem. We use extensively the two main types of enlargement of filtration (initial and progressive), as those two settings lead to tractable formula. The book is almost self-contained and uses tools from various fields aside from enlargement of filtration theory, such as from stochastic calculus, to convex analysis, to optimal stochastic control, to backward stochastic differential equations, etc.

Chapter 1 sets the standard utility maximization framework, without asymmetric information. We recall the different methods of resolution, using the convex duality theory or using the dynamic programming principle. The chapter ends with some examples in a Brownian and in a Brownian–Poisson setting. Chapter 2 recalls fundamental results in the theory of enlargement of filtration. We mainly focus on initial enlargement and on progressive enlargement of filtration. After introducing and discussing the density hypothesis (Jacod's hypothesis), we give some technical results about martingale measures and martingale decomposition. Chapter 3 applies results and tools of the previous chapters, in the framework of a financial market subject to counterparty risks. In this setting, the portfolio value may have an instantaneous loss at the default time of the counterparty, with a regime change of the price dynamics of the assets in the portfolio. The optimization problem is solved by decomposing it into two parts: the after-default part and the before-default one. We first consider a standard investor who just observes the default when it arrives, and then for the insider who possesses more information on the counterparty default. We provide a numerical comparison between the standard investor and the insider. Chapter 4 considers a financial market model with discontinuous risky assets, on which investors differently informed can invest. Mainly, two types of private information are considered. The first type ("full strong" information) consists of the knowledge, from the beginning, of an extra information about the outcome of some variable of the prices. For the second type ("noisy strong" information), the insider's information is perturbed by an independent noise changing throughout time. We characterize the optimal strategy of investors depending on their information, and provide theoretical and numerical comparison in some examples.

Acknowledgments

We warmly thank Monique Pontier, Areski Cousin and the anonymous referee who have carefully read this work and sent us many comments. We also thank our collaborators and colleagues for fruitful discussions on this topic.

Optimization Problems

Stochastic portfolio optimization is a central topic in financial mathematics. In a portfolio optimization problem, we consider a finite family of investable assets whose prices are described by a stochastic process $S = (S_t^1, \ldots, S_t^n)_{0 \leq t \leq T}$ valued in $\mathbb{R}^n$ ($n \in \mathbb{N}$, $n \geq 1$), where T is a positive real number, which denotes the time horizon. An investment strategy is described by a stochastic process $\phi = (\phi^1, \ldots, \phi^n)$, where for $u \in [0, T]$, ϕ_u^i denotes the quantity of investment in the ith asset. The value process X of the portfolio can then be represented by the following form

$$X_t = X_0 + \int_0^t \phi_u \cdot dS_u = X_0 + \sum_{i=1}^n \int_0^t \phi_u^i dS_u^i, \qquad [1.1]$$

where X_0 denotes the initial wealth and $\cdot$ denotes the scalar product in $\mathbb{R}^n$. The aim of a portfolio optimization problem is to maximize the expectation of some utility functional acting on X_T with ϕ runs over certain family of "admissible investment strategies".

In the classic literature, the price process S is often supposed to be adapted with respect to a Brownian filtration, which verifies a stochastic diffusion equation, and admissible investment strategies are predictable processes. Under this framework, various methods, such as the duality method and the dynamic programming principle, have been developed to solve the above stochastic optimization problem. However, in a large family of financial problems, it is not adequate to describe the financial market by a Brownian filtration. It is in particular the case while the financial market is sensitive to default risks or default contagion risks. In such situations, the asset prices may jump at a random time, which could either be deterministic or totally inaccessible with respect to the information on the usual variation of the stocks. Moreover, in the study of asymmetric information, one needs to consider investment strategies with restricted or supplementary information. In the study of portfolio optimization problem under such situations, new tools are needed. Note that a common feature of the two situations described above is the exotic filtration which appears either in the description of the asset prices, or in the choice of admissible investment strategies.

The purpose of this chapter is to present recent progresses on stochastic portfolio optimization with exotic filtrations. In particular, we explain how to apply the tools of the enlargement of filtrations to solve the optimization problem.

1.1. Portfolio optimization problem

Throughout the chapter, let $(\Omega, \mathcal{G}, \mathbb{P})$ be a probability space and $\mathbb{G} = (\mathcal{G}_t)_{t \geq 0}$ be a filtration of the σ-algebra $\mathcal{G}$, which describes the market information. We assume that the filtration $\mathbb{G}$ satisfies the usual conditions (right-continuous and complete). Let $T > 0$ be a positive real number representing the time-horizon. We consider a portfolio of one risk-free asset together with n risky assets in the financial market, whose prices are described by an n-dimensional stochastic process $S = (S^1, \ldots, S^n)$ on $[0, T]$. We assume that the process S is a $(\mathbb{G}, \mathbb{P})$-semimartingale. For simplicity, we assume that the prices are discounted, and hence the price S^0 of the risk-free asset is constant 1.

1.1.1. Portfolio value

For any $\mathbb{G}$-predictable stochastic process $\phi = (\phi^1, \ldots, \phi^n)$ on $(0, T]$ valued in $\mathbb{R}^n$ such that ϕ^i is integrable with respect to dS^i on $[0, T]$ (in the sense of [DEL 80, VIII.75]) for any $i \in \{1, \cdots, n\}$, we let X^ϕ be the wealth process associated with the strategy ϕ as follows:

$$dX_t^\phi = \phi_t \cdot dS_t = \sum_{i=1}^n \phi_t^i dS_t^i, \qquad [1.2]$$

with an initial condition $X_0^\phi = X_0$, $X_0 > 0$. The value process is given by a stochastic integral

$$X_t^\phi = X_0 + \sum_{i=1}^{n} \int_0^t \phi_u^i dS_u^i. \qquad [1.3]$$

The stochastic process X^ϕ should be considered as the value process of a self-financing portfolio consisting of the risk-free asset $S^0 = 1$ and the assets $S^1, \ldots, S^n$, with the investment strategy ϕ which represents the quantity of the financial assets held in the portfolio. Note that the self-financing property implies that the quantity ϕ^0 invested in the risk-free asset verifies the relation

$$\phi_t^0 = X_t^\phi - \phi_t \cdot S_t = X_t^\phi - \sum_{i=1}^{n} \phi_t^n S_t^n. \qquad [1.4]$$

We also consider the following proportional version of portfolio. For any $\mathbb{G}$-predictable stochastic process $\pi = (\pi^1, \ldots, \pi^n)$ on $(0, T]$ valued in $\mathbb{R}^n$ such that π^i/S_-^i is integrable with respect to dS^i on $[0, T]$ for any $i \in \{1, \cdots, n\}$, the stochastic integral

$$\int_0^t \pi_u \cdot \frac{dS_u}{S_{u-}} := \sum_{i=1}^{n} \int_0^t \frac{\pi_u^i}{S_{u-}^i} dS_u^i, \quad t \in [0, T]$$

is well-defined and forms a $(\mathbb{G}, \mathbb{P})$-semimartingale (see [DEL 80, VIII.75]). The investment strategy π represents the proportion of the wealth invested in each financial asset. We denote by X^π the strong solution to the following stochastic differential equation

$$\frac{dX_t^\pi}{X_{t-}^\pi} = \pi_t \cdot \frac{dS_t}{S_{t-}} := \sum_{i=1}^{n} \pi_t^i \frac{dS_t^i}{S_{t-}^i}, \quad X_0^\pi = X_0, \qquad [1.5]$$

which can be written as (see [JAC 03, S I.4f])

$$X^\pi = X_0 \mathcal{E} \left(\int_0^t \pi_u \cdot \frac{dS_u}{S_{u-}}, \ t \in [0, T] \right) \qquad [1.6]$$

where for any semimartingale Y on $[0, T]$, $\mathcal{E}(Y)$ denotes the Doléans–Dade exponential of the process Y, given by

$$\mathcal{E}(Y)_t = \exp\left(Y_t - Y_0 - \frac{1}{2}\langle Y, Y \rangle_t\right) \prod_{s \le t}(1 + \Delta Y_s)e^{-\Delta Y_s}, \quad t \in [0, T].$$

The proportional investment on the risk-free asset is thus given by

$$\pi^0 = 1 - \sum_{i=1}^{n} \pi^i. \tag{1.7}$$

In many practical cases, for example when the price processes S^i are continuous or when the jumps of the process

$$\int_0^t \pi_u \cdot \frac{dS_u}{S_{u-}}, \quad t \in [0, T]$$

are strictly bounded from below by -1, the portfolio wealth X^π in the proportional form is positive. In the circumstance where only positive portfolio value is allowed, the proportional form of investment strategy is more adapted to the study of optimization problems.

The proportional and the quantitative forms of investment strategy are related, as explained below. Let

$$\phi_t := X_t^\pi\left(\pi_t * \frac{1}{S_{t-}}\right) = X_t^\pi\left(\frac{\pi_t^1}{S_{t-}^1}, \cdots, \frac{\pi_t^n}{S_{t-}^n}\right), \quad t \in (0, T], \tag{1.8}$$

where $*$ denotes the coordinate-by-coordinate product of vectors, namely, for all vectors $x = (x_1, \cdots, x_n)$ and $y = (y_1, \cdots, y_n)$ in $\mathbb{R}^n$,

$$x * y := (x_1 y_1, \cdots, x_n y_n). \tag{1.9}$$

Then, we have

$$dX_t^\pi = \phi_t \cdot dS_t.$$

Namely, X^π identifies with the portfolio value process of the investment strategy ϕ according to the previous model [1.2]. However, given a portfolio in the quantitative form leading to a value process in $\mathbb{R}$ (and not necessarily positive), it is not always possible to find an investment strategy in the proportional form, which allows us to reproduce the corresponding portfolio value.

1.1.2. *Optimization problem*

The aim of the optimization problem is to determine the supremum in the following form

$$V_0(X_0) := \sup_{\pi \in \mathcal{A}} \mathbb{E}^{\mathbb{P}}[G_T U(X_T^\pi) + F_T^\pi], \quad X_0^\pi = X_0, \qquad [1.10]$$

where X_0 is the initial wealth of the portfolio, X^π is defined by the stochastic differential equation [1.5]. In the above formula, $\mathcal{A}$ is a family of proportional investment strategies $\pi = (\pi^1, \cdots, \pi^n)$ such that π^i/S_-^i is integrable with respect to dS^i for any $i \in \{1, \cdots, n\}$ and the the corresponding value process X^π is positive, $U : \mathbb{R}_+ \to \mathbb{R}$ is a utility function, G_T is a positive $\mathcal{G}_T$-measurable random variable, which represents a multiplicative random utility weight, and F_T^π is an integrable $\mathcal{G}_T$-measurable random variable, which represents an additive random utility weight and may depend on the initial portfolio value X_0 and the investment strategy π. The investment strategies in the family $\mathcal{A}$ are called *admissible strategies* for the optimization problem [1.10] . Note that the admissible strategy set $\mathcal{A}$ may vary according to different constraints of the optimization problem. Typically, the additive random utility weight F_T^π can be chosen to be a stochastic integral

$$\int_0^T f(t, X_{t-}^\pi)\, dY_t,$$

where f is a Borel function in two variables and Y is a $(\mathbb{G}, \mathbb{P})$-semimartingale. Examples of utility functions are discussed in the next section. We assume that, for any investment strategy $\pi \in \mathcal{A}$, the random variable $G_T U(X_T^\pi)$ is integrable.

We can also consider the dynamic variant of the above optimization problem. Let t be an element of $[0, T]$ and X_t be a positive $\mathcal{G}_t$-measurable random variable, we let

$$V_t(X_t) := \operatorname*{ess\,sup}_{\pi \in \mathcal{A}} \mathbb{E}^{\mathbb{P}}[G_T U(X_T^\pi) + F_T^\pi \mid \mathcal{G}_t], \quad X_t^\pi = X_t. \qquad [1.11]$$

More generally, if σ is a $\mathbb{G}$-stopping time, which is bounded from above by T, we can consider the following dynamic optimization problem

$$V_\sigma(X_\sigma) := \operatorname*{ess\,sup}_{\pi \in \mathcal{A}} \mathbb{E}^{\mathbb{P}}[G_T U(X_T^\pi) + F_T^\pi \mid \mathcal{G}_\sigma], \quad X_\sigma^\pi = X_\sigma, \qquad [1.12]$$

where X_σ is a positive $\mathcal{G}_\sigma$-measurable random variable, which describes the wealth of the portfolio at time σ, and X^π is the strong solution to the stochastic differential equation [1.2] on the stochastic interval $[\![\sigma, T]\!]$ with the initial condition $X_\sigma^\pi = X_\sigma$. The choices of admissible investment strategies and the random utility weights G_T and F_T^π will be presented progressively in the coming chapters, according to different situations under which we consider the above optimization problems (see, for example, theorem 3.1 in Chapter 3).

In some circumstances, negative values of portfolio are allowed, where utility functions defined on $\mathbb{R}$ are considered. In such case, the quantitative representation of investment strategies is more adequate and we use formula [1.2] to compute the portfolio value. The portfolio optimization can be formulated as:

$$V_0(X_0) := \sup_{\phi \in \mathcal{A}'} \mathbb{E}^{\mathbb{P}}[G_T U(X_T^\phi) + F_T^\phi], \quad X_0^\phi = X_0, \qquad [1.13]$$

where $\mathcal{A}'$ is a family of investment strategies $\phi = (\phi_1, \cdots, \phi_n)$ such that ϕ_i is integrable with respect to dS^i on $[0, T]$ for any $i \in \{1, \cdots, n\}$, X^ϕ is the portfolio value of the strategy ϕ which is defined by the relation [1.2], and G_T and F_T^ϕ are, respectively, the additive and the multiplicative utility weights. The dynamic versions of the optimization problem can be proposed in a similar way. If σ is a $\mathbb{G}$-stopping time bounded from above by T and X_σ is an integrable $\mathcal{G}_\sigma$-measurable random variable, we let

$$V_\sigma(X_\sigma) := \operatorname*{ess\,sup}_{\phi \in \mathcal{A}'} \mathbb{E}^{\mathbb{P}}[G_T U(X_T^\phi) + F_T^\phi \mid \mathcal{G}_\sigma], \quad X_\sigma^\phi = X_\sigma, \qquad [1.14]$$

where X^ϕ denotes the stochastic process

$$X_t^\phi = X_\sigma + \sum_{i=1}^n \int_\sigma^t \phi_u^i dS_u^i, \quad \sigma \le t \le T$$

defined on the stochastic interval $[\![\sigma, T]\!]$.

Note that to each optimization problem for investment strategies in the proportional form as [1.10], we can associate *via* the relation [1.8] an equivalent optimization problem for investment strategies in the quantitative form [1.13]. However, the positivity constraint for the portfolio value often becomes more complicated in the setting of [1.13] and the resolution of the optimization problem becomes more sophisticated. In such circumstance, it is preferable to discuss the resolution of the optimization problem in the setting of [1.10].

1.1.3. *Examples of utility functions*

The utility function plays an important role in the optimization problem. It represents the risk aversion of the investor relatively to the gains or losses. In financial mathematics, the utility functions are widely used in portfolio optimization. We refer the readers to Dana and Jeanblanc [DAN 03] and to Pham [PHA 09] for a panoramic presentation on utility functions and applications in financial mathematics.

In this chapter, we mainly consider utility functions $U : (0, +\infty) \to \mathbb{R}$ which satisfies to the *Inada conditions*, namely, U is strictly concave, of class C^1 on $(0, +\infty)$, and such that

$$\lim_{x \to 0+} U'(x) = +\infty, \qquad \lim_{x \to +\infty} U'(x) = 0.$$

The function U' is then positive, continuous and strictly decreasing on $(0, +\infty)$. We denote by $I : \mathbb{R}_+ \to \mathbb{R}_+$ the inverse function of U'. It is a strictly decreasing function such that

$$\lim_{y \to 0+} I(y) = +\infty, \qquad \lim_{y \to +\infty} I(y) = 0.$$

Recall that the *Legendre transform* (or *dual function*) of the utility function U is defined as

$$\forall y \in (0, +\infty), \quad \widetilde{U}(y) := \sup_{x > 0} \Big(U(x) - xy \Big).$$

Under the Inada conditions, it can be computed as:

$$\widetilde{U}(y) = U(I(y)) - yI(y). \qquad [1.15]$$

The logarithmic and the power utility functions (see the description below) are examples of utility functions that satisfy the Inada conditions.

We also consider utility functions defined on $\mathbb{R}$ which satisfy *modified Inada conditions*: such a utility function is strictly concave, of class C^1 on $\mathbb{R}$ and such that

$$\lim_{x \to -\infty} U'(x) = +\infty, \quad \lim_{x \to +\infty} U'(x) = 0.$$

The Legendre transform of such a utility function is defined in a similar way as

$$\widetilde{U}(y) := \sup_{x \in \mathbb{R}} \left(U(x) - xy \right).$$

The equality [1.15] also holds in this case. Note that the exponential utility functions explained below satisfy the modified Inada conditions.

In the following, we recall several examples of utility functions.

1.1.3.1. *Logarithmic utility function*

The logarithmic utility function is of the form

$$\forall x \in (0, +\infty), \quad U(x) = \log x.$$

We have $U'(x) = 1/x$ and hence $I(y) = 1/y$ for any $y \in (0, +\infty)$. Moreover,

$$U(I(y)) = \log(1/y) = -U(y). \tag{1.16}$$

Therefore, the Legendre transform of U is

$$\widetilde{U}(y) = U(I(y)) - yI(y) = -\log(y) - y \cdot (1/y) = -1 - \log(y).$$

A special feature of the logarithmic utility function is that $U(xy) = \log(x) + U(y)$ for $x, y \in (0, +\infty)$. In particular, the optimal value function

$$V_\sigma(X_\sigma) = \operatorname{ess\,sup}_{\pi \in \mathcal{A}} \mathbb{E}^{\mathbb{P}}[G_T U(X_T^\pi) + F_T^\pi \,|\, \mathcal{G}_\sigma], \quad X_\sigma^\pi = X_\sigma,$$

verifies the following relation

$$V_\sigma(X_\sigma) = \log(X_\sigma)\mathbb{E}^{\mathbb{P}}[G_T|\mathcal{G}_\sigma] + V_\sigma(1) \tag{1.17}$$

for any positive $\mathcal{G}_\sigma$-measurable random variable X_σ such that $G_T \log(X_\sigma)$ is integrable. In fact, if we denote by $X^{\pi,1}$ the solution to the stochastic differential equation [1.2] on the stochastic interval $[\![\sigma, T]\!]$ with the initial condition $X_\sigma^{\pi,1} = 1$, then the relation $X^\pi = X_\sigma X^{\pi,1}$ holds. Therefore, we have

$$\log(X_T^\pi) = \log(X_\sigma) + \log(X_T^{\pi,1}),$$

which leads to the equality [1.17].

1.1.3.2. *Power utility function*

The logarithmic utility function can be considered as a limit case of power utility function. Let p be a real number, $p < 1$ and $p \neq 0$. The power utility function of parameter p is

$$\forall\, x \in (0, +\infty), \quad U(x) = \frac{x^p}{p}.$$

The family of power utility functions is the only family of utility functions with a constant relative risk aversion, namely

$$-x \cdot \frac{U''(x)}{U'(x)}$$

is a constant (the logarithmic utility function, which also satisfies this relation, is considered as the limit case with $p = 0$ in the family). Therefore, a power utility function is also called a CRRA (abbreviation for "*constant relative risk aversion*") utility function. Note that we have

$$U(\lambda x) = p\, U(\lambda) U(x)$$

for all λ and x in $(0, +\infty)$. This property is called *isoelasticity*, which is important in solving the optimization problem.

A direct computation shows that $U'(x) = x^{p-1}$ and hence $I(y) = y^{1/(p-1)}$ for any $y \in (0, +\infty)$. Therefore, we have

$$\forall\, y \in (0, +\infty), \quad U(I(y)) = \frac{y^{p/(p-1)}}{p}. \tag{1.18}$$

The Legendre transform for the power utility function is given by

$$\widetilde{U}(y) = U(I(y)) - yI(y) = \left(\frac{1}{p} - 1\right)y^{p/(p-1)}.$$

Note that the power utility function $U(x) = x^p/p$ satisfies the relation $U(xy) = y^p U(x)$. Therefore, in the case where the additive random utility weight F_T^π is zero, the optimal value function

$$V_\sigma(X_\sigma) = \operatorname*{ess\,sup}_{\pi \in \mathcal{A}} \mathbb{E}^{\mathbb{P}}[G_T U(X_T^\pi) \,|\, \mathcal{G}_\sigma], \quad X_\sigma^\pi = X_\sigma,$$

satisfies the relation

$$V_\sigma(X_\sigma) = X_\sigma^p V_\sigma(1) \qquad\qquad\qquad [1.19]$$

for any positive $\mathcal{G}_\sigma$-measurable random variable X_σ such that $G_T X_\sigma^p$ is integrable. This comes from the relation $U(X_T^\pi) = U(X_T^{\pi,1})X_\sigma^p$, where $X^{\pi,1}$ is the solution to the stochastic differential equation [1.2] on the stochastic interval $[\![\sigma, T]\!]$ with the initial condition $X_\sigma^{\pi,1} = 1$.

1.1.3.3. *Exponential utility function*

Let γ be a positive real number. By exponential utility function of parameter γ, we refer to the function

$$U(x) = -\mathrm{e}^{-\gamma x}, \quad x \in \mathbb{R}.$$

We have $U'(x) = \gamma\mathrm{e}^{-\gamma x}$ and hence

$$I(y) = -\frac{1}{\gamma}(\log y - \log\gamma).$$

In particular, we have

$$\forall\, y \in (0, +\infty), \quad U(I(y)) = -y/\gamma. \qquad\qquad [1.20]$$

Therefore, the Legendre transform of the exponential utility function is

$$\widetilde{U}(y) = U(I(y)) - yI(y) = \frac{y}{\gamma}\left(\log\frac{y}{\gamma} - 1\right).$$

Compared to the logarithmic and the power utility functions, the optimization with exponential utility function has a special feature: the portfolio is allowed to take negative values. We refer the readers to Rouge and El Karoui [ROU 00] for exponential utility maximization with applications in the pricing of financial instruments. Note that the optimal value function in the exponential utility case has also a special form. We consider the investment strategy in the quantity form, and thus the portfolio value process is given as in the formula [1.3], and we consider the portfolio optimization problem (with the zero additive utility weight)

$$V_\sigma(X_\sigma) := \operatorname*{ess\,sup}_{\phi \in \mathcal{A}'} \mathbb{E}^{\mathbb{P}}[G_T U(X_T^\phi) \mid \mathcal{G}_\sigma], \quad X_\sigma^\phi = X_\sigma.$$

Note that the exponential utility function satisfies the relation $U(x + y) = e^{-\gamma y} U(x)$ for x and y in $\mathbb{R}$. Therefore, we have

$$V_\sigma(X_\sigma) = e^{-\gamma X_\sigma} V_\sigma(0).$$

This comes from the relation $U(X_T^\phi) = e^{-\gamma X_\sigma} U(X_T^{\phi,0})$, where $X^{\phi,0}$ the stochastic process

$$X_t^{\phi,0} = \sum_{i=1}^n \int_\sigma^t \phi_u^i dS_u^i, \quad \sigma \le t \le T$$

defined on the stochastic interval $[\![\sigma, T]\!]$.

1.2. Duality approach

In this section, we present the duality method in the stochastic optimization problem [1.12]. Recall that the financial market is described by a probability space $(\Omega, \mathcal{G}, \mathbb{P})$ equipped with a filtration $\mathbb{G} = (\mathcal{G}_t)_{t \ge 0}$ satisfying the usual conditions. We consider a portfolio consisting of n assets, whose prices are described by a $\mathbb{G}$-adapted process $S = (S^1, \ldots, S^n)$ valued in $\mathbb{R}_+^n$. For simplicity, we again assume that the prices are discounted, and hence the price of the risk-free asset is constant and equal to 1.

ASSUMPTION 1.1.– We assume that the market is free of arbitrage opportunity, namely, there exists at least one probability measure $\mathbb{Q}$ (which we fix in the sequel) on the measurable space $(\Omega, \mathcal{G})$, which is equivalent to the probability measure $\mathbb{P}$ and such that the price process S is a $(\mathbb{G}, \mathbb{Q})$-martingale on $[0, T]$, where $T > 0$ is the time horizon.

Let σ be a $\mathbb{G}$-stopping time, which is bounded from above by T. From a dynamic point of view for the portfolio investment, we consider σ as the intermediary time of the investment. Let X_σ be a positive $\mathcal{G}_\sigma$-measurable integrable random variable, which denotes the portfolio value at time σ.

We say that a $\mathbb{G}$-predictable process $\pi = (\pi^1, \ldots, \pi^n)$ is a (proportional) *investment strategy* if the predictable process π^i/S^i_- is integrable on $[0, T]$ with respect to S^i. In this case, the following stochastic differential equation

$$\frac{dX_t^\pi}{X_{t-}^\pi} = \pi_t \cdot \frac{dS_t}{S_{t-}} = \sum_{i=1}^{n} \pi_t^i \frac{dS_t^i}{S_{t-}^i}, \quad X_\sigma^\pi = X_\sigma \qquad [1.21]$$

has a unique solution on the stochastic interval $[\![\sigma, T]\!]$. The process X^π represents the portfolio value corresponding to the investment strategy π. Note that the process X^π only depends on the value of the investment strategy π on the stochastic interval $]\!]\sigma, T]\!]$. Therefore, by abuse of notion, we say that a stochastic process on the stochastic interval $]\!]\sigma, T]\!]$ is an investment strategy if it can be extended to a stochastic process on $[0, T]$ which is an investment strategy. By the assumption 1.1, the process X^π is a $(\mathbb{G}, \mathbb{Q})$-supermartingale on $[\![\sigma, T]\!]$ (since it is a non-negative local martingale). In particular, we have

$$\mathbb{E}^{\mathbb{Q}}[X_T^\pi \mid \mathcal{G}_\sigma] \leq X_\sigma. \qquad [1.22]$$

The aim of the portfolio optimization is to find the following essential supremum in the space of $\mathcal{G}_\sigma$-measurable random variables:

$$V_\sigma^{\mathbb{P}}(G_T, X_\sigma) = \operatorname*{ess\,sup}_{\pi \in \mathcal{A}} \mathbb{E}^{\mathbb{P}}[G_T U(X_T^\pi) \mid \mathcal{G}_\sigma], \qquad [1.23]$$

where $\mathcal{A}$ is a family of (proportional) investment strategies, U is a utility function which satisfies the Inada conditions and G_T is a positive $\mathcal{G}_T$-measurable random variable. With the notation of section 1.1, we assume that the additive utility weight F_T^π is zero for any $\pi \in \mathcal{A}$. If π^* is an investment strategy in $\mathcal{A}$ such that the above essential supremum is attained, namely

$$V_\sigma^{\mathbb{P}}(G_T, X_\sigma) = \mathbb{E}^{\mathbb{P}}[G_T U(X_T^{\pi^*}) \mid \mathcal{G}_\sigma] \quad \mathbb{P}\text{-a.s.},$$

we say that π^* is an *optimal strategy* on $]\!]\sigma, T]\!]$.

1.2.1. *Change of probability measures*

Let $\mathbb{P}'$ be a probability measure which is equivalent to $\mathbb{P}$. Let M be the $(\mathbb{G}, \mathbb{P})$-martingale on $[0, T]$ which represents the Radon–Nikodym derivative of the probability measure $\mathbb{P}'$ with respect to $\mathbb{P}$ on $(\mathcal{G}_t)_{0 \leq t \leq T}$. For any $t \in [0, T]$, we have $d\mathbb{P}' = M_t d\mathbb{P}$ on $\mathcal{G}_t$. By Doob's optimal stopping theorem, we obtain that M_σ is the Radon–Nikodym derivative of $\mathbb{Q}$ with respect to $\mathbb{P}$ on $\mathcal{G}_\sigma$. Hence, we have

$$\mathbb{E}^{\mathbb{P}}\left[G_T U(X_T^\pi) \,\Big|\, \mathcal{F}_\sigma\right] = M_\sigma \mathbb{E}^{\mathbb{P}'}\left[\frac{G_T}{M_T} U(X_T^\pi) \,\Big|\, \mathcal{F}_\sigma\right].$$

In particular, the following relation holds

$$V_\sigma^{\mathbb{P}}(G_T, X_\sigma) = M_\sigma V_\sigma^{\mathbb{P}'}(G_T/M_T, X_\sigma).$$

Therefore, by using the change of probability measure, we can transform the optimization problem [1.23] to a similar problem under any equivalent probability, and in particular under the martingale probability $\mathbb{Q}$.

1.2.2. *Dual optimization problem*

In this section, we solve the optimization problem [1.23]. Let Z be the process of Radon–Nikydom derivatives of $\mathbb{Q}$ with respect to $\mathbb{P}$ on $(\mathcal{G}_t)_{0 \leq t \leq T}$. Let X_T be a $\mathcal{G}_T$-measurable random variable. We say that X_T is *realized* by an investment strategy π if one has $X_T^\pi = X_T$ a.s. (with $X_\sigma^\pi = X_\sigma$).

THEOREM 1.1.– We assume that, for any $y > 0$, the random variable $I(yZ_T/G_T)$ is integrable with respect to the probability measure $\mathbb{Q}$. Let $\mathcal{A}$ be a family of proportional investment strategies. Then, the following inequality holds

$$V_\sigma^{\mathbb{P}}(G_T, X_\sigma) \leq \mathbb{E}^{\mathbb{P}}\left[G_T U\left(I\left(\frac{\widehat{Y}_\sigma Z_T}{G_T}\right)\right) \,\Big|\, \mathcal{G}_\sigma\right] \quad \mathbb{P}\text{-a.s.}, \qquad [1.24]$$

where the $\mathcal{G}_\sigma$-measurable random variable $\widehat{Y}_\sigma$ is determined by the following equation

$$\mathbb{E}^{\mathbb{Q}}\left[I\left(\widehat{Y}_\sigma \frac{Z_T}{G_T}\right) \,\Big|\, \mathcal{G}_\sigma\right] = \mathbb{E}^{\mathbb{P}}\left[\frac{Z_T}{Z_\sigma} I\left(\widehat{Y}_\sigma \frac{Z_T}{G_T}\right) \,\Big|\, \mathcal{G}_\sigma\right] = X_\sigma \quad \mathbb{P}\text{-a.s.. } [1.25]$$

Moreover, if the random variable $I(\widehat{Y}_\sigma Z_T/G_T)$ is realized by some proportional investment strategy π^* in $\mathcal{A}$, then the equality in the formula [1.24] holds, and π^* is a proportional optimal investment strategy, namely, the essential supremum in [1.23] is attained by π^*.

PROOF.– Let $\widetilde{U}$ be the Legendre transform of the utility function U. Recall that

$$\forall y \in (0, +\infty), \quad \widetilde{U}(y) = \sup_{x>0} \Big(U(x) - xy \Big).$$

Let π be a proportional investment strategy in $\mathcal{A}$. For any positive $\mathcal{G}_\sigma$-measurable random variable Y_σ, by definition of the Legendre transform we have

$$U(X_T^\pi) \leq \frac{Y_\sigma Z_T}{G_T} X_T^\pi + \widetilde{U}\Big(\frac{Y_\sigma Z_T}{G_T}\Big).$$

Therefore,

$$\mathbb{E}^{\mathbb{Q}}\Big[\frac{G_T}{Z_T} U(X_T^\pi) \,\Big|\, \mathcal{G}_\sigma\Big] \leq Y_\sigma \mathbb{E}^{\mathbb{Q}}[X_T^\pi | \mathcal{F}_\sigma] + \mathbb{E}^{\mathbb{Q}}\Big[\frac{G_T}{Z_T} \widetilde{U}\Big(\frac{Y_\sigma Z_T}{G_T}\Big) \,\Big|\, \mathcal{G}_\sigma\Big].$$

By [1.22], we have

$$\mathbb{E}^{\mathbb{Q}}\Big[\frac{G_T}{Z_T} U(X_T^\pi) \,\Big|\, \mathcal{G}_\sigma\Big] \leq Y_\sigma X_\sigma + \mathbb{E}^{\mathbb{Q}}\Big[\frac{G_T}{Z_T} \widetilde{U}\Big(\frac{Y_\sigma Z_T}{G_T}\Big) \,\Big|\, \mathcal{G}_\sigma\Big].$$

Note that the right-hand side of the formula is equal to

$$Y_\sigma X_\sigma + \mathbb{E}^{\mathbb{Q}}\Big[\frac{G_T}{Z_T} U\Big(I\Big(\frac{Y_\sigma Z_T}{G_T}\Big)\Big) - Y_\sigma I\Big(\frac{Y_\sigma Z_T}{G_T}\Big) \,\Big|\, \mathcal{G}_\sigma\Big]$$

since

$$\forall y \in (0, +\infty), \quad \widetilde{U}(y) = U(I(y)) - yI(y).$$

If $\widehat{Y}_\sigma$ is a solution to equation [1.25], we have

$$\mathbb{E}^{\mathbb{Q}}\Big[\widehat{Y}_\sigma I\Big(\frac{\widehat{Y}_\sigma Z_T}{G_T}\Big) \,\Big|\, \mathcal{G}_\sigma\Big] = \widehat{Y}_\sigma X_\sigma,$$

and hence we obtain

$$\mathbb{E}^{\mathbb{Q}}\left[\frac{G_T}{Z_T}U(X_T^\pi)\,\Big|\,\mathcal{G}_\sigma\right] \le \mathbb{E}^{\mathbb{Q}}\left[\frac{G_T}{Z_T}U\Big(I\Big(\frac{\widehat{Y}_\sigma Z_T}{G_T}\Big)\Big)\,\Big|\,\mathcal{G}_\sigma\right],$$

or equivalently

$$\mathbb{E}^{\mathbb{P}}[G_T U(X_T^\pi)\,|\,\mathcal{G}_\sigma] \le \mathbb{E}^{\mathbb{P}}\left[G_T U\Big(I\Big(\frac{\widehat{Y}_\sigma Z_T}{G_T}\Big)\Big)\,\Big|\,\mathcal{G}_\sigma\right].$$

Therefore, we obtain the inequality [1.24]. The existence of a solution to equation [1.25] can be obtained by a measurable selection argument by applying lemma 1.1 below to the function

$$F : I \times \Omega \to \mathbb{R}_+, \quad F(y,\cdot) = I(yZ_T/G_T).$$

Finally, if there exists certain proportional investment strategy π^* in $\mathcal{A}$ such that

$$I\Big(\widehat{Y}_\sigma \frac{Z_T}{G_T}\Big) = X_T^{\pi^*},$$

then we have

$$\mathbb{E}^{\mathbb{P}}\left[G_T U\Big(I\Big(\frac{\widehat{Y}_\sigma Z_T}{G_T}\Big)\Big)\,\Big|\,\mathcal{G}_\sigma\right] = \mathbb{E}^{\mathbb{P}}[G_T U(X_T^{\pi^*})\,|\,\mathcal{G}_\sigma],$$

namely, the upper bound in [1.24] is actually attained by the investment strategy π^*. The theorem is thus proved. $\qquad\square$

The following measurable selection lemma is used in the proof of the above theorem.

LEMMA 1.1.– Let $(\Omega, \mathcal{G}, \mathbb{P})$ be a probability space and $\mathcal{F}$ be a sub-σ-algebra of $\mathcal{G}$. Let $F : (0, +\infty) \times \Omega \to (0, +\infty)$ be a positive $\mathcal{B}((0, +\infty)) \otimes \mathcal{G}$-measurable function. Assume that the following conditions are satisfied:

1) for any $\omega \in \Omega$, the function $F(\cdot, \omega)$ on $(0, +\infty)$ is decreasing and continuous, and verifies

$$\lim_{y \to 0+} F(y, \omega) = +\infty, \quad \lim_{y \to +\infty} F(y, \omega) = 0;$$

2) for any $y \in (0, +\infty)$, the random variable $F(y, \cdot)$ is integrable.

Then, for any $\mathcal{F}$-measurable positive random variable Z, there exists an $\mathcal{F}$-measurable random variable Y valued in $[0, +\infty[$ such that

$$\mathbb{E}^{\mathbb{P}}[F(Y(\cdot), \cdot) \mid \mathcal{F}] = Z, \ \mathbb{P}\text{-a.s.}$$

PROOF.– Let I_0 be the set of all positive rational numbers. Since I_0 is countable, we can write it as a sequence $(y_n)_{n \geq 0}$. We then construct by induction a sequence of random variables $(Z_n)_{n \geq 0}$ which verifies the following conditions:

1) $Z_n = \mathbb{E}[F(y_n, \cdot) \mid \mathcal{F}] \ \mathbb{P}\text{-a.s.}$;

2) if $y_n \leq y_m$, then $Z_n(\omega) \geq Z_m(\omega)$ for any $\omega \in \Omega$ $(n, m \in \mathbb{N})$;

3) for any $\omega \in \Omega$, $\inf_{n \geq 0} Z_n(\omega) = 0$ and $\sup_{n \geq 0} Z_n(\omega) = +\infty$.

We first prove the lemma under the supplementary condition that there exists $N \in \mathbb{N}$ such that $Z \leq Z_N$. For any $n \in \mathbb{N}$, let $T_n := y_n \mathbb{1}_{\{Z > Z_n\}} + (+\infty) \mathbb{1}_{\{Z \leq Z_n\}}$. We choose Y to be the random variable $\inf_{n \geq 0} T_n$. Clearly, the random variable Y is $\mathcal{F}$-measurable and takes values in $[0, +\infty[$. The monotone convergence theorem for conditional expectations shows that

$$\mathbb{E}[F(Y(\cdot), \cdot) \mid \mathcal{F}] = U \lim_{n \to +\infty} \mathbb{E}[F(T_n(\cdot), \cdot) \mid \mathcal{F}]$$

$$= \sup_{n \geq 0} \left(\mathbb{1}_{\{Z > Z_n\}} Z_n \right) \leq Z, \ \mathbb{P}\text{-a.s.}$$

Moreover, if S is an $\mathcal{F}$-measurable random variable taking finitely many values in I_0 and such that $S < Y$, then we have $\mathbb{E}[F(S(\cdot), \cdot) \mid \mathcal{F}] \geq Z$, $\mathbb{P}$-a.s. Otherwise, we can find $i \in \mathbb{N}$ such that the random set $\{S = y_i\} \cap \{Z_i < Z\}$ is not negligible (and hence not empty), which leads to a contradiction. Under the supplementary assumption, the random variable Y is bounded from below by y_N. We can thus construct an increasing sequence $(S_n)_{n \geq 0}$ of $\mathcal{F}$-measurable random variables taking finitely many values in I_0 and such that $y_N/2 \leq S_n < Y$ for any $n \in \mathbb{N}$, which converges pointwise to Y. The sequence $(F(S_n(\cdot), \cdot))_{n \geq 0}$ is thus dominated by the integrable random variable $F(y_N/2, \cdot)$ and converges to $F(Y(\cdot), \cdot)$. The dominating convergence theorem thus implies that $\mathbb{E}[F(Y(\cdot), \cdot) \mid \mathcal{F}] \geq Z$, $\mathbb{P}$-a.s.

For a general positive random variable Z, we choose a sequence of $\mathcal{F}$-measurable random variables $(Y_n)_{n \geq 0}$ such that

$$\mathbb{E}[F(Y_n(\cdot), \cdot) \mid \mathcal{F}] = \min(Z, Z_n), \ \mathbb{P}\text{-a.s.}.$$

We then take $Y = \inf_{n \geq 0} Y_n$. By the monotone convergence theorem, we obtain

$$\mathbb{E}[F(Y(\cdot), \cdot) \mid \mathcal{F}] = \sup_{n \geq 0} \mathbb{E}[F(Y_n(\cdot), \cdot) \mid \mathcal{F}] = Z, \quad \mathbb{P}\text{-a.s.}$$

since $\lim_{y \to 0+} F(y, \cdot) = +\infty$ (and hence $\sup_{n \geq 0} Z_n = +\infty$). The lemma is thus proved. □

REMARK 1.1.– The typical situation where theorem 1.1 can be used to determine the optimal investment strategy is the case where the market is complete. In this case, the filtration $\mathbb{G}$ is generated by the process S and any positive $\mathcal{G}_T$-measurable random variable satisfying suitable integrability condition (according to the filtration $\mathbb{G}$) can be realized as the terminal value of certain admissible investment strategy. For simplicity, we consider the initial time optimization problem (namely, $\sigma = 0$) and suppose that the σ-algebra $\mathcal{G}_0$ is trivial. In the case where the market is not complete, in general, the random variable $I(\widehat{Y}_0 Z_T / G_T)$ in theorem 1.1 is not replicable by an admissible investment strategy. In this case, we need to consider the set $\mathcal{M}$ of Radon–Nikodym derivatives on $\mathcal{G}_T$ (with respect to $\mathbb{P}$) of all equivalent martingale measures of the process S and take $(\widehat{Y}_0, \widehat{Z}_T)$ to be the couple that minimizes

$$\inf_{Z_T \in \mathcal{M}} \mathbb{E}^{\mathbb{P}}\left[G_T \widetilde{U}\left(\frac{Y_0 Z_T}{G_T}\right) \right]. \tag{1.26}$$

Then, the optimal investment strategy is the one which replicates $I(\widehat{Y}_0 \widehat{Z}_T / G_T)$, where $(\widehat{Y}_0, \widehat{Z}_T)$ minimizes the dual optimization problem [1.26]. We refer the readers to El Karoui and Quenez [ELK 95] for more details. In Chapter 4, we will discuss the resolution of the optimization problem in the framework of incomplete market in some concrete situations.

We also consider the case of investment strategies in the quantity form. We fix a $\mathbb{G}$-stopping time $\sigma \leq T$ and an integrable $\mathcal{G}_\sigma$-measurable random variable X_σ. We say a $\mathbb{G}$-predictable process $\phi = (\phi^1, \ldots, \phi^n)$ is an investment strategy if each ϕ^i is integrable on $[0, T]$ with respect to dS^i and if the stochastic process

$$X_t^\phi = X_\sigma + \sum_{i=1}^{n} \int_\sigma^t \phi_u^i \, dS_u^i, \quad t \in [\![\sigma, T]\!]$$

is a $(\mathbb{G}, \mathbb{Q})$-supermartingale on $[\![\sigma, T]\!]$. We say that a random variable X_T is realized by an investment strategy ϕ if one has

$$X_T^\phi = X_\sigma + \sum_{i=1}^n \int_\sigma^T \phi_u^i \, dS_u^i = X_T.$$

Let U be a utility function on $\mathbb{R}$ which satisfies the modified Inada conditions, and I be the inverse function of U'. The same method as in theorem 1.1 leads to the following result.

THEOREM 1.2.– We assume that, for any $y > 0$, the random variable $I(yZ_T/G_T)$ is integrable with respect to the probability measure $\mathbb{Q}$. Let $\mathcal{A}'$ be a family of investment strategies and let

$$V_\sigma^\mathbb{P}(G_T, X_\sigma) := \operatorname*{ess\,sup}_{\phi \in \mathcal{A}'} \mathbb{E}^\mathbb{P}[G_T U(X_T^\phi)|\mathcal{G}_\sigma]$$

Then, the following inequality holds

$$V_\sigma^\mathbb{P}(G_T, X_\sigma) \leq \mathbb{E}^\mathbb{P}\left[G_T U\left(I\left(\frac{\widehat{Y}_\sigma Z_T}{G_T}\right)\right) \,\Big|\, \mathcal{G}_\sigma\right] \quad \mathbb{P}\text{-a.s.}, \qquad [1.27]$$

where the $\mathcal{G}_\sigma$-measurable random variable $\widehat{Y}_\sigma$ is determined by the following equation

$$\mathbb{E}^\mathbb{Q}\left[I\left(\widehat{Y}_\sigma \frac{Z_T}{G_T}\right) \,\Big|\, \mathcal{G}_\sigma\right] = \mathbb{E}^\mathbb{P}\left[\frac{Z_T}{Z_\sigma} I\left(\widehat{Y}_\sigma \frac{Z_T}{G_T}\right) \,\Big|\, \mathcal{G}_\sigma\right] = X_\sigma \quad \mathbb{P}\text{-a.s..} \; [1.28]$$

Moreover, if the random variable $I(\widehat{Y}_\sigma Z_T/G_T)$ is realized by some investment strategy ϕ^* in $\mathcal{A}'$, then the equality in the formula [1.24] holds, and ϕ^* is an optimal investment strategy, namely, the essential supremum in [1.23] is attained by ϕ^*.

1.2.3. *Examples*

In this section, we apply theorem 1.1 to some explicit utility functions. We will make precise different cases of the filtration $\mathbb{G}$ in the next chapter.

1.2.3.1. *Logarithmic utility*

We assume that U is the logarithmic utility function. We consider the following optimization problem

$$V_\sigma^\mathbb{P}(G_T, X_\sigma) = \operatorname*{ess\,sup}_{\pi \in \mathcal{A}} \mathbb{E}^\mathbb{P}[G_T \log(X_T^\pi) \mid \mathcal{G}_\sigma],$$

where σ is a $\mathbb{G}$-stopping time, $\sigma \leq T$, X_σ is a positive $\mathcal{G}_\sigma$-measurable random variable and $\mathcal{A}$ is a family of proportional investment strategies. The portfolio value process X^π is determined by the stochastic differential equation

$$\frac{dX_t^\pi}{X_{t-}^\pi} = \pi_t \cdot \frac{dS_t}{S_{t-}} := \sum_{i=1}^n \pi_t^i \frac{dS_t^i}{S_{t-}^i}, \quad X_\sigma^\pi = X_\sigma \qquad [1.29]$$

Note that we have $U(I(y)) = -\log y$ for any $y \in (0, +\infty)$. Moreover, equation [1.25] becomes

$$\mathbb{E}^\mathbb{Q}\!\left[\widehat{Y}_\sigma^{-1} \frac{G_T}{Z_T} \,\middle|\, \mathcal{G}_\sigma\right] = \frac{\mathbb{E}^\mathbb{P}[G_T \mid \mathcal{G}_\sigma]}{Z_\sigma \widehat{Y}_\sigma} = X_\sigma.$$

The solution of the equation is given by

$$\widehat{Y}_\sigma = \frac{G_\sigma}{X_\sigma Z_\sigma} \quad \text{with} \quad G_\sigma := \mathbb{E}^\mathbb{P}[G_T \mid \mathcal{G}_\sigma]. \qquad [1.30]$$

In particular, we have

$$I(\widehat{Y}_\sigma Z_T / G_T) = \frac{Z_\sigma X_\sigma}{G_\sigma} \cdot \frac{G_T}{Z_T}. \qquad [1.31]$$

Therefore, we obtain the following result.

PROPOSITION 1.1.– We assume that the utility function U is the logarithmic function and that the random variable G_T is integrable with respect to the probability measure $\mathbb{P}$. For any family $\mathcal{A}$ of proportional investment strategies, we have

$$V_\sigma^\mathbb{P}(G_T, X_\sigma) \leq \mathbb{E}^\mathbb{P}[G_T \log(G_T / Z_T) \mid \mathcal{G}_\sigma]$$
$$- G_\sigma \log(G_\sigma / Z_\sigma) + G_\sigma \log(X_\sigma). \qquad [1.32]$$

If there exists an investment strategy π^* in $\mathcal{A}$ such that

$$\frac{X_T^{\pi^*}}{X_\sigma} = \frac{G_T/Z_T}{G_\sigma/Z_\sigma}$$

then the equality holds in the above upper bound, and π^* is an optimal proportional investment strategy.

PROOF.– The upper bound [1.32] is a direct consequence of [1.24] and [1.30], where we use the fact that

$$U\left(I\left(\frac{\widehat{Y}_\sigma Z_T}{G_T}\right)\right) = -\log(\widehat{Y}_\sigma Z_T/G_T)$$

$$= \log(G_T/Z_T) - \log(G_\sigma/Z_\sigma) + \log(X_\sigma).$$

The second assertion results from the second assertion of theorem 1.1 and the relation [1.31]. □

1.2.3.2. *Power utility*

We assume that the utility function U is the power utility function:

$$U(x) = \frac{x^p}{p}, \quad x \in (0, +\infty),$$

where $p < 1$, $p \neq 0$. We consider the following optimization problem

$$V_\sigma^{\mathbb{P}}(G_T, X_\sigma) = \operatorname*{ess\,sup}_{\pi \in \mathcal{A}} \frac{1}{p}\mathbb{E}^{\mathbb{P}}[G_T(X_T^\pi)^p \mid \mathcal{G}_\sigma].$$

The portfolio value process X^π is determined as in [1.36]. Note that we have $I(y) = y^{1/(p-1)}$, and hence equation [1.25] becomes

$$\mathbb{E}^{\mathbb{Q}}\left[\left(\widehat{Y}_\sigma \frac{Z_T}{G_T}\right)^{1/(p-1)} \Big| \mathcal{G}_\sigma\right] = \widehat{Y}_\sigma^{1/(p-1)}\mathbb{E}^{\mathbb{Q}}\left[\left(\frac{Z_T}{G_T}\right)^{1/(p-1)} \Big| \mathcal{G}_\sigma\right] = X_\sigma.$$

The solution of this equation is given by

$$\widehat{Y}_\sigma = \left(\frac{X_\sigma Z_\sigma}{\mathbb{E}^{\mathbb{P}}[Z_T^{p/(p-1)}/G_T^{1/(p-1)} \mid \mathcal{G}_\sigma]}\right)^{p-1}. \qquad [1.33]$$

In particular, we have

$$I(\widehat{Y}_\sigma Z_T/G_T) = (\widehat{Y}_\sigma Z_T/G_T)^{1/(p-1)} = \frac{X_\sigma Z_\sigma (Z_T/G_T)^{1/(p-1)}}{\mathbb{E}^{\mathbb{P}}[Z_T^{p/(p-1)}/G_T^{1/(p-1)} \mid \mathcal{G}_\sigma]}. \quad [1.34]$$

Therefore, we obtain the following result.

PROPOSITION 1.2.– Let U be the power utility function of parameter p. Assume that the random variable $Z_T^{p/(p-1)}/G_T^{1/(p-1)}$ is integrable with respect to the probability measure $\mathbb{P}$. For any family $\mathcal{A}$ of proportional investment strategies, we have

$$V_\sigma^{\mathbb{P}}(G_T, X_\sigma) \le \frac{X_\sigma^p}{p} \cdot \frac{Z_\sigma^p}{\mathbb{E}^{\mathbb{P}}[Z_T^{p/(p-1)}/G_T^{1/(p-1)} \mid \mathcal{G}_\sigma]^{p-1}}. \quad [1.35]$$

If there exists an investment strategy π^* in $\mathcal{A}$ such that

$$\frac{X_T^{\pi^*}}{X_\sigma} = \frac{Z_\sigma(Z_T/G_T)^{1/(p-1)}}{\mathbb{E}^{\mathbb{P}}[Z_T^{p/(p-1)}/G_T^{1/(p-1)} \mid \mathcal{G}_\sigma]}$$

then the equality holds in the above upper bound, and π^* is an optimal proportional investment strategy.

PROOF.– By [1.18], we have

$$\mathbb{E}^{\mathbb{P}}\left[G_T U\left(I\left(\frac{\widehat{Y}_\sigma Z_T}{G_T}\right)\right) \Big| \mathcal{G}_\sigma\right] = \frac{1}{p}\mathbb{E}^{\mathbb{P}}\left[G_T\left(\frac{\widehat{Y}_\sigma Z_T}{G_T}\right)^{p/(p-1)} \Big| \mathcal{G}_\sigma\right].$$

By [1.33], we obtain

$$\mathbb{E}^{\mathbb{P}}\left[G_T U\left(I\left(\frac{\widehat{Y}_\sigma Z_T}{G_T}\right)\right) \Big| \mathcal{G}_\sigma\right] = \frac{X_\sigma^p}{p} \cdot \frac{Z_\sigma^p}{\mathbb{E}^{\mathbb{P}}[Z_T^{p/(p-1)}/G_T^{1/(p-1)} \mid \mathcal{G}_\sigma]^{p-1}}.$$

Thus, the upper bound [1.35] follows from [1.24]. The second assertion results from the second assertion of theorem 1.1 and the relation [1.34].   □

1.2.3.3. *Exponential utility*

We assume that the utility function U is the exponential utility function:

$$U(x) = -\mathrm{e}^{-\gamma x}, \quad x \in (0, +\infty),$$

where $\gamma > 0$. We consider the following optimization problem

$$V_\sigma^\mathbb{P}(G_T, X_\sigma) = \operatorname*{ess\,sup}_{\phi \in \mathcal{A}'} \mathbb{E}^\mathbb{P}[-G_T \exp(-\gamma X_T^\phi) \,|\, \mathcal{G}_\sigma],$$

where σ is a $\mathbb{G}$-stopping time, $\sigma \leq T$, X_σ is an integrable $\mathcal{G}_\sigma$-measurable random variable and $\mathcal{A}'$ is a family of investment strategies in the quantity form. The portfolio value process X^ϕ is given by

$$X_t^\phi = X_\sigma + \int_\sigma^t \phi_u \cdot dS_u := \sum_{i=1}^n \int_0^t \phi_u^i dS_u^i \qquad [1.36]$$

Note that $I(y) = -(\log(y/\gamma))/\gamma$ for any $y > 0$, and hence equation [1.25] becomes

$$-\frac{1}{\gamma}\mathbb{E}^\mathbb{Q}[\log(\widehat{Y}_\sigma Z_T/\gamma G_T) \,|\, \mathcal{G}_\sigma] = -\frac{1}{\gamma}\Big(\log(\widehat{Y}_\sigma)$$

$$+ \mathbb{E}^\mathbb{Q}[\log(Z_T/\gamma G_T) \,|\, \mathcal{G}_\sigma]\Big) = X_\sigma.$$

The solution to this equation is given by

$$\begin{aligned}
\widehat{Y}_\sigma &= \exp(-\gamma X_\sigma - \mathbb{E}^\mathbb{Q}[\log(Z_T/\gamma G_T) \,|\, \mathcal{G}_\sigma]) \\
&= \exp(-\gamma X_\sigma - Z_\sigma^{-1}\mathbb{E}^\mathbb{P}[Z_T \log(Z_T/\gamma G_T) \,|\, \mathcal{G}_\sigma]).
\end{aligned} \qquad [1.37]$$

In particular, we have

$$I(\widehat{Y}_\sigma Z_T/G_T) = X_\sigma + \frac{1}{\gamma Z_\sigma}\mathbb{E}^\mathbb{P}\Big[Z_T \log\Big(\frac{Z_T}{\gamma G_T}\Big)\Big|\mathcal{G}_\sigma\Big] - \frac{1}{\gamma}\log\Big(\frac{Z_T}{\gamma G_T}\Big). \quad [1.38]$$

Therefore, we obtain the following result.

PROPOSITION 1.3.– Let U be the exponential utility function of parameter p. Assume that the random variable $Z_T \log(Z_T/\gamma G_T)$ is integrable with respect to the probability measure $\mathbb{P}$. For any family $\mathcal{A}'$ of investment strategies, we have

$$V_\sigma^\mathbb{P}(G_T, X_\sigma) \leq -Z_\sigma \exp(-\gamma X_\sigma - Z_\sigma^{-1} \mathbb{E}^\mathbb{P}[Z_T \log(Z_T/G_T) \,|\, \mathcal{G}_\sigma]). \quad [1.39]$$

If there exists an investment strategy ϕ^* in $\mathcal{A}'$ such that

$$X_T^{\phi^*} - X_\sigma = \frac{1}{\gamma Z_\sigma} \mathbb{E}^\mathbb{P}\left[Z_T \log\left(\frac{Z_T}{\gamma G_T}\right) \,\Big|\, \mathcal{G}_\sigma\right] - \frac{1}{\gamma} \log\left(\frac{Z_T}{\gamma G_T}\right)$$

then the equality holds in the above upper bound, and ϕ^* is an optimal investment strategy.

PROOF.– By [1.20], we have

$$\mathbb{E}^\mathbb{P}\left[G_T U\left(I\left(\frac{\widehat{Y}_\sigma Z_T}{G_T}\right)\right) \,\Big|\, \mathcal{G}_\sigma\right] = -\frac{1}{\gamma} \mathbb{E}^\mathbb{P}\left[\widehat{Y}_\sigma Z_T \,\Big|\, \mathcal{G}_\sigma\right] = -\frac{\widehat{Y}_\sigma Z_\sigma}{\gamma}.$$

By [1.33], we obtain

$$\mathbb{E}^\mathbb{P}\left[G_T U\left(I\left(\frac{\widehat{Y}_\sigma Z_T}{G_T}\right)\right) \,\Big|\, \mathcal{G}_\sigma\right] =$$
$$-\frac{Z_\sigma \exp(-\gamma X_\sigma - Z_\sigma^{-1} \mathbb{E}^\mathbb{P}[Z_T \log(Z_T/\gamma G_T) \,|\, \mathcal{G}_\sigma])}{\gamma}.$$

Thus, the upper bound [1.35] follows from [1.24]. The second assertion results from the second assertion of theorem 1.1 and the relation [1.38]. $\qquad \square$

1.3. Dynamic programming principle

Let $\mathcal{A}$ be a family of proportional investment strategies. If t_1 and t_2 are two real numbers, $0 \leq t_1 \leq t_2 \leq T$, we denote by $\mathcal{A}_{t_1, t_2}$ the set of all stochastic processes ψ on the interval $(t_1, t_2]$ which can be written as the restriction of a proportional investment strategy $\pi \in \mathcal{A}$ on this interval. If ψ is an element in $\mathcal{A}_{t_1, t_2}$, we say that ψ is an admissible investment strategy on $(t_1, t_2]$. If π is an element in $\mathcal{A}$ whose restriction on $(t_1, t_2]$ coincides with ψ, we say that π is an admissible proportional investment strategy *extending* ψ.

Given an integrable $\mathcal{G}_{t_1}$-measurable random variable X_{t_1} and an admissible proportional investment strategy ψ on $(t_1, t_2]$, we denote by X^ψ the process on $[t_1, t_2]$ which is the solution of the stochastic differential equation

$$\frac{dX_u^\psi}{X_{u-}^\psi} = \psi_t \cdot \frac{dS_u}{S_{u-}}, \quad \text{for } u \in (t_1, t_2], \quad X_{t_1}^\psi = X_{t_1} \text{ given.} \qquad [1.40]$$

If $\pi \in \mathcal{A}$ is a proportional investment strategy extending ψ and if X^π is a corresponding portfolio value process (with certain initial portfolio value) such that $X_{t_1}^\pi = X_{t_1}$, then we have $X^\pi = X^\psi$ on $[t_1, t_2]$.

DEFINITION 1.1.– *We say that the proportional investment strategy family $\mathcal{A}$ satisfies the* gluing *property if for any triplet t_1, t_2, t_3 of real numbers such that $0 \leq t_1 \leq t_2 \leq t_3 \leq T$, the natural map from $\mathcal{A}_{t_1,t_3}$ to $\mathcal{A}_{t_1,t_2} \times \mathcal{A}_{t_2,t_3}$ sending any element of $\mathcal{A}_{t_1,t_3}$ to its restrictions on $(t_1, t_2]$ and on $(t_2, t_3]$, is a bijection. Namely, any pair of admissible strategies φ and ψ in $\mathcal{A}_{t_1,t_2}$ and $\mathcal{A}_{t_2,t_3}$ glue together to a unique admissible proportional strategy in $\mathcal{A}_{t_1,t_3}$.*

We observe from the above definition that, if the strategy family $\mathcal{A}$ satisfies the gluing property, then for any finite family $(t_i)_{i=0}^{n+1}$ of real numbers such that

$$0 = t_0 \leq t_1 \leq \cdots \leq t_{n+1} = T$$

and any element $(\psi_i)_{i=0}^n \in \mathcal{A}_{t_0,t_1} \times \cdots \times \mathcal{A}_{t_n,t_{n+1}}$, there exists a (unique) proportional investment strategy $\pi \in \mathcal{A}$ such that the restriction of π on $(t_i, t_{i+1}]$ identifies with ψ_i.

A typical example of proportional investment strategy family is the set of all $\mathbb{G}$-predictable processes which satisfies certain integrability condition (with respect to the price process S) on $[0, T]$. Then, the gluing property corresponds to the fact that the integrability on $[0, T]$ is equivalent to the integrability on the intervals in a subdivision of $[0, T]$.

DEFINITION 1.2.– *Let $\mathcal{A}$ be a family of proportional investment strategies, which satisfies the gluing property. For fixed initial portfolio value X_0, we associate with any proportional investment strategy $\pi \in \mathcal{A}$ a $(\mathbb{G}, \mathbb{P})$-semimartingale $F^\pi(X_0)$ on $[0, T]$ such that $F_t^\pi(X_0)$ is integrable for any $t \in [0, T]$. The process $F^\pi(X_0)$ is called an* additive utility weight. *We say that the $F^\pi(X_0)$ is admissible if for any pair t_1, t_2 of elements in $[0, T]$,*

$0 \leq t_1 \leq t_2 \leq T$ and for $\psi \in \mathcal{A}_{t_1,t_2}$ being the restriction of π on $(t_1, t_2]$, the process

$$F_t^{\psi}(X_{t_1}) := (F_t^{\pi}(X_0) - F_{t_1}^{\pi}(X_0))_{t_1 \leq t \leq t_2} \qquad [1.41]$$

on $[t_1, t_2]$ only depends on the value $X_{t_1} = X_{t_1}^{\pi}$ of the portfolio at time t_1 and the restriction ψ of the strategy π on $(t_1, t_2]$.

REMARK 1.2.– Let F be an additive utility weight which is admissible. Let t_1, t_2 and t_3 be elements of $[0, T]$ such that $t_1 \leq t_2 \leq t_3$. If ψ is an element of $\mathcal{A}_{t_1,t_3}$ and φ is the restriction of ψ on $(t_2, t_3]$, then for any $\mathcal{F}_{t_2}$-measurable random variable X_{t_2} which can be realized as the portfolio value at time t_2 of certain proportional investment strategy π (with initial portfolio value X_0), we have

$$\forall t \in [t_2, t_3], \quad F_t^{\varphi}(X_{t_2}) = F_t^{\pi}(X_0) - F_{t_2}^{\pi}(X_0)$$

and

$$\forall t \in [t_1, t_3], \quad F_t^{\psi}(X_{t_1}) = F_t^{\pi}(X_0) - F_{t_1}^{\pi}(X_0),$$

where $X_{t_1} = X_{t_1}^{\pi}$. Therefore, for any $t \in [t_2, t_3]$, we have

$$\begin{aligned}
F_t^{\varphi}(X_{t_2}) &= F_t^{\pi}(X_0) - F_{t_2}^{\pi}(X_0) \\
&= (F_t^{\pi}(X_0) - F_{t_1}^{\pi}(X_0)) - (F_{t_2}^{\pi}(X_0) - F_{t_1}^{\pi}(X_0)) \\
&= F_t^{\psi}(X_{t_1}) - F_{t_2}^{\psi}(X_{t_1}).
\end{aligned} \qquad [1.42]$$

EXAMPLE 1.1.– Let f be a continuous function on $\mathbb{R}_+^2$ and M be a $(\mathbb{G}, \mathbb{P})$-semimartingale. We assume that, for any $\pi \in \mathcal{A}$, the process $f(t, X_{t-}^{\pi})^2$ is locally integrable with respect to $\langle M \rangle$. Then, the stochastic integral

$$F_t^{\pi}(X_0) = \int_0^t f(s, X_{s-}^{\pi}) dM_s$$

is well-defined. If $t_1 \leq t_2$ are two elements of $[0, T]$, then we have

$$F_t^{\pi}(X_0) - F_{t_1}^{\pi}(X_0) = \int_{t_1}^t f(s, X_{s-}^{\pi}) dM_s \text{ on } [t_1, t_2],$$

which only depends on the value of $X_{t_1}^{\pi}$ and the restriction of the proportional investment strategy π on $(t_1, t_2]$.

In the following, we consider a family of proportional investment strategies, which satisfies the gluing property, and an admissible additive utility weight F. Let t be an element of $[0, T]$. For any $\mathcal{G}_t$-measurable random variable X_t which can be realized as the portfolio value at time t of certain investment strategy in $\mathcal{A}$, we denote by $V_t(X_t)$ the following essential supremum

$$V_t(X_t) := \operatorname*{ess\,sup}_{\psi \in \mathcal{A}_{t,T}} \mathbb{E}^{\mathbb{P}} \left[G_T U(X_T^\psi) + F_T^\psi(X_t) \,\Big|\, \mathcal{G}_t \right],$$

where X^ψ and $F^\psi(X_t)$ are defined in [1.40] and [1.41]. Note that, for any $\mathcal{G}_T$-measurable random variable X_T which can be realized as the terminal portfolio value of a proportional investment strategy in $\mathcal{A}$, we have

$$V_T(X_T) = G_T U(X_T), \quad \mathbb{P}\text{-a.s.}$$

Note that for $\psi \in \mathcal{A}_{T,T}$ we always have $F_T^\psi(X_T) = 0$ by definition.

The following result is important in the dynamic programming approach of the optimization problem (see [ELK 95]).

THEOREM 1.3.– Let t_1 and t_2 be two real numbers such that $0 \leq t_1 \leq t_2 \leq T$. Let X_{t_1} be a $\mathcal{G}_{t_1}$-measurable random variable which can be realized as the portfolio value at t_1 of some proportional investment strategy in $\mathcal{A}$. Then, we have

$$V_{t_1}(X_{t_1}) = \operatorname*{ess\,sup}_{\varphi \in \mathcal{A}_{t_1,t_2}} \mathbb{E}^{\mathbb{P}} \left[V_{t_2}(X_{t_2}^\varphi) + F_{t_2}^\varphi(X_{t_1}) \,\big|\, \mathcal{G}_{t_1} \right], \quad \mathbb{P}\text{-a.s.,} \qquad [1.43]$$

where $X_{t_1}^\varphi = X_{t_1}$. Moreover, for any initial portfolio value X_0 and any proportional investment strategy $\pi \in \mathcal{A}$, the process $(V_t(X_t^\pi) + F_t^\pi(X_0))_{0 \leq t \leq T}$ is a $(\mathbb{G}, \mathbb{P})$-supermartingale on $[0, T]$. Finally, $\pi^* \in \mathcal{A}$ is an optimal proportional investment strategy for the optimization problem

$$V_0(X_0) = \sup_{\pi \in \mathcal{A}} \mathbb{E}^{\mathbb{P}}[G_T U(X_T^\pi) + F_T^\pi(X_0)] \qquad [1.44]$$

if and only if the process $(V_t(X_t^{\pi^*}) + F_t^{\pi^*}(X_0))_{0 \leq t \leq T}$ is an $(\mathbb{G}, \mathbb{P})$-martingale.

PROOF.– Let φ be an element in $\mathcal{A}_{t_1,t_2}$. By definition, we have

$$V_{t_2}(X_{t_2}^{\varphi}) = \operatorname*{ess\,sup}_{\substack{\psi \in \mathcal{A}_{t_2,T} \\ X_{t_2}^{\psi} = X_{t_2}^{\varphi}}} \mathbb{E}^{\mathbb{P}}\big[V_T(X_T^{\psi}) + F_T^{\psi}(X_{t_2}) \,\big|\, \mathcal{F}_{t_2}\big], \quad \mathbb{P}\text{-a.s.}$$

Consider an element ψ in $\mathcal{A}_{t_2,T}$. By the gluing property, there exists an element π in $\mathcal{A}_{t_1,T}$ whose restrictions on $(t_1,t_2]$ and on $(t_2,T]$ identify with φ and ψ, respectively. The process X^{π} (with $X_{t_1}^{\pi} = X_{t_1}$) then coincides with X^{φ} on $[t_1,t_2]$, and with X^{ψ} on $[t_2,T]$. Let $X_{t_2} := X_{t_2}^{\pi} = X_{t_2}^{\varphi}$. By the relations $F_{t_2}^{\varphi}(X_{t_1}) = F_{t_2}^{\pi}(X_{t_1})$ and $F_T^{\psi}(X_{t_2}) = F_T^{\pi}(X_{t_1}) - F_{t_2}^{\pi}(X_{t_1})$ (see remark 1.2), we obtain

$$\mathbb{E}^{\mathbb{P}}\big[\mathbb{E}[V_T(X_T^{\psi}) + F_T^{\psi}(X_{t_2}) \,|\, \mathcal{G}_{t_2}] + F_{t_2}^{\varphi}(X_{t_1}) \,\big|\, \mathcal{G}_{t_1}\big]$$
$$= \mathbb{E}^{\mathbb{P}}\big[V_T(X_T^{\pi}) + F_T^{\pi}(X_{t_1}) \,|\, \mathcal{G}_{t_1}\big] \leq V_{t_1}(X_{t_1}).$$

Since ψ is arbitrary, we deduce

$$\mathbb{E}^{\mathbb{P}}[V_{t_2}(X_{t_2}^{\varphi}) + F_{t_2}^{\varphi}(X_{t_1}) \,|\, \mathcal{G}_{t_1}] \leq V_{t_1}(X_{t_1}).$$

Therefore,

$$V_{t_1}(X_{t_1}) \geq \operatorname*{ess\,sup}_{\varphi \in \mathcal{A}_{t_1,t_2}} \mathbb{E}[V_{t_2}(X_{t_2}^{\varphi}) + F_{t_2}^{\varphi}(X_{t_1})) \,|\, \mathcal{G}_{t_1}] \quad \mathbb{P}\text{-a.s.}$$

Conversely, any $\pi \in \mathcal{A}_{t_1,T}$ induces by restriction two admissible strategies $\varphi \in \mathcal{A}_{t_1,t_2}$ and $\psi \in \mathcal{A}_{t_1,T}$, respectively. Still from the relation (with $X_{t_2} := X_{t_2}^{\pi}$)

$$\mathbb{E}^{\mathbb{P}}[V_T(X_T^{\pi}) + F_T^{\pi}(X_{t_1}) \,|\, \mathcal{G}_{t_2}] = \mathbb{E}^{\mathbb{P}}[V_T(X_T^{\psi}) + F_T^{\psi}(X_{t_2}) \,|\, \mathcal{G}_{t_2}] + F_{t_2}^{\varphi}(X_{t_1})$$

we obtain

$$\mathbb{E}^{\mathbb{P}}[V_T(X_T^{\pi}) + F_T^{\pi}(X_{t_1}) \,|\, \mathcal{G}_{t_2}] \leq V_{t_2}(X_{t_2}^{\varphi}) + F_{t_2}^{\varphi}(X_{t_1}),$$

and hence

$$\mathbb{E}^{\mathbb{P}}[V_T(X_T^{\pi}) + F_T^{\pi}(X_{t_1}) \,|\, \mathcal{G}_{t_1}] \leq \mathbb{E}^{\mathbb{P}}[V_{t_2}(X_{t_2}^{\varphi}) + F_{t_2}^{\varphi}(X_{t_1}) \,|\, \mathcal{G}_{t_1}].$$

Since π is arbitrary, we deduce

$$V_{t_1}(X_{t_1}) \leq \operatorname*{ess\,sup}_{\varphi \in \mathcal{A}_{t_1,t_2}} \mathbb{E}[V_{t_2}(X_{t_2}^{\varphi}) + F_{t_2}^{\varphi}(X_{t_1}) \,|\, \mathcal{G}_{t_1}].$$

The relation [1.43] is thus proved.

The second assertion can be deduced from the first one. Let s and t be two elements of $[0, T]$ such that $s < t$, and π be a proportional admissible investment strategy in $\mathcal{A}$. We denote by φ the restriction of π on the interval $(s, t]$. By [1.43], we have

$$V_s(X_s^\pi) \geq \mathbb{E}^{\mathbb{P}}[V_t(X_t^\pi) + F_t^\varphi(X_s^\pi) \mid \mathcal{G}_s].$$

Thus, we obtain

$$V_s(X_s^\pi) + F_s^\pi(X_0) \geq \mathbb{E}^{\mathbb{P}}[V_t(X_t^\pi) + F_t^\pi(X_0) \mid \mathcal{G}_s]$$

since $F_t^\varphi(X_s) = F_t^\pi(X_0) - F_s^\varphi(X_0)$. Therefore, the process $(V(t, X_t^\pi) + F_t^\pi(X_0))_{0 \leq t \leq T}$ is a $(\mathbb{G}, \mathbb{P})$-supermartingale.

We now prove the last assertion. Assume that π^* is an optimal investment strategy, then we have

$$V_0(X_0) = \mathbb{E}^{\mathbb{P}}[V_T(X_T^{\pi^*}) + F_T^{\pi^*}(X_0)]. \tag{1.45}$$

Since the process $(V_t(X_t^{\pi^*}) + F_t^{\pi^*}(X_0))_{0 \leq t \leq T}$ is a supermartingale, we obtain that it is actually a martingale. Conversely, if π^* is an element in $\mathcal{A}$ such that the process $(V(t, X_t^{\pi^*}) + F_t^{\pi^*}(X_0))_{0 \leq t \leq T}$ is a $(\mathbb{G}, \mathbb{P})$-martingale, then the equality [1.45] holds, which implies that the supremum in [1.44] is attained by the investment strategy π^*. $\qquad\square$

1.4. Several explicit examples

In this section, we apply the general dynamical programming principle to concrete situations.

1.4.1. *Brownian setting*

In this section, we suppose that the filtration $\mathbb{G}$ is generated by a standard Brownian motion W. Recall the martingale representation theorem states that any càdlàg $(\mathbb{G}, \mathbb{P})$-local martingale M can be written as:

$$M_t = M_0 + \int_0^t \xi_s dW_s,$$

where ξ is a $\mathbb{G}$-predictable process such that $\int_0^T \xi_s^2 ds < +\infty$ almost surely. We assume for simplicity that the portfolio contains a single risky asset, whose price process S is driven by the stochastic differential equation

$$dS_t = S_t(\mu_t dt + \sigma_t dW_t),$$

where μ and $\sigma > 0$ are $\mathbb{G}$-predictable process such that

$$\mathbb{E}^{\mathbb{P}}\left[\int_0^T \left(|\mu_t| + |\sigma_t|^2 + \left|\frac{\mu_t}{\sigma_t}\right|^2 \right) dt \right] < +\infty.$$

We also assume that the following Novikov's condition is satisfied

$$\mathbb{E}^{\mathbb{P}}\left[\exp\left(\frac{1}{2} \int_0^T \left|\frac{\mu_t}{\sigma_t}\right|^2 dt \right) \right] < +\infty.$$

In this case, the market is complete, and the unique martingale probability measure $\mathbb{Q}$ is given by

$$\frac{d\mathbb{Q}}{d\mathbb{P}}\bigg|_{\mathcal{G}_T} = \exp\left(\int_0^T \frac{\mu_t}{\sigma_t} dW_t - \frac{1}{2} \int_0^T \frac{\mu_t^2}{\sigma_t^2} dt \right).$$

We denote by Z the process

$$Z_t = \exp\left(- \int_0^t \frac{\mu_s}{\sigma_s} dW_s - \frac{1}{2} \int_0^t \frac{\mu_s^2}{\sigma_s^2} ds \right), \quad t \in [0, T]. \tag{1.46}$$

It is a $(\mathbb{G}, \mathbb{P})$-martingale. Let $\mathcal{A}$ be the set of $\mathbb{G}$-predictable processes π such that

$$\mathbb{E}^{\mathbb{P}}\left[\int_0^T (|\mu_t \pi_t| + |\sigma_t \pi_t|^2) dt \right] < +\infty.$$

Clearly, $\mathcal{A}$ satisfies the gluing property in definition 1.1. Note that for any $\pi \in \mathcal{A}$, the value process X^π satisfies the stochastic differential equation

$$\frac{dX_t^\pi}{X_t^\pi} = \pi_t \frac{dS_t}{S_t} = \pi_t(\mu_t dt + \sigma_t dW_t).$$

Thus, the process X^π can be written as:

$$X_t^\pi = X_0 \exp\left(\int_0^t \pi_s \sigma_s dW_s + \int_0^t \left(\pi_s \mu_s - \frac{1}{2}|\pi_s \sigma_s|^2\right)ds\right).$$

We consider the following optimization problem

$$V_0(X_0) = \sup_{\pi \in \mathcal{A}} \mathbb{E}^\mathbb{P}[G_T U(X_T^\pi)],$$

where G_T is the terminal value of an exponential martingale

$$G_t = G_0 \exp\left(\int_0^t b_s dW_s - \frac{1}{2}\int_0^t b_s^2 ds\right),$$ [1.47]

where

$$\mathbb{E}^\mathbb{P}\left[\exp\left(\frac{1}{2}\int_0^T b_s^2 ds\right)\right] < +\infty.$$

1.4.1.1. Logarithmic utility

We assume that U is the logarithmic utility function. By proposition 1.1 (with $\sigma = 0$), we have

$$V_0(X_0) = \mathbb{E}^\mathbb{P}[G_T \log(G_T/Z_T)] + G_0 \log(X_0/G_0).$$

By Itô's formula, we obtain from [1.47] and [1.46] that

$$G_T \log(G_T/Z_T) - G_0 \log(G_0/Z_0)$$
$$= \frac{1}{2}\int_0^T G_t\left(b_t^2 + \frac{\mu_t^2}{\sigma_t^2} + 2b_t\frac{\mu_t}{\sigma_t}\right)dt + \int_0^T G_t\left(b_t + \frac{\mu_t}{\sigma_t} + b_t \log\frac{G_t}{Z_t}\right)dW_t.$$

Therefore, if

$$\mathbb{E}\left[\int_0^T G_t^2\left(b_t + \frac{\mu_t}{\sigma_t} + b_t \log(G_t/Z_t)\right)^2 dt\right] < +\infty,$$

then we have

$$V_0(X_0) = \frac{1}{2}\int_0^T \mathbb{E}^\mathbb{P}\left[G_t\left(b_t + \frac{\mu_t}{\sigma_t}\right)^2\right]dt + G_0 \log(X_0).$$ [1.48]

Similarly, for $t \in [0, T]$ one has

$$V_t(X_t) = \mathbb{E}^{\mathbb{P}}[G_T \log(G_T/Z_T)|\mathcal{G}_t] + G_t \log(X_t Z_t/G_t)$$

$$= \tfrac{1}{2} \int_t^T \mathbb{E}^{\mathbb{P}}\left[G_t\left(b_t + \tfrac{\mu_t}{\sigma_t}\right)^2\right]dt + G_t \log(X_t)$$

for any $\mathcal{G}_t$-measurable random variable X_t which can be written as the portfolio value at time t of some investment strategy.

1.4.1.2. Power utility

We assume that U is the power utility function $U(x) = x^p/p$. By proposition 1.2, we have

$$V_0(X_0) = \frac{X_0^p}{p} \mathbb{E}^{\mathbb{P}}\left[Z_T^{p/(p-1)} G_T^{-1/(p-1)}\right]^{1-p}.$$

Note that

$$\frac{Z_t^{p/(p-1)}}{G_t^{1/(p-1)}} = \frac{1}{G_0^{1/(p-1)}} \exp\left(-\frac{1}{p-1}\int_0^t \left(b_s + p\frac{\mu_s}{\sigma_s}\right)dW_s\right.$$

$$\left. + \frac{1}{2(p-1)}\int_0^t \left(b_s^2 - p\frac{\mu_s^2}{\sigma_s^2}\right)ds\right).$$

In particular, if the processes μ, σ and b are deterministic, then we have

$$V_0(X_0) = G_0 \exp\left(-\frac{p}{2}\int_0^T \left(b_t + \frac{\mu_t}{\sigma_t}\right)^2 dt\right)\frac{X_0^p}{p}.$$

Similarly, for $t \in [0, T]$ we have

$$V_t(X_t) = \frac{(X_t Z_t)^p}{p} \mathbb{E}^{\mathbb{P}}\left[Z_T^{p/(p-1)}/G_T^{1/(p-1)} \mid \mathcal{G}_t\right]^{1-p},$$

which is equal to

$$G_t \exp\left(-\frac{p}{2}\int_t^T \left(b_s + \frac{\mu_s}{\sigma_s}\right)^2 ds\right)\frac{X_t^p}{p}$$

if the processes μ, σ and b are deterministic.

1.4.1.3. *Exponential utility*

We assume that U is the exponential utility function, namely, $U(x) = -e^{-\gamma x}$. In this case by proposition 1.3, we have

$$V_0(X_0) = \frac{1}{\gamma} e^{-\gamma X_0} \exp\left(-\mathbb{E}^{\mathbb{P}}\left[Z_T \log\left(\frac{Z_T}{\gamma G_T}\right)\right]\right)$$

$$= e^{-\gamma X_0} \exp\left(-\mathbb{E}^{\mathbb{P}}\left[Z_T \log\left(\frac{Z_T}{G_T}\right)\right]\right).$$

Note that we have

$$d\log(Z_t/G_t) = -(b_t + \mu_t/\sigma_t)dW_t + \frac{1}{2}(b_t^2 - \mu_t^2/\sigma_t^2)dt$$

and

$$dZ_t = -Z_t\frac{\mu_t}{\sigma_t}dW_t.$$

Therefore,

$$d\left(Z_t \log\left(\frac{Z_t}{G_T}\right)\right) = -Z_t\left(b_t + \frac{\mu_t}{\sigma_t} + \frac{\mu_t}{\sigma_t}\log\left(\frac{Z_t}{G_t}\right)\right)dW_t + \frac{Z_t}{2}\left(b_t + \frac{\mu_t}{\sigma_t}\right)^2 dt.$$

In particular, if

$$\mathbb{E}\left[\int_0^T Z_t^2\left(b_t + \frac{\mu_t}{\sigma_t} + \frac{\mu_t}{\sigma_t}\log\left(\frac{Z_t}{G_t}\right)\right)^2 dt\right] < +\infty,$$

then we have

$$V_0(X_0) = -e^{-\gamma X_0}\exp\left(-\frac{1}{2}\int_0^T \mathbb{E}^{\mathbb{P}}\left[Z_t\left(b_t + \frac{\mu_t}{\sigma_t}\right)^2\right]dt\right).$$

Similarly, for $t \in [0, T]$, we have

$$V_t(X_t) = -Z_t\exp(-\gamma X_t - Z_t^{-1}\mathbb{E}^{\mathbb{P}}[Z_T\log(Z_T/G_T)\,|\,\mathcal{G}_t])$$

$$= -e^{-\gamma X_t}Z_t\exp\left(-\frac{1}{2Z_t}\int_t^T \mathbb{E}^{\mathbb{P}}\left[Z_s\left(b_s + \frac{\mu_s}{\sigma_s}\right)^2\,\Big|\,\mathcal{F}_t\right]ds\right).$$

1.4.2. *Brownian setting with additive utility weight*

We keep the notation of the previous section. Here, we consider the optimization problem

$$V_0(X_0) = \sup_{\pi \in \mathcal{A}} \mathbb{E}^{\mathbb{P}}[G_T U(X_T^{\pi}) + F_T^{\pi}(X_0)],$$

where $F_T^{\pi}(X_0)$ is an additive utility weight satisfying the gluing property (see definition 1.2). For the resolution of this optimization problem, we consider its dynamic version

$$V_t(X_t) = \operatorname*{ess\,sup}_{\varphi \in \mathcal{A}_{t,T}} \mathbb{E}^{\mathbb{P}}[G_T U(X_T^{\varphi}) + F_T^{\varphi}(X_t) \mid \mathcal{G}_t],$$

with

$$F_T^{\varphi}(X_t) = F_T^{\pi}(X_0) - F_t^{\pi}(X_0),$$

where π is a proportional investment strategy on $[0,T]$ extending φ such that $X_t^{\pi} = X_t^{\varphi}$. By theorem 1.3, if π is a proportional investment strategy in $\mathcal{A}$, then the process $(V_t(X_t^{\pi}) + F_t^{\pi}(X_0))_{t \in [0,T]}$ is a $(\mathbb{G}, \mathbb{P})$-supermartingale. It is a $(\mathbb{G}, \mathbb{P})$-martingale if $\pi = \pi^*$ is the optimal proportional investment strategy.

1.4.2.1. *Logarithmic utility*

We assume that U is the logarithmic utility function and that the additive utility weight is of the form

$$F_t^{\pi}(X_0) = \int_0^t c_s \log(X_s^{\pi}) \, ds,$$

where c is a càdlàg $\mathbb{G}$-adapted processes. In this case, for any $\pi \in \mathcal{A}$ we have

$$\begin{aligned}
&V_t(X_t^{\pi}) + F_t^{\pi}(X_0) \\
&= G_t \log(X_t^{\pi}) + \int_0^t c_s \log(X_s^{\pi}) \, ds + \log(X_t^{\pi})\mathbb{E}\left[\int_t^T c_s \, ds \big| \mathcal{G}_t\right] \\
&\quad +\operatorname*{ess\,sup}_{\varphi \in \mathcal{A}_{t,T}} \mathbb{E}^{\mathbb{P}}\left[G_T \log\left(\frac{X_T^{\varphi}}{X_t^{\pi}}\right) + \int_t^T c_s \log\left(\frac{X_s^{\varphi}}{X_t^{\pi}}\right) ds \mid \mathcal{G}_t\right],
\end{aligned}$$

where $X_t^{\varphi} = X_t^{\pi}$. Note that the process $(X_s^{\varphi}/X_t^{\pi})_{s \in [t,T]}$ only depends on the investment strategy φ on $(t,T]$ but not on X_t^{π}. For $t \in [0,T]$, let

$$Y_t := \operatorname*{ess\,sup}_{\varphi \in \mathcal{A}_{t,T}} \mathbb{E}^{\mathbb{P}}\left[G_T \log(X_T^{\varphi,1}) + \int_t^T c_s \log(X_s^{\varphi,1}) \, ds \mid \mathcal{G}_t\right],$$

where the process $X^{\varphi,1}$ is described by the stochastic differential equation

$$dX_u^{\varphi,1} = X_u^{\varphi,1}\varphi_u \frac{dS_u}{S_u}, \quad X_t^{\varphi,1} = 1.$$

Then, we obtain that, for any $\pi \in \mathcal{A}$, the process defined for all $t \in [0, T]$

$$Y_t + \log(X_t^\pi) + \int_0^t c_s \log(X_s^\pi)ds + \log(X_t^\pi)\mathbb{E}^{\mathbb{P}}\left[\int_t^T c_s\, ds \,\bigg|\, \mathcal{G}_t\right]$$

$$[1.49]$$

is a $(\mathbb{G}, \mathbb{P})$-supermartingale. In particular (by taking $\pi = 0$), we obtain that the process Y itself is a $(\mathbb{G}, \mathbb{P})$-supermartingale. Hence, there exists $\xi \in L_{\text{loc}}^2(W)$ and a decreasing $\mathbb{G}$-adapted process A such that

$$dY_t = \xi_t dW_t + dA_t.$$

We let H be the martingale

$$H_t := \mathbb{E}^{\mathbb{P}}\left[\int_0^T c_s ds \,\bigg|\, \mathcal{G}_t\right], \quad t \in [0, T],$$

which is written as

$$H_t = \int_0^t \eta_s dW_s,$$

where $\eta \in L_{\text{loc}}^2(W)$. Note that

$$\log(X_t^\pi) = \log(X_0) + \int_0^t \pi_s \sigma_s dW_s + \int_0^t \left(\pi_s \mu_s - \frac{1}{2}(\pi_s \sigma_s)^2\right)ds,$$

which leads to

$$d(G_t \log(X_t^\pi)) = G_t(\log(X_t^\pi)b_t + \pi_t \sigma_t)dW_t$$

$$+ G_t \left(b_t \pi_t \sigma_t + \pi_t \mu_t - \frac{1}{2}(\pi_t \sigma_t)^2\right)dt$$

since $dG_t = b_t G_t dW_t$ (see equation [1.47]). Hence, we obtain that the finite variation part A^π in the Doob–Meyer decomposition of [1.49] is given by

$$dA_t^\pi = dA_t + \pi_t(G_t b_t \sigma_t + \mu_t C_t + \eta_t \sigma_t)dt - \frac{\pi_t^2}{2}\sigma_t^2 C_t dt,$$

where

$$C_t = G_t + H_t - \int_0^t c_s ds, \quad t \in [0, T].$$

Note that A^π is non-increasing for any $\pi \in \mathcal{A}$, and is zero when $\pi = \pi^*$ is the optimal investment strategy. Hence, we obtain

$$dA_t = -\frac{(G_t b_t \sigma_t + \mu_t C_t + \eta_t \sigma_t)^2}{2\sigma_t^2 C_t}dt,$$

and the optimal investment strategy π^* maximizes

$$\pi_t(G_t b_t \sigma_t + \mu_t C_t + \eta_t \sigma_t) - \frac{\pi_t^2}{2}\sigma_t^2 C_t,$$

namely,

$$\pi_t^* = \frac{G_t b_t \sigma_t + \mu_t C_t + \eta_t \sigma_t}{\sigma_t^2 C_t}.$$

Note that $Y_T = 0$. Therefore, the process Y is given for all $t \in [0, T]$

$$Y_t = A_t - \mathbb{E}^{\mathbb{P}}[A_T|\mathcal{G}_t] = \mathbb{E}^{\mathbb{P}}\left[\int_t^T \frac{(G_s b_s \sigma_s + \mu_s C_s + \eta_s \sigma_s)^2}{2\sigma_s^2 C_s}ds \,\middle|\, \mathcal{G}_t\right]$$

In particular, we have

$$V_0(X_0) = G_0 \log(X_0) + \log(X_0)\mathbb{E}^{\mathbb{P}}\left[\int_0^T c_s ds\right]$$
$$+ \mathbb{E}^{\mathbb{P}}\left[\int_0^T \frac{(G_s b_s \sigma_s + \mu_s C_s + \eta_s \sigma_s)^2}{2\sigma_s^2 C_s}ds\right]. \qquad [1.50]$$

Note that in the case where the additive utility weight is zero (namely, $c_t = 0$, $t \in [0, T]$), we have $C = G$ and hence we recover the result of [1.48] obtained by the duality method.

1.4.2.2. *Power utility*

We assume that $U(x) = x^p/p$ is the power utility function, where $p < 1$, $p \neq 0$. We also suppose that the additive utility weight is of the form

$$F_t^\pi(X_0) = \int_0^t c_s(X_s^\pi)^p \, ds,$$

where c is a càdlàg $\mathbb{G}$-adapted process. For any $\pi \in \mathcal{A}$, we have

$$
\begin{aligned}
&V_t(X_t^\pi) + F_t^\pi(X_0) \\
&= \operatorname*{ess\,sup}_{\varphi \in \mathcal{A}_{t,T}} \mathbb{E}^{\mathbb{P}} \left[\frac{G_T}{p}(X_T^\varphi)^p + \int_t^T c_s(X_s^\varphi)^p \, ds \,\middle|\, \mathcal{G}_t \right] + \int_0^t c_s(X_s^\pi)^p ds \\
&= (X_t^\pi)^p \operatorname*{ess\,sup}_{\varphi \in \mathcal{A}_{t,T}} \mathbb{E}^{\mathbb{P}} \left[\frac{G_T}{p}\left(\frac{X_T^\varphi}{X_t^\pi}\right)^p + \int_t^T c_s\left(\frac{X_s^\varphi}{X_t^\pi}\right)^p ds \,\middle|\, \mathcal{G}_t \right] + \int_0^t c_s(X_s^\pi)^p ds,
\end{aligned}
\tag{1.51}
$$

with the convention $X_t^\varphi = X_t^\pi$. Note that the process $(X_s^\varphi/X_t^\pi)_{s \in [t,T]}$ only depends on the investment strategy φ on $(t, T]$. Let

$$Y_t := \operatorname*{ess\,sup}_{\varphi \in \mathcal{A}_{t,T}} \mathbb{E}^{\mathbb{P}} \left[\frac{G_T}{p}(X_T^{\varphi,1})^p + \int_t^T c_s(X_s^{\varphi,1})^p \, ds \,\middle|\, \mathcal{G}_t \right], \tag{1.52}$$

where the process $X^{\varphi,1}$ is determined by the stochastic differential equation on $[t, T]$

$$dX_u^{\varphi,1} = X_u^{\varphi,1} \varphi_u \frac{dS_u}{S_u}, \quad X_t^{\varphi,1} = 1.$$

With this notation, the formula [1.51] can be rewritten as:

$$V_t(X_t^\pi) + F_t^\pi(X_0) = (X_t^\pi)^p Y_t + \int_0^t c_s(X_s^\pi)^p ds.$$

Therefore, the process $\left((X_t^\pi)^p Y_t + \int_0^t c_s(X_s^\pi)^p ds, t \in [0,T]\right)$ is a $(\mathbb{G}, \mathbb{P})$-supermartingale for any π. In particular (by taking $\pi = 0$), the process $(Y_t + \int_0^t c_s ds, t \in [0,T])$ is a $(\mathbb{G}, \mathbb{P})$-supermartingale. Hence, there exists $\xi \in L_{\mathrm{loc}}^2(W)$ and a decreasing $\mathbb{G}$-adapted process A such that

$$dY_t = \xi_t dW_t + dA_t - c_t dt. \tag{1.53}$$

Note that

$$d(X_t^\pi)^p = p(X_t^\pi)^{p-1} dX_t^\pi + \tfrac{1}{2} p(p-1)(X_t^\pi)^p \pi_t^2 \sigma_t^2 dt$$
$$= p\pi_t(X_t^\pi)^p \Big(\sigma_t dW_t + (\mu_t + \tfrac{1}{2}(p-1)\pi_t \sigma_t^2) dt \Big).$$

Hence, we obtain

$$d(Y_t(X_t^\pi)^p) + c_t(X_t^\pi)^p dt$$
$$= Y_t d(X_t^\pi)^p + (X_t^\pi)^p dY_t + d\langle (X^\pi)^p, Y \rangle_t + c_t(X_t^\pi)^p dt$$
$$= (X_t^\pi)^p \big((\xi_t + p\pi_t \sigma_t Y_t) dW_t + p((\mu_t Y_t + \xi_t \sigma_t)\pi_t$$
$$- \tfrac{1}{2}(1-p)\sigma_t^2 \pi_t^2 Y_t) dt + dA_t \big).$$

Therefore, the optimal investment strategy π^* maximizes

$$(\mu_t Y_t + \xi_t \sigma_t)\pi_t - \frac{1}{2}(1-p)\sigma_t^2 Y_t \pi_t^2.$$

In other words, we have

$$\pi_t^* = \frac{\mu_t Y_t + \xi_t \sigma_t}{(1-p)\sigma_t^2 Y_t},$$

and

$$dA_t = \Big(-\frac{p(\mu_t Y_t + \xi_t \sigma_t)^2}{2(1-p)\sigma_t^2 Y_t} \Big) dt.$$

Therefore, the process Y satisfies the backward stochastic differential equation

$$dY_t = \Big(-c_t - \frac{p(\mu_t Y_t + \xi_t \sigma_t)^2}{2(1-p)\sigma_t^2 Y_t} \Big) dt + \xi_t dW_t, \quad Y_T = G_T/p.$$

1.4.2.3. *Exponential utility*

We assume that U is the exponential utility function $U(x) = -e^{-\gamma x}$. We assume in addition that additive utility weight is of the form

$$F_t^\pi(X_0) = \int_0^t c_s \exp(-\gamma X_s^\pi) ds,$$

where c is a càdlàg $\mathbb{G}$-adapted process. We introduce the change of variables by taking

$$\widetilde{\mathcal{A}} = \left\{ \pi X^\pi \,\middle|\, \pi \in \mathcal{A} \right\}.$$

For $\alpha \in \widetilde{\mathcal{A}}$, let $\widetilde{X}^\alpha$ be the solution of the stochastic differential equation

$$d\widetilde{X}_t^\alpha = \alpha_t \frac{dS_t}{S_t} = \alpha_t(\mu_t dt + \sigma_t dW_t), \quad \widetilde{X}_0^\alpha = X_0.$$

Note that $\widetilde{X}^\alpha = X^\pi$ provided that $\alpha = \pi X^\pi$. Hence, we have

$$V_t(X_t^\pi) = \widetilde{V}_t(\widetilde{X}_t^\alpha) := \operatorname*{ess\,sup}_{\beta \in \widetilde{\mathcal{A}}_{t,T}} \mathbb{E}^{\mathbb{P}} \left[-e^{-\gamma \widetilde{X}_T^\beta} + \int_t^T c_s e^{-\gamma \widetilde{X}_s^\beta} ds \,\middle|\, \mathcal{G}_s \right],$$

where $\widetilde{\mathcal{A}}_{t,T}$ denotes the restriction on $(t, T]$ of the investment strategies in $\widetilde{\mathcal{A}}$. Therefore,

$$
\begin{aligned}
&V_t(X_t^\pi) + F_t^\pi(X_0) \\
&= \operatorname*{esssup}_{\beta \in \widetilde{\mathcal{A}}_{t,T}} \mathbb{E}^{\mathbb{P}} \left[-e^{-\gamma \widetilde{X}_T^\beta} + \int_t^T c_s e^{-\gamma \widetilde{X}_s^\beta} ds \,\middle|\, \mathcal{G}_t \right] + \int_0^t c_s e^{-\gamma X_s^\pi} ds \\
&= e^{-\gamma X_t^\pi} \operatorname*{esssup}_{\beta \in \widetilde{\mathcal{A}}_{t,T}} \mathbb{E}^{\mathbb{P}} \left[-e^{-\gamma(\widetilde{X}_T^\beta - X_t^\pi)} + \int_t^T c_s e^{-\gamma(\widetilde{X}_s^\beta - X_t^\pi)} ds \,\middle|\, \mathcal{G}_t \right] \\
&\quad + \int_0^t c_s e^{-\gamma X_s^\pi} ds.
\end{aligned}
$$

We let

$$Y_t = \operatorname*{ess\,sup}_{\beta \in \widetilde{\mathcal{A}}_{t,T}} \mathbb{E}^{\mathbb{P}} \left[-G_T e^{-\gamma \widetilde{X}_T^{\beta,0}} + \int_t^T c_s e^{-\gamma \widetilde{X}_s^{\beta,0}} ds \,\middle|\, \mathcal{G}_t \right],$$

where the process $\widetilde{X}^{\beta,0}$ on $[t, T]$ is determined by the stochastic differential equation

$$d\widetilde{X}_s^{\beta,0} = \beta_s(\mu_s ds + \sigma_s dW_s), \quad \widetilde{X}_t^{\beta,0} = 0.$$

Thus, the process $\left(e^{-\gamma X_t^\pi} Y_t + \int_0^t c_s e^{-\gamma X_s^\pi} ds, \ t \in [0, T] \right)$ is a $(\mathbb{G}, \mathbb{P})$-supermartingale for any π. In particular, the process $\left(Y_t + \int_0^t c_s ds, t \in [0, T] \right)$

is a $(\mathbb{G}, \mathbb{P})$-supermartingale. Hence, there exists $\xi \in L^2_{\text{loc}}(W)$ and a decreasing $\mathbb{G}$-adapted process A such that

$$dY_t = \xi_t dW_t + dA_t - c_t dt.$$

Note that

$$
\begin{aligned}
d\,e^{-\gamma X^\pi_t} &= -\gamma e^{-\gamma X^\pi_t}\big(\pi_t X^\pi_t(\mu_t dt + \sigma_t dW_t)\big) \\
&\quad + \tfrac{1}{2}\gamma^2 e^{-\gamma X^\pi_t}\pi_t^2(X^\pi_t)^2\sigma_t^2 dt \\
&= e^{-\gamma X^\pi_t}\Big(-\gamma\pi_t X^\pi_t \sigma_t dW_t - \Big(\gamma\pi_t X^\pi_t \mu_t \\
&\quad - \tfrac{1}{2}\gamma^2\pi_t^2(X^\pi_t)^2\sigma_t^2\Big)dt\Big),
\end{aligned}
$$

which leads to

$$
d(e^{-\gamma X^\pi_t}Y_t) + c_t e^{-\gamma X^\pi_t}dt = e^{-\gamma X^\pi_t}\Big((\xi_t - \gamma Y_t \pi_t X^\pi_t \sigma_t)dW_t \\
- \Big(\pi_t(\gamma Y_t X^\pi_t \mu_t + \gamma\xi_t X^\pi_t \sigma_t) - \tfrac{1}{2}\pi_t^2\gamma^2 Y_t(X^\pi_t)^2\sigma_t^2\Big)dt + dA_t\Big).
$$

Therefore, we have

$$\pi^* = \frac{Y_t\mu_t + \xi_t\sigma_t}{\gamma Y_t X^\pi_t \sigma_t^2},$$

and

$$dA_t = \frac{(Y_t\mu_t + \xi_t\sigma_t)^2}{Y_t\sigma_t^2}dt.$$

Therefore, the process Y satisfies the following backward stochastic differential equation

$$dY_t = \Big(-c_t + \frac{(Y_t\mu_t + \xi_t\sigma_t)^2}{Y_t\sigma_t^2}\Big)dt + \xi_t dW_t, \quad Y_T = -G_T.$$

1.5. Brownian-Poisson filtration with general utility weights

In this section, we consider the portfolio optimization problem under the Brownian–Poisson filtration. Let W be an m-dimensional Brownian motion and N be an m'-dimensional Poisson process. Let Λ be the compensator process of N and $M = N - \Lambda$ be the compensated Poisson process. Let λ be the density process of Λ, namely,

$$\Lambda_t = \int_0^t \lambda_s ds.$$

We assume that W and N are independent and that the filtration $\mathbb{G}$ is generated by W and N. Recall that the martingale representation theorem (see Brémaud [BRÉ 81] for the Poisson setting and Jacod-Shiryaev [JAC 03] for the Brownian-Poisson setting) asserts that any square integrable $(\mathbb{G}, \mathbb{P})$-martingale X can be written in the form:

$$X_t = X_0 + \int_0^t \xi_t \cdot (W_t, M_t), \quad t \in [0, T],$$

where $\xi = (\xi^W, \xi^M)$ is an $(m + m')$-dimensional $\mathbb{G}$-predictable processes. We consider a portfolio of n assets (with $n \leq m + m'$) whose price process is determined by the following stochastic differential equation

$$dS_t = S_{t-} * \left(\mu_t dt + \sigma_t (dW_t, dM_t)' \right),$$

where μ is an n-dimensional $\mathbb{G}$-predictable process on $[0, T]$, and $\sigma = (\sigma^W, \sigma^M)$ is a $\mathbb{G}$-predictable process on $[0, T]$ valued in $\mathbb{R}^{n \times (m+m')}$.

Let $\mathcal{A}$ be the set of $\mathbb{G}$-predictable processes π on $[0, T]$ valued in $\mathbb{R}^n$ such that

$$\mathbb{E}^{\mathbb{P}} \left[\int_0^T (|\pi_t \cdot \mu_t| + \|(\sigma_t^W)' \pi_t\|^2 + \|(\sigma_t^M)' \pi_t\|) dt \right] < +\infty$$

and that the entries of the matrix $\pi_t \sigma_t^M$ are all > -1.

For $\pi \in \mathcal{A}$, let X^π be the portfolio value associated with the investment strategy π, namely, X^π is determined by the following stochastic differential equation

$$dX_t^\pi = X_{t-}^\pi ((\pi_t \cdot \mu_t) dt + \pi_t \cdot \sigma_t^W dW_t + \pi_t \cdot \sigma_t^M dM_t), \quad X_0^\pi = X_0.$$

In particular, we have

$$\frac{\Delta X_t^\pi}{X_{t-}^\pi} = \pi_t \cdot \sigma_t^M \Delta N_t. \qquad [1.54]$$

We consider the following optimization problem

$$V_0(X_0) = \sup_{\pi \in \mathcal{A}} \mathbb{E}^{\mathbb{P}}[G_T U(X_T^\pi) + F_T^\pi(X_0)],$$

where the additive utility weight $F^\pi(X_0)$ is of the form

$$F_t^\pi(X_0) = \int_0^t f(s, \pi_s, X_s^\pi)ds, \quad t \in [0, T]$$

where $f(t, \cdot, \cdot)$ is a $\mathbb{G} \otimes \mathcal{B}(\mathbb{R}^n) \otimes \mathcal{B}(\mathbb{R})$-adapted process. We also consider the dynamic version of the optimization problem

$$V_t(X_t) = \operatorname*{ess\,sup}_{\varphi \in \mathcal{A}_{t,T}} \mathbb{E}^{\mathbb{P}}[G_T U(X_T^\varphi) + F_T^\varphi(X_0) \mid \mathcal{G}_t],$$

with $\mathcal{A}_{t,T}$ being the set of the restriction on $[t, T]$ of investment strategies in $\mathcal{A}$, where X^φ is determined by the following stochastic differential equation

$$dX_s^\varphi = X_{s-}^\varphi((\varphi_s \cdot \mu_s)ds + \varphi_s \cdot \sigma_s^W dW_s + \varphi_s \cdot \sigma_s^M dM_s), \quad X_t^\varphi = X_t,$$

and

$$F_T^\varphi(X_t) = \int_t^T f(s, \varphi_s, X_s^\varphi)ds.$$

By theorem 1.3, for any investment strategy $\pi \in \mathcal{A}$, the process

$$V_t(X_t^\pi) + F_t^\pi(X_0) = V_t(X_t^\pi) + \int_0^t f(s, \pi_s, X_s^\pi)ds$$

is a $(\mathbb{G}, \mathbb{P})$-supermartingle. It is a $(\mathbb{G}, \mathbb{P})$-martingale if and only if π is the optimal investment strategy. We assume that the $(\mathbb{G}, \mathbb{P})$-martingale

$$G_t = \mathbb{E}[G_T \mid \mathcal{G}_t], \quad t \in [0, T]$$

satisfies the following stochastic differential equation

$$dG_t = G_{t-}\left(b_t^W \cdot dW_t + b_t^M \cdot dM_t\right),$$

where $b = (b^W, b^M)$ is a $\mathbb{G}$-predictable process valued in $\mathbb{R}^{m+m'}$.

1.5.1. *Logarithmic utility*

In this section, we assume that $U(x) = \log(x)$. We assume that the additive utility weight is of the form

$$F_T^\pi(X_0) = \int_0^T \left(c_t \log(X_t^\pi) + g(t, \pi_t) \right) dt.$$

For $t \in [0, T]$, let

$$Y_t = \operatorname*{ess\,sup}_{\varphi \in \mathcal{A}_{t,T}} \mathbb{E}^{\mathbb{P}} \left[G_T \log(X_T^{\varphi,1}) + \int_t^T \left(c_s \log(X_s^{\varphi,1}) + g(s, \varphi_s) \right) ds \,\bigg|\, \mathcal{G}_t \right],$$

where $X^{\varphi,1}$ is the solution of the following stochastic differential equation on $[t, T]$,

$$dX_s^{\varphi,1} = X_{s-}^{\varphi,1} \left((\varphi_s \cdot \mu_s) ds + \varphi_s \cdot \sigma_s^W dW_s + \varphi_s \cdot \sigma_s^M dM_s \right), \quad X_t^{\varphi,1} = 1.$$

We can then rewrite $V_t(X_t^\pi)$ as

$$V_t(X_t^\pi) = \log(X_t^\pi) G_t + \log(X_t^\pi) \mathbb{E}^{\mathbb{P}} \left[\int_t^T c_s \, ds \,\bigg|\, \mathcal{G}_t \right] + Y_t.$$

Hence,

$$V_t(X_t^\pi) + F_t^\pi(X_0) = \log(X_t^\pi) \left(G_t + \mathbb{E}^{\mathbb{P}} \left[\int_0^T c_s ds \,\bigg|\, \mathcal{G}_t \right] \right) \\ - \log(X_t^\pi) \int_0^t c_s ds + \int_0^t \left(c_s \log(X_s^\pi) + g(s, \pi_s) \right) ds + Y_t.$$

We let H be the martingale

$$H_t = \mathbb{E}^{\mathbb{P}} \left[\int_0^T c_s ds \,\bigg|\, \mathcal{G}_t \right],$$

which is written as

$$H_t = H_0 + \int_0^t \eta_s^W dW_s + \int_0^t \eta_s^M dM_s.$$

Since the process $(V_t(X_t^\pi) + F_t^\pi(X_0),\ t \in [0, T])$ is a $(\mathbb{G}, \mathbb{P})$-martingale for any investment strategy π, we obtain (by taking $\pi = 0$) that the process

$$\int_0^t g(s, 0)ds + Y_t, \quad t \in [0, T]$$

is a $(\mathbb{G}, \mathbb{P})$-supermartingale. Then, there exists a decreasing process A and an $(m + m')$-dimensional $\mathbb{G}$-predictable process $\xi = (\xi^W, \xi^M)$ such that

$$dY_t + g(t, 0)dt = \xi_t^W \cdot dW_t + \xi_t^M \cdot dM_t + dA_t.$$

By Itô's formula for semimartingales, we have

$$\log(X_t^\pi) = \log(X_0) + \int_0^t \frac{dX_s^\pi}{X_{s-}^\pi} - \frac{1}{2} \int_0^t \|(\sigma_s^W)'\pi_s\|^2 dt$$
$$+ \sum_{s \le t} \left(\log\left(\frac{X_s^\pi}{X_{s-}^\pi}\right) - \frac{\Delta X_s^\pi}{X_{s-}^\pi} \right).$$

By [1.54], we have

$$\sum_{s \le t} \left(\log\left(\frac{X_s^\pi}{X_{s-}^\pi}\right) - \frac{\Delta X_s^\pi}{X_{s-}^\pi} \right) = \int_0^t \left(\log(1 + (\sigma_s^M)'\pi_s) - (\sigma_s^M)'\pi_s \right) \cdot dN_s,$$

where for $(x_1, \cdots, x_{m'})$, the expression

$$\log(1 + (x_1, \cdots, x_{m'})) - (x_1, \cdots, x_{m'})$$

denotes the vector

$$(\log(1 + x_1) - x_1, \cdots, \log(1 + x_{m'}) - x_{m'}).$$

Therefore, we obtain

$$d(\log(X_t^\pi)) = \pi_t \cdot \sigma_t^W dW_t + \log(1 + (\sigma_t^M)'\pi_t) \cdot dM_t$$
$$- \frac{1}{2} \int_0^t \|(\sigma_s^W)'\pi_s\|^2 dt + \left(\pi_t \cdot \mu_t + \left(\log(1 + (\sigma_s^M)'\pi_s) \right) \right.$$
$$\left. - (\sigma_s^M)'\pi_s) \cdot \lambda_t \right) dt$$

We deduce that

$$
\begin{aligned}
&d((G_t + H_t)\log(X_t^\pi)) \\
&= (G_{t-} + H_{t-})d\log(X_t^\pi) + \log(X_{t-}^\pi)(dG_t + dH_t) \\
&+ ((G_{t-}b_t^W + \eta_t^W) \cdot (\sigma_t^W)'\pi_t)dt + (\log(1 + (\sigma_t^M)'\pi_t) * (G_{t-}b_t^M + \eta_t^M)) \cdot dN_t \\
&= ((G_{t-} + H_{t-})(\sigma_t^W)'\pi_t + \log(X_{t-}^\pi)(G_{t-}b_t^W + \eta_t^W)) \cdot dW_t \\
&+ \Big[(G_{t-} + H_{t-})\log(1 + (\sigma_t^M)'\pi_t) + \log(X_{t-}^\pi)(G_{t-}b_t^M + \eta_t^M) \\
&\quad + \big(\log(1 + (\sigma_t^M)'\pi_t) * (G_{t-}b_t^M + \eta_t^M)\big)\Big] \cdot dM_t \\
&+ \Big[(G_{t-} + H_{t-})\Big(\pi_t \cdot \mu_t + \big(\log(1 + (\sigma_s^M)'\pi_s) - (\sigma_s^M)'\pi_s\big) \cdot \lambda_t - \tfrac{1}{2}\|(\sigma_t^W)'\pi_t\|^2\Big) \\
&+ ((G_{t-}b_t^W + \eta_t^W) \cdot (\sigma_t^W)'\pi_t) + \big(\log(1 + (\sigma_t^M)'\pi_t) * (G_{t-}b_t^M + \eta_t^M)\big) \cdot \lambda_t\Big]dt.
\end{aligned}
$$

We let $C_t := \int_0^t c_s ds$ for $t \in [0,T]$. Then,

$$
\begin{aligned}
&d(\log(X_t^\pi)C_t) = C_t d\log X_t^\pi + \log X_t^\pi c_t dt \\
&= C_t\pi_t \cdot \sigma_t^W dW_t + C_t\log(1 + (\sigma_t^M)'\pi_t) \cdot dM_t + \log X_t^\pi c_t dt \\
&+ C_t\Big(\pi_t \cdot \mu_t + \big(\log(1 + (\sigma_t^M)'\pi_t) - (\sigma_t^M)'\pi_t\big) \cdot \lambda_t - \tfrac{1}{2}\|(\sigma_t^W)'\pi_t\|^2\Big)dt.
\end{aligned}
$$

Therefore, we obtain that

$$
dA_t = a_t dt,
$$

with

$$
\begin{aligned}
a_t = \operatorname{esssup}_{\pi \in \mathcal{A}}\Big[&g(t,\pi_t) - g(t,0) + (G_{t-} + H_{t-} - C_t) \\
&\cdot\Big(\pi_t \cdot \mu_t - \tfrac{1}{2}\|(\sigma_t^W)'\pi_t\|^2 + \big(\log(1 + (\sigma_t^M)'\pi_t) - (\sigma_t^M)'\pi_t\big) \cdot \lambda_t\Big) \\
&+ \big(\log(1 + (\sigma_t^M)'\pi_t) * (G_{t-}b_t^M + \eta_t^M)\big) \cdot \lambda_t + ((G_{t-}b_t^W + \eta_t^W) \cdot (\sigma_t^W)'\pi_t)\Big].
\end{aligned}
$$

Enlargement of Filtration

The enlargement of filtration plays a key role in both the study of credit risks and asymmetric information risks. In the study of credit risks, we often consider a subfiltration of the market filtration, representing the market information which is not directly related with the default event. Then, the market filtration corresponds to the progressive enlargement of the auxiliary subfiltration by the default event. In the study of asymmetric information risks, we consider insiders who possess more information than usual investors in the market. Hence, the information filtration of the insider is in general larger than the market filtration. According to different types of insiders, such filtration could be an initial enlargement of the market filtration, corresponding to the information that the insider acquires from the beginning, or a progressive enlargement by an observation filtration, corresponding to the information that the insider acquires along the timeline.

In this chapter, we recall some results in the theory of enlargement of filtration. For simplicity, we fix a finite time horizon $T > 0$. Let $(\Omega, \mathcal{G}, \mathbb{P})$ be a complete probability space and $\mathbb{F} = (\mathcal{F}_t)_{t \in [0,T]}$ be a filtration of the σ-algebra $\mathcal{G}$ satisfying the usual conditions. By *initial enlargement* of $\mathbb{F}$, we refer to a filtration of the form

$$\mathbb{F} \vee \mathcal{G}_0 := (\mathcal{F}_t \vee \mathcal{G}_0)_{t \in [0,T]},$$

where $\mathcal{G}_0$ is a sub-σ-algebra of $\mathcal{G}$. In practice, $\mathcal{G}_0$ is often given by the σ-algebra of a random variable. By *progressive enlargement* of $\mathbb{F}$, we refer to a filtration of the form

$$\mathbb{F} \vee \mathbb{D} := (\mathcal{F}_t \vee \mathcal{D}_t)_{t \in [0,T]},$$

where $\mathbb{D} = (\mathcal{D}_t)_{t\in[0,T]}$ is another filtration of $\mathcal{G}$. A typical example of $\mathbb{D}$ is the filtration associated with the default process $D = (\mathbb{1}_{\{\tau \leq t\}})_{t\in[0,T]}$ of a random time τ. In this case, the progressive enlargement $\mathbb{F} \vee \mathbb{D}$ is the smallest filtration containing $\mathbb{F}$ such that the random time τ becomes a stopping time.

The stochastic calculus in the context of enlargement of filtration is much more complex than the usual study within a fixed filtration. In fact, in general, it is not clear that an $\mathbb{F}$-semimartingale remains a semimartingale if we consider it as an adapted process with respect to the enlarged filtration. The fundamental works of Jacod [JAC 85] (see also, Jeulin [JEU 80]) highlight the importance of the $\mathbb{F}$-conditional density in the semimartingale property in the context of the initial enlargement of filtration. Jacod's approach has been widely used in the study of insider information risks. See, for example, the works of Grorud and Pontier [GRO 98], and Amendinger's thesis [AME 99].

In the study of credit risks, the research has been more focused on the modeling of the default mechanism (the structural approach), or the compensator of the default process (the intensity-based approach). We refer the readers to the paper of Elliott, Jeanblanc and Yor [ELL 00] and the book of Bielecki and Rutkowski [BIE 02] for the application of the theory of enlargement of filtrations to the credit risks. Besides the intensity approach, the density approach of Jacod provides a suitable generalization of default modeling since the default intensity is not enough to describe the impact of the default event on the financial market (see [ELK 10]).

The chapter is organized as follows. We first introduce and discuss the density hypothesis. We then give some technical results about martingale measures and martingale decomposition in the framework of initial and noisy initial enlargement of filtration, and finally for progressive enlargement of filtration. Throughout the chapter, we fix a complete probability space $(\Omega, \mathcal{G}, \mathbb{P})$, a finite time horizon $T > 0$ and a reference filtration $\mathbb{F} = (\mathcal{F}_t)_{t\in[0,T]}$.

2.1. Conditional law and density hypothesis

Let L be a $\mathcal{G}$-measurable map from Ω to a Polish space E (equipped with its Borel σ-algebra $\mathcal{E}$). We denote by η^L the probability law of L. It is a Borel probability measure on E which sends any Borel subset A of E to $\mathbb{P}(L \in A)$.

Let $\mathcal{F}$ be a sub-σ-algebra of $\mathcal{G}$. It is a classical result in the theory of disintegration (see, for example, Kallenberg [KAL 02] theorem 5.4) that there exists a regular version of the $\mathcal{F}$-conditional probability law of L, which is a map $\mathbb{P}(L \in \cdot \mid \mathcal{F})$ from $\Omega \times \mathcal{E}$ to $[0, 1]$, sending $(\omega, A) \in \Omega \times \mathcal{E}$ to $\mathbb{P}(L \in A \mid \mathcal{F})(\omega)$, which verifies the following conditions:

1) for any $\omega \in \Omega$, $(A \in \mathcal{E}) \mapsto \mathbb{P}(L \in A \mid \mathcal{F})(\omega)$ is a Borel probability measure on E;

2) for any Borel set A in E, the random variable $(\omega \in \Omega) \mapsto \mathbb{P}(L \in A \mid \mathcal{F})(\omega)$ is $\mathcal{G}$-measurable, which is $\mathbb{P}$-almost surely equal to the $\mathcal{F}$-conditional expectation $\mathbb{E}^{\mathbb{P}}[\mathbb{1}_A(L) \mid \mathcal{F}]$.

Note that the Polish space E admits a countable topological basis. Hence, the Borel σ-algebra $\mathcal{E}$ is generated by a countable family of elements. In particular, two regular versions of the $\mathcal{F}$-conditional probability law of L only differ on a $\mathbb{P}$-negligible subset of Ω.

DEFINITION 2.1.– *We say that the random variable L satisfies the* conditional density hypothesis *(with respect to the filtration $\mathbb{F}$) if there exists a (strictly) positive $\mathcal{F}_T \otimes \mathcal{E}$-measurable function $p_T(\cdot)$ on $\Omega \times E$ such that*

$$\eta_T^L(d\ell) = p_T(\ell)\, \eta^L(d\ell), \quad \mathbb{P}\text{-a.s.},$$

where η_T^L denotes a regular version of the $\mathcal{F}_T$-conditional probability law of L. In other words, the $\mathcal{F}_T$-conditional probability law of L is equivalent to the probability law of L. The random function $p_T(\cdot)$ is called the $\mathcal{F}_T$-conditional density *of the random variable L under the probability measure $\mathbb{P}$.*

REMARK 2.1.– Note that the above definition does not depend on the choice of the regular version of the $\mathcal{F}_T$-conditional probability law of L since any pair of such regular versions only differ on a $\mathbb{P}$-negligible set. Moreover, a non-negative $\mathcal{F}_T \otimes \mathcal{E}$-measurable function $p_T(\cdot)$ is the $\mathcal{F}_T$-conditional density of L under the probability $\mathbb{P}$ if and only if it is the Radon–Nikodym derivative of the measure $X_T(\cdot) \mapsto \mathbb{E}^{\mathbb{P}}[X_T(L)]$ on $\mathcal{F}_T \otimes \mathcal{E}$ with respect to the product measure $\mathbb{P} \otimes \eta^L$. In particular, $p_T(\cdot)$ is unique up to a $\mathbb{P} \otimes \eta^L$-negligible function.

The following proposition shows that the density hypothesis is invariant under change of probability measure. This property is important for the applications in financial mathematics.

PROPOSITION 2.1.– We assume that the random variable L satisfies the conditional density hypothesis and admits $p_T(\cdot)$ as its $\mathcal{F}_T$-conditional density under the probability $\mathbb{P}$. Let $\mathbb{P}'$ be a probability measure on $(\Omega, \mathcal{G})$ which is equivalent to $\mathbb{P}$ and let $q_T(L)$ be the Radon–Nikodym derivative $d\mathbb{P}'/d\mathbb{P}$ on

$\mathcal{F}_T \vee \sigma(L)$. Then, the random variable L also admits an $\mathcal{F}_T$-conditional density under the probability $\mathbb{P}'$, which is given by

$$p'_T(x) = \frac{p_T(x)q_T(x)}{\mathbb{E}^{\mathbb{P}}[p_T(x)q_T(x)]} \cdot \frac{1}{\int_E q_T(\ell)p_T(\ell)\eta^L(d\ell)}, \quad x \in E. \qquad [2.1]$$

PROOF.– For any non-negative Borel function f on E, we have

$$\mathbb{E}^{\mathbb{P}'}[f(L) \mid \mathcal{F}_T] = \frac{\mathbb{E}^{\mathbb{P}}[f(L)q_T(L) \mid \mathcal{F}_T]}{\mathbb{E}^{\mathbb{P}}[q_T(L) \mid \mathcal{F}_T]} = \frac{\int_E f(\ell)q_T(\ell)p_T(\ell)\eta^L(d\ell)}{\int_E q_T(\ell)p_T(\ell)\eta^L(d\ell)}.$$

Moreover, we have

$$\mathbb{E}^{\mathbb{P}'}[f(L)] = \mathbb{E}^{\mathbb{P}}[f(L)q_T(L)] = \mathbb{E}^{\mathbb{P}}\left[\int_E f(\ell)q_T(\ell)p_T(\ell)\eta^L(d\ell)\right]$$
$$= \int_E f(\ell)\mathbb{E}^{\mathbb{P}}[q_T(\ell)p_T(\ell)]\eta^L(d\ell).$$

Therefore, the $\mathcal{F}_T$-conditional law of L under the probability $\mathbb{P}'$ is equivalent to the $\mathbb{P}'$-probability law of L and the corresponding Radon–Nikodym density is $p'_T(\cdot)$.   □

The density hypothesis allows us to construct a new probability measure on $(\Omega, \mathcal{G})$ under which the random variable L is independent of $\mathcal{F}_T$. This construction is a key point in Jacod's approach to the semimartingale problem in the initial enlargement of filtration.

PROPOSITION 2.2.– Assume that the random variable L satisfies the conditional density hypothesis with respect to the filtration $\mathbb{F}$ and let $p_T(\cdot)$ be the $\mathcal{F}_T$-conditional density of L. Then, we have $\mathbb{E}^{\mathbb{P}}[p_T(L)^{-1}] = 1$. Moreover, if we let $\mathbb{Q}$ be the probability measure on $(\Omega, \mathcal{G})$ such that $d\mathbb{Q} = p_T(L)^{-1}d\mathbb{P}$, then the following assertions hold:

1) $\mathbb{Q}$ identifies with $\mathbb{P}$ on $\mathcal{F}_T$ and on $\sigma(L)$;

2) the σ-algebra $\sigma(L)$ and $\mathcal{F}_T$ are independent under $\mathbb{Q}$.

PROOF.– By definition, we have

$$\mathbb{E}^{\mathbb{P}}[p_T(L)^{-1}] = \mathbb{E}^{\mathbb{P}}\left[\int_E p_T(\ell)^{-1}\eta_T^L(d\ell)\right]$$
$$= \mathbb{E}^{\mathbb{P}}\left[\int_E p_T(\ell)^{-1}p_T(\ell)\eta^L(d\ell)\right] = 1.$$

Therefore, the probability measure $\mathbb{Q}$ is well-defined.

Let X_T be a non-negative $\mathcal{F}_T$-measurable random variable and f be a non-negative Borel function on E. We have

$$\mathbb{E}^{\mathbb{Q}}[X_T f(L)] = \mathbb{E}^{\mathbb{P}}[X_T f(L) p_T(L)^{-1}] = \mathbb{E}^{\mathbb{P}}\left[X_T \int_E f(\ell) p_T(\ell)^{-1} \eta_T^L(d\ell)\right]$$
$$= \mathbb{E}^{\mathbb{P}}[X_T] \int_E f(\ell) \eta^L(d\ell) = \mathbb{E}^{\mathbb{P}}[X_T] \cdot \mathbb{E}^{\mathbb{P}}[f(L)].$$

If we take $X_T = 1$, we obtain $\mathbb{E}^{\mathbb{Q}}[f(L)] = \mathbb{E}^{\mathbb{P}}[f(L)]$. If we take f as the constant function with value 1, we obtain $\mathbb{E}^{\mathbb{Q}}[X_T] = \mathbb{E}^{\mathbb{P}}[X_T]$. Hence, the probability measures $\mathbb{P}$ and $\mathbb{Q}$ coincide on $\mathcal{F}_T$ and on $\sigma(L)$. This also implies that

$$\mathbb{E}^{\mathbb{Q}}[X_T f(L)] = \mathbb{E}^{\mathbb{Q}}[X_T] \mathbb{E}^{\mathbb{Q}}[f(L)].$$

Namely, $\mathcal{F}_T$ and $\sigma(L)$ are independent under the probability measure $\mathbb{Q}$.

$\square$

REMARK 2.2.– We can actually prove the equivalence between the conditional density hypothesis and the existence of an equivalent probability measure that coincides with $\mathbb{P}$ on $\mathcal{F}_T$ and $\sigma(L)$ and under which $\mathcal{F}_T$ and $\sigma(L)$ are independent. In fact, if such an equivalent probability measure exists, then under this probability measure the $\mathcal{F}_T$-conditional law of L almost surely identifies with the probability law of L. Therefore, the conditional density hypothesis is trivially satisfied with the constant conditional density 1. By proposition 2.1, we find that the conditional density hypothesis is satisfied with respect to the initial probability measure. Moreover, the probability measure $\mathbb{Q}$ constructed in proposition 2.2 is the only one that is identical to $\mathbb{P}$ on $\mathcal{F}_T$. We refer the readers to Grorud and Pontier [GRO 98] for more details and for the applications in the modeling of insider information.

COROLLARY 2.1.– If the random variable L satisfies the conditional density hypothesis, then for any intermediate time $t \in [0, T]$ the $\mathcal{F}_t$-conditional law of L is equivalent to the probability law of L. Moreover, if $p_T(\cdot)$ is the $\mathcal{F}_T$-conditional density of L and if $p_t(\cdot)$ is an $\mathcal{F}_t \otimes \mathcal{E}$-measurable function such that $p_t(x) = \mathbb{E}^{\mathbb{P}}[p_T(x) \,|\, \mathcal{F}_t]$ $\mathbb{P}$-a.s. for any $x \in E$, then $p_t(\cdot)$ is the $\mathcal{F}_t$-conditional density of L, and the Radon–Nikodym density $d\mathbb{Q}/d\mathbb{P}$ on $\mathcal{F}_t \vee \sigma(L)$ is $p_t(L)^{-1}$.

PROOF.– Under the probability measure $\mathbb{Q}$ constructed in the previous proposition, the random variable L is independent of $\mathcal{F}_T$, hence it is also independent of $\mathcal{F}_t$. In particular, its $\mathcal{F}_t$-conditional probability law coincides with the probability law under the probability measure $\mathbb{Q}$. Since the density hypothesis is invariant under any change of probability measure (see proposition 2.1), we obtain that the random variable L satisfies the density hypothesis at time t.

We claim that $p_t(L)$ is the Radon–Nikodym derivative $d\mathbb{P}/d\mathbb{Q}$ on $\mathcal{F}_t \vee \sigma(L)$. In fact, if $X_t(\cdot)$ is a non-negative $\mathcal{F}_t \otimes \mathcal{E}$-measurable function, then by the independence between $\mathcal{F}_T$ and $\sigma(L)$ we have

$$\mathbb{E}^{\mathbb{Q}}[p_t(L)X_t(L)] = \int_E \mathbb{E}^{\mathbb{Q}}[p_t(\ell)X_t(\ell)]\eta^L(d\ell) = \int_E \mathbb{E}^{\mathbb{P}}[p_t(\ell)X_t(\ell)]\eta^L(d\ell),$$

where we have also used the fact that $\mathbb{Q}$ coincides with $\mathbb{P}$ on $\mathcal{F}_T$ and on $\sigma(L)$. Since $p_t(\ell) = \mathbb{E}^{\mathbb{P}}[p_T(\ell) \mid \mathcal{F}_t]$ $\mathbb{P}$-a.s., we obtain

$$
\begin{aligned}
\mathbb{E}^{\mathbb{Q}}[p_t(L)X_t(L)] &= \int_E \mathbb{E}^{\mathbb{P}}[p_T(\ell)X_t(\ell)]\eta^L(d\ell) \\
&= \mathbb{E}^{\mathbb{P}}\left[\int_E X_t(\ell)\eta_T^L(d\ell) \right] = \mathbb{E}^{\mathbb{P}}[X_t(L)].
\end{aligned}
$$

Finally, since the constant function 1 is the $\mathcal{F}_t$-conditional density of L under the probability $\mathbb{Q}$, by remark 2.1(b) we obtain that $p_t(\cdot)$ is the $\mathcal{F}_t$-conditional density of L under the probability $\mathbb{P}$. We actually apply the formula [2.1] and the following facts

$$\int_E p_t(x)\eta^L(dx) = \mathbb{E}^{\mathbb{P}}\left[\int_E p_T(x)\eta^L(dx) \,\Big|\, \mathcal{F}_t \right] = 1 \quad \mathbb{P}\text{-a.s.,} \qquad [2.2]$$

$$\mathbb{E}^{\mathbb{P}}[p_t(x)] = \mathbb{E}^{\mathbb{P}}[p_T(x)] = 1 \quad \eta\text{-a.e.,} \qquad [2.3]$$

to determine the $\mathcal{F}_t$-conditional density of L under $\mathbb{P}$. Both formulas result from the relation

$$\int_E f(x)p_T(x)\,\eta^L(dx) = \int_E f(x)\,\eta_T^L(dx) = \mathbb{E}^{\mathbb{P}}[f(L) \mid \mathcal{F}_T] \quad \mathbb{P}\text{-a.s.} \qquad [2.4]$$

which is valid for any non-negative Borel function f on E. In fact, if we take f as the constant function 1 in [2.4], we obtain

$$\int_E p_T(x)\,\eta^L(dx) = 1 \quad \mathbb{P}\text{-a.s.,}$$

which implies [2.2]. Moreover, if we take the expectation with respect to $\mathbb{P}$ on both sides of [2.4], we obtain

$$\int_E f(x)\mathbb{E}^{\mathbb{P}}[p_T(x)]\,\eta^L(dx) = \mathbb{E}^{\mathbb{P}}[f(L)] = \int_E f(x)\,\eta^L(dx),$$

which leads to [2.3]. The corollary is thus proved. $\qquad\qquad\square$

REMARK 2.3.– According to Jacod [JAC 85, lemma 1.8], there exists a càdlàg stochastic process $(p_t(\cdot))_{t\in[0,T]}$ on the measurable space $(\Omega\times E, \mathcal{A}\otimes\mathcal{E})$, which is $(\mathcal{F}_t\otimes\mathcal{E})_{t\in[0,T]}$-adapted, such that

1) $p_t(\cdot)$ is a regular version of the $\mathcal{F}_t$-conditional density of L;

2) for any $x\in E$, $(p_t(x))_{t\in[0,T]}$ is a càdlàg $(\mathbb{P},\mathbb{F})$-martingale.

We call it a *càdlàg martingale version* of the conditional density process of L.

EXAMPLE 2.1.– Let $\mathbb{F}$ be the filtration associated with a Brownian motion W. Consider the random variable $L = (\lambda/\sqrt{T})W_T + \sqrt{1-\lambda^2}Y$, where $\lambda \in (0,1)$ and Y is a random variable which follows the standard Gaussian law and which is independent of $\mathcal{F}_T$. Note that the random variable L also follows the standard Gaussian law. Moreover, the $\mathcal{F}_T$-conditional law of L is $N((\lambda/\sqrt{T})W_T, 1 - \lambda^2)$. Therefore, the random variable L satisfies the conditional density hypothesis with the $\mathcal{F}_T$-conditional density

$$p_T(x) = \frac{1}{\sqrt{1-\lambda^2}}\exp\left(\frac{x^2}{2} - \frac{(x - \lambda W_T/\sqrt{T})^2}{2(1-\lambda^2)}\right).$$

We refer the readers to Karatzas and Pikovsky [PIK 96] for more details and applications in portfolio optimization.

2.2. Initial enlargement of filtration

One way to enlarge the reference filtration $\mathbb{F}$ is to consider the *initial enlargement* of the filtration $\mathbb{F}$ by the random variable L, namely, the filtration $\mathbb{G} = (\mathcal{G}_t)_{t\in[0,T]}$ where

$$\forall t \in [0,T], \quad \mathcal{G}_t = \mathcal{F}_t \vee \sigma(L).$$

Note that any $\mathcal{G}_t$-measurable random variable can be written in the form $X_t(L)$, where $X_t(\cdot)$ is an $\mathcal{F}_t \otimes \mathcal{E}$-measurable function on $\Omega \times E$. This enlarged filtration typically models the information flow of an insider whose private information consists of the knowledge of the random variable L from the beginning, which is called an *initial strong information*. For example, L may be a functional of the price process S.

DEFINITION 2.2.– *The initial enlargement of the filtration* $\mathbb{F}$ *by the random variable* L *is the filtration* $\mathbb{G} = (\mathcal{G}_t)_{t \in [0,T]}$ *where*

$$\forall t \in [0, T], \quad \mathcal{G}_t = \mathcal{F}_t \vee \sigma(L).$$

The following proposition describes the predictable σ-algebra of the enlarged filtration $\mathbb{G}$.

PROPOSITION 2.3.– Let $\mathcal{P}(\mathbb{F})$ be the predictable σ-algebra of $\mathbb{F}$. A stochastic process Z is $\mathbb{G}$-predictable if and only if it can be written in the form $X(L)$, where $X(\cdot)$ is a $\mathcal{P}(\mathbb{F}) \otimes \mathcal{E}$-measurable function. In particular, the predictable σ-algebra of the filtration $\mathbb{G}$ identifies with $\mathcal{P}(\mathbb{F}) \vee \sigma(L)$, where we consider L as a constant stochastic process.

PROOF.– Recall that the $\mathbb{F}$-predictable σ-algebra is generated by the stochastic sets of the form $A \times [0, +\infty)$ with $A \in \mathcal{F}_0$ or of the form $B \times [s, t)$ with $0 < s < t \leq T$ and $B \in \mathcal{F}_{s-} := \bigcup_{u<s} \mathcal{F}_u$. The assertion of the proposition then follows from the fact that $\mathcal{G}_{t-} = \mathcal{F}_{t-} \vee \sigma(L)$ for any $t \in [0, T]$. □

In the remaining of the section, we assume that:

HYPOTHESES 2.1.– L satisfies the conditional density hypothesis at time $T > 0$ with respect to the filtration $\mathbb{F}$ (see definition 2.1).

We denote by $(p_t(\cdot))_{t \in [0,T]}$ a càdlàg martingale version of the conditional density process of L (see remark 2.3). Note that under the conditional density hypothesis, the enlargement filtration $\mathbb{G}$ is right-continuous (see Amendinger [AME 00] proposition 3.3), and hence verifies the usual conditions.

2.2.1. *Martingales of the enlarged filtration*

We will use the auxiliary product space $\Omega \times E$ and the change of probability measure on this space to study the initial enlargement of filtration. Let $\Gamma : \Omega \to \Omega \times E$ be the graph map of L, which sends $\omega \in \Omega$ to $(\omega, L(\omega))$. If $Y(\cdot)$ is a random variable on the product space $\Omega \times E$, then $Y(L)$ identifies with the composed map $Y(\cdot) \circ \Gamma$. In particular, the random variable L identifies with the second projection $\varpi : \Omega \times E \to E$ composed of the map Γ.

Let $\mathbb{P}'$ be the probability measure on $(\Omega \times E, \mathcal{G} \otimes \mathcal{E})$ such that, for any non-negative $\mathcal{G} \otimes \mathcal{E}$-measurable function Y on $\Omega \times E$, we have

$$\int_{\Omega \times E} Y(\omega, x)\, \mathbb{P}'(d\omega, dx) := \mathbb{E}^{\mathbb{P}}[Y(L)] = \int_{\Omega} Y(\omega, L(\omega))\, \mathbb{P}(d\omega). \quad [2.5]$$

We observe that the random variable ϖ on the probability space $(\Omega \times E, \mathcal{G} \otimes \mathcal{E}, \mathbb{P}')$ shares some common properties of the random variable L on $(\Omega, \mathcal{G}, \mathbb{P})$ and we can use it as a model to understand the random variable L and the initial enlargement of filtration $\mathbb{G}$.

PROPOSITION 2.4.– The probability law of ϖ under $\mathbb{P}'$ identifies with the probability law η^L under $\mathbb{P}$.

PROOF.– Let f be a non-negative Borel function on E. We have

$$\begin{aligned}
\mathbb{E}^{\mathbb{P}}[f(L)] &= \int_{\Omega} f(L(\omega))\, \mathbb{P}(d\omega) = \int_{\Omega \times E} f(x)\, \mathbb{P}'(d\omega, dx) \\
&= \int_{\Omega \times E} f(\varpi(\omega, x))\, \mathbb{P}'(d\omega, dx) = \mathbb{E}^{\mathbb{P}'}[f(\varpi)],
\end{aligned}$$

where the second equality comes from [2.5]. The proposition is thus proved. $\square$

The proposition shows that the second marginal law of the probability measure $\mathbb{P}'$ identifies with the probability law of L. Moreover, if X is a $\mathcal{G}$-measurable function, viewed as a random variable on $(\Omega \times E, \mathcal{G} \otimes \mathcal{E})$ sending (ω, x) to $X(\omega)$, then we have $\mathbb{E}^{\mathbb{P}}[X] = \mathbb{E}^{\mathbb{P}'}[X]$. Therefore, the first marginal law of the probability measure $\mathbb{P}'$ identifies with $\mathbb{P}$. Therefore, we may consider $\mathbb{P}'$ as a coupling of the probability measures $\mathbb{P}$ and η^L. We denote by $\mathbb{P}^{\circ}$ the product measure $\mathbb{P} \otimes \eta^L$ on $\Omega \times E$. The following proposition describes the relation between $\mathbb{P}'$ and $\mathbb{P}^{\circ}$.

PROPOSITION 2.5.– For any $t \in [0, T]$, the probability measure $\mathbb{P}'$ on $(\Omega \times E, \mathcal{F}_t \otimes \mathcal{E})$ is absolutely continuous with respect to $\mathbb{P}^{\circ}$, and admits $p_t(\cdot)$ as the Radon–Nikodym density $d\mathbb{P}'/d\mathbb{P}^{\circ}$ on $\mathcal{F}_t \otimes \mathcal{E}$.

PROOF.– Let $Y_t(\cdot)$ be a non-negative $\mathcal{F}_t \otimes \mathcal{E}$-measurable function on $\Omega \times E$. We have

$$\mathbb{E}^{\mathbb{P}'}[Y_t(\cdot)] = \mathbb{E}^{\mathbb{P}}[Y_t(L)] = \mathbb{E}^{\mathbb{Q}}[Y_t(L)p_t(L)],$$

where $\mathbb{Q}$ is the equivalent probability measure defined in proposition 2.2. Moreover, the random variable L is independent of $\mathcal{F}_t$ under the probability $\mathbb{Q}$ and the probability measures $\mathbb{P}$ and $\mathbb{Q}$ coincide on $\mathbb{F}_t$. Hence, we have

$$\begin{aligned}
\mathbb{E}^{\mathbb{Q}}[Y_t(L)p_t(L)] &= \int_{\Omega \times E} Y_t(\cdot)p_t(\cdot)\, d(\mathbb{Q} \otimes \eta^L) \\
&= \int_{\Omega \times E} Y_t(\cdot)p_t(\cdot)\, d(\mathbb{P} \otimes \eta^L) = \mathbb{E}^{\mathbb{P}^\circ}[Y_t(\cdot)p_t(\cdot)].
\end{aligned}$$

The proposition is thus proved.   □

Denote by $\mathbb{F} \otimes \mathcal{E}$ the filtration $(\mathcal{F}_t \otimes \mathcal{E})_{t \in [0,T]}$ on the product space $\Omega \times E$. Proposition 2.5 implies that the process $(p_t(\cdot))_{t \in [0,T]}$ is an $(\mathbb{F} \otimes \mathcal{E}, \mathbb{P}^\circ)$-martingale. More generally, we have the following criterion for $\mathbb{F} \otimes \mathcal{E}$-martingales.

PROPOSITION 2.6.– Let $X(\cdot)$ be an $\mathbb{F} \otimes \mathcal{E}$-adapted process on $[0,T]$. Then, it is an $(\mathbb{F} \otimes \mathcal{E}, \mathbb{P}')$-martingale if and only if the process $X(\cdot)p(\cdot)$ is an $(\mathbb{F} \otimes \mathcal{E}, \mathbb{P}^\circ)$-martingale.

PROOF.– Let s and t be two real numbers, $0 \leq s < t \leq T$. We have

$$\mathbb{E}^{\mathbb{P}'}[X_t(\cdot) \mid \mathcal{F}_s \otimes \mathcal{E}] = \mathbb{E}^{\mathbb{P}^\circ}\left[\frac{X_t(\cdot)p_t(\cdot)}{p_s(\cdot)} \,\Big|\, \mathcal{F}_s \otimes \mathcal{E}\right].$$

Therefore, $\mathbb{E}^{\mathbb{P}'}[X_t(\cdot) \mid \mathcal{F}_s \otimes \mathcal{E}] = X_s(\cdot)$ if and only if $\mathbb{E}^{\mathbb{P}^\circ}[X_t(\cdot)p_t(\cdot) \mid \mathcal{F}_s \otimes \mathcal{E}] = X_s(\cdot)p_s(\cdot)$.   □

PROPOSITION 2.7.– Let $X(\cdot)$ be an $\mathbb{F} \otimes \mathcal{E}$-adapted process on $[0,T]$ such that $(X_t(x)p_t(x))_{t \in [0,T]}$ is an $(\mathbb{F}, \mathbb{P})$-martingale for any $x \in E$. Then,

1) $X(\cdot)$ is an $(\mathbb{F} \otimes \mathcal{E}, \mathbb{P}')$-martingale.

2) $X(L)$ is an $(\mathbb{F}, \mathbb{P})$-martingale.

PROOF.–

1) Under the product probability measure $\mathbb{P}^\circ$, we have

$$\forall x \in E, \quad \mathbb{E}^{\mathbb{P}^\circ}[X_t(\cdot)p_t(\cdot) \mid \mathcal{F}_s \otimes \mathcal{E}](x) = X_s(x)p_s(x)$$

for $0 \leq s < t \leq T$. Therefore, $(X_t(\cdot)p_t(\cdot))_{t \in [0,T]}$ is an $(\mathbb{F} \otimes \mathcal{E}, \mathbb{P}^\circ)$-martingale. By proposition 2.6, we obtain that $X(\cdot)$ is an $(\mathbb{F} \otimes \mathcal{E}, \mathbb{P}')$-martingale.

2) By [2.5], for any $\mathcal{G} \otimes \mathcal{E}$-measurable function $Y(\cdot)$ we have $\mathbb{E}^{\mathbb{P}'}[Y(\cdot)] = \mathbb{E}^{\mathbb{P}}[Y(L)]$. In particular, for $0 \leq s < t \leq T$ and any bounded $\mathcal{F}_s \otimes \mathcal{E}$-measurable function $Y_s(\cdot)$ we have

$$\mathbb{E}^{\mathbb{P}}[Y_s(L)X_t(L)] = \mathbb{E}^{\mathbb{P}'}[Y_s(\cdot)X_t(\cdot)] = \mathbb{E}^{\mathbb{P}'}[Y_s(\cdot)X_s(\cdot)] = \mathbb{E}^{\mathbb{P}}[Y_s(L)X_s(L)]$$

since $X(\cdot)$ is an $(\mathbb{F} \otimes \mathcal{E}, \mathbb{P}')$-martingale. Therefore, $X(L)$ is an $(\mathbb{F}, \mathbb{P})$-martingale. $\qquad\square$

REMARK 2.4.– By using the equivalent probability measure $\mathbb{P}^\circ$, we can prove that any $(\mathbb{F} \otimes \mathcal{E}, \mathbb{P}^\circ)$-martingale admits a version $X(\cdot)$ such that $(X_t(x))_{t \in [0,T]}$ is a càdlàg $(\mathbb{F}, \mathbb{P})$-martingale for any $x \in E$. Similarly, any $(\mathbb{F} \otimes \mathcal{E}, \mathbb{P}')$-martingale admits a version $X(\cdot)$ such that $(X_t(x)p_t(x))_{x \in E}$ is a càdlàg $(\mathbb{F}, \mathbb{P})$-martingale for any $x \in E$. We refer the readers to a work of Meyer [MEY 79] on martingales depending on a parameter for more details. In particular, the filtrations $\mathbb{F} \otimes \mathcal{E}$ and $\mathbb{G}$ are right continuous (for the right continuity of the filtration $\mathbb{G}$, see [AME 00] proposition 3.3).

The following proposition gives an explicit form of the conditional expectation with respect to the filtration $\mathbb{G}$.

PROPOSITION 2.8.– Let $X_T(\cdot)$ be a non-negative $\mathcal{F}_T \otimes \mathcal{E}$-measurable random variable. For $t \in [0, T]$, we have

$$\mathbb{E}^{\mathbb{P}}[X_T(L) \mid \mathcal{F}_t \vee \sigma(L)] = \mathbb{E}^{\mathbb{P}}\left[\frac{X_T(x)p_T(x)}{p_t(x)} \,\Big|\, \mathcal{F}_t\right]_{x=L} \qquad [2.6]$$

PROOF.– Let $Y_t(\cdot)$ be a non-negative $\mathcal{F}_t \otimes \mathcal{E}$-measurable random variable. By [2.5], we have

$$\mathbb{E}^{\mathbb{P}}[X_T(L)Y_t(L)] = \mathbb{E}^{\mathbb{P}'}[X_T(\cdot)Y_t(\cdot)] = \mathbb{E}^{\mathbb{P}^\circ}[X_T(\cdot)Y_t(\cdot)p_T(\cdot)].$$

Moreover, we have

$$\begin{aligned}
&\mathbb{E}^{\mathbb{P}}\left[\mathbb{E}^{\mathbb{P}}\left[\tfrac{X_T(x)p_T(x)}{p_t(x)} \,\Big|\, \mathcal{F}_t\right]_{x=L} Y_t(L)\right] \\
&= \mathbb{E}^{\mathbb{P}'}\left[\mathbb{E}^{\mathbb{P}^\circ}\left[\tfrac{X_T(\cdot)p_T(\cdot)}{p_t(\cdot)} \,\Big|\, \mathcal{F}_t \otimes \mathcal{E}\right] Y_t(\cdot)p_t(\cdot)\right] \\
&= \mathbb{E}^{\mathbb{P}^\circ}\left[\mathbb{E}^{\mathbb{P}^\circ}\left[X_T(\cdot)p_T(\cdot) \mid \mathcal{F}_t \otimes \mathcal{E}\right] Y_t(\cdot)\right] = \mathbb{E}^{\mathbb{P}^\circ}[X_T(\cdot)p_T(\cdot)Y_t(\cdot)].
\end{aligned}$$

Therefore, the equality [2.6] is proved. $\qquad\square$

The following result due to Jacod shows that any local $\mathbb{F}$-martingale is a $\mathbb{G}$-semimartingale and gives its decomposition into the sum of a local $\mathbb{G}$-martingale and a $\mathbb{G}$-predictable process of finite variation.

PROPOSITION 2.9.– Let X be a local $(\mathbb{F}, \mathbb{P})$-martingale on $[0, T]$. Then, it is a $\mathbb{G}$-semimartingale. Moreover, its decomposition in the filtration $\mathbb{G}$ is given by

$$X_t = \widetilde{X}_t + \int_{]0,t]} \frac{d\langle p(x), X\rangle_s^{\mathbb{F},\mathbb{P}}}{p_{s-}(x)}\bigg|_{x=L},$$

where $\widetilde{X}$ is a local $(\mathbb{G}, \mathbb{P})$-martingale.

PROOF.– For any $t \in [0, T]$, let

$$A_t = \int_{]0,t]} \frac{d\langle p(x), X \rangle_s^{\mathbb{F},\mathbb{P}}}{p_{s-}(x)} \bigg|_{x=L}.$$

Let $\mathbb{Q}$ be the probability measure on $(\Omega, \mathcal{G})$ such that $d\mathbb{Q}/d\mathbb{P} = p_t(L)^{-1}$ on $\mathcal{G}_t$. Note that $\mathbb{Q}$ coincides with $\mathbb{P}$ on $\mathbb{F}$. Hence, X is a local $(\mathbb{F}, \mathbb{Q})$-martingale, and hence a local $(\mathbb{G}, \mathbb{Q})$-martingale since L is independent of $\mathbb{F}$ under the probability $\mathbb{Q}$. Note that $p(L)$ is also an $(\mathbb{G}, \mathbb{Q})$-martingale. Moreover, for any locally bounded $\mathbb{G}$-predictable process $Y(L)$, we have

$$\int_{]0,t]} Y_s(L) \, d\langle p(L), X \rangle_s^{\mathbb{G},\mathbb{Q}} = \int_{]0,t]} Y_s(x) \, d\langle p(x), X \rangle_s \bigg|_{x=L}. \qquad [2.7]$$

To show that $\widetilde{X} = X - A$ is a local $(\mathbb{G}, \mathbb{P})$-martingale, it suffices to show that $p(L)\widetilde{X} = p(L)(X - A)$ is a local $(\mathbb{G}, \mathbb{Q})$-martingale. We have

$$p_t(L)\widetilde{X}_t - p_0(L)\widetilde{X}_0 = \int_{]0,t]} p_{s-}(L) \, (dX_s - dA_s)$$
$$+ \widetilde{X}_{s-} \, dp_s(L) + d[p(L), X]_s - d[p(L), A]_s.$$

Note that

$$\int_{]0,t]} p_{s-}(L) dA_s = \int_{]0,t]} d\langle p(x), X \rangle_s \bigg|_{x=L} = \langle p(L), X \rangle_t^{\mathbb{G},\mathbb{Q}}.$$

Moreover, since $p(L)$ is a local $(\mathbb{G}, \mathbb{Q})$-martingale and A is a $\mathbb{G}$-predictable process, by [JAC 03, Chapter I, proposition 4.49] we obtain that $[p(L), A]$ is a local $(\mathbb{G}, \mathbb{Q})$-martingale. Therefore,

$$p_t(L)\widetilde{X}_t = p_0(L)\widetilde{X}_0 + \int_{]0,t]} p_{s-}(L) \, dX_s + \widetilde{X}_{s-} \, dp_s(L)$$
$$+ \left([p(L), X]_t - \langle p(L), X \rangle_t^{\mathbb{G},\mathbb{Q}} \right) - [p(L), A]_t, \quad t \in [0, T]$$

is a local $(\mathbb{G}, \mathbb{Q})$-martingale. The proposition is thus proved. $\qquad \square$

2.2.2. *Example of a Brownian-Poisson filtration and information drift*

We specify here the former results in a mixed diffusive-jump market model that will be considered in Chapter 4. We consider the filtration $\mathbb{F}$ generated by an m-dimensional standard Brownian motion W and an m'-dimensional Poisson process which are independent. We consider the initial enlargement $\mathbb{G}$ of $\mathbb{F}$ by a random variable L which admits an $\mathbb{F}$-conditional density $(p_t(\cdot))_{t \in [0,T]}$.

Under the enlarged filtration $\mathbb{G}$, the Brownian motion W and the compensated Poisson process M are no longer local martingales. Nevertheless, as shown by Jacod [JAC 79] and recalled previously, under assumption 2.1, they remain semimartingales. The bounded variation part in their semimartingale decomposition in $\mathbb{G}$ is called the *information drift*. The information drift is a key process in the resolution of the optimization problem for an insider and in the computation of the information value.

In this mixed diffusive-jump model, we apply the martingale representation theorem to the càdlàg martingale version of the conditional density of L:

$$dp_t(l) = \alpha_t(l).dW_t + \beta_t(l).dM_t \qquad [2.8]$$

where for all l, $t \to \alpha_t(l)$ and $t \to \beta_t(l)$ are $\mathbb{F}$-predictable processes.

Applying proposition 2.9, we obtain the following result (that is also proved in proposition 12 of [GRO 00]),

LEMMA 2.1.– If $X_t = X_0 + \int_0^t u_s dW_s + \int_0^t v_s dM_s$ is an $(\mathbb{F}, \mathbb{P})$-local martingale, then $\tilde{X}_t = X_t - \int_0^t \frac{1}{p_{s-}(L)}(\alpha_s(l).u_s + (\lambda_s * \beta_s(l).v_s)_{|l=L} ds$ is a $(\mathbb{G}, \mathbb{P})$-local martingale.

In particular, $\widetilde{W}_. := W_. - \int_0^\cdot \frac{\alpha_s(L)}{p_{s-}(L)} ds$ is a $(\mathbb{G}, \mathbb{P})$-Brownian motion and $\widetilde{M}_. := N_. - \int_0^\cdot \lambda_s * (I_{m'} + \frac{\beta_s(L)}{p_{s-}(L)}) ds$ is the compensated process of a $(\mathbb{G}, \mathbb{P})$-Poisson process with intensity $(\lambda_. * I_{m'} + \frac{\beta_.(L)}{p_.(L)}))$.

DEFINITION 2.3.– *The information drift is the $\mathbb{G}$-predictable vector process*

$$\rho_s^1 := \frac{\alpha_s(L)}{p_{s-}(L)}, \ \frac{\rho_s^2}{\lambda_s} := \frac{\beta_s(L)}{p_{s-}(L)} + I_{m'}.$$

The information drift will be useful in Chapter 4 to compute risk neutral probabilities and optimal strategies for an insider having the information flow $\mathbb{G}$. With this notation, the $(\mathbb{G}, \mathbb{P})$-Brownian motion $\widetilde{W}_{\cdot} = W_{\cdot} - \int_0^{\cdot} \rho_s^1 ds$ and the compensated process of the $(\mathbb{G}, \mathbb{P})$-Poisson process $\widetilde{M}_{\cdot} := N_{\cdot} - \int_0^{\cdot} \rho_s^2 ds$.

2.2.3. *Noisy initial enlargements*

A more realistic framework is to enlarge dynamically the filtration $\mathbb{F}$ by a dynamic perturbation L_s of a random variable L. This typically models the case of an agent whose additional information changes through time. Her/his knowledge is perturbed by an independent noise, and becomes clearer to her/him as time evolves.

HYPOTHESES 2.2.– $L_s = \mathcal{L}(L, \mathcal{B}_s)$ with

$\mathcal{L} : \mathbb{R}^2 \to \mathbb{R}$ is a given measurable function;

$\mathcal{B} = \{\mathcal{B}_t, 0 \leq t \leq T\}$ is independent of $\mathcal{F}_T$;

– L is a $\mathcal{F}_T$-measurable random variable such that:

$\mathbb{P}(L \in \cdot|\mathcal{F}_t)(\omega) \ll \mathbb{P}(L \in \cdot)$ for all $t \in [0, T[$ for $\mathbb{P}$-almost all $\omega \in \Omega$.

$\mathbb{G}$ denotes the right-continuous enlarged filtration

$$(\mathcal{G}_t = \cap_{u>t} (\mathcal{F}_u \vee \sigma(L_s, s \leq u)))_{t \in [0,T[}.$$

L contains the additional information available to the insider and $\mathcal{B}$ represents an additional noise that perturbs this side-information. Therefore, we expect in general that $\mathcal{B}_T = 0$ and that the variance of the noise decreases to zero as revelation time T approaches.

Recalling the martingale representation of the conditional density of L (see [2.8]), we have

THEOREM 2.1.– We assume hypotheses 2.2 and for all $t \in [0, T[$

$$E_{\mathbb{P}} \left(||\frac{\alpha_t(L)}{p_t(L)}|| + ||\lambda_t * (I_{m'} + \frac{\lambda_t . \beta_t(L)}{p_{t-}(L)})|| \right) < +\infty$$

and $\left(I_n + \frac{\beta_t(L)}{p_{t-}(L)} \right)$ has positive components. Setting $\rho_t^1 = E_{\mathbb{P}} \left(\frac{\alpha_t(L)}{p_t(L)} \mid \mathcal{G}_t \right)$ and $\rho_t^2 = E_{\mathbb{P}} \left(\left(\lambda_t * (I_{m'} + \frac{\beta_t(L)}{p_{t-}(L)}) \right) \mid \mathcal{G}_t \right),$ we assume that

$\int_0^T \left(||\rho_t^1|| + ||\rho_t^2|| \right) dt < +\infty$ $\mathbb{P}$ almost surely. Then, $\widetilde{W}_. := W_. - \int_0^. \rho_s^1 ds$ is a $(\mathbb{G}, \mathbb{P})$-Brownian motion and $\widetilde{M}_. := N_. - \int_0^. \rho_s^2 ds$ is the compensated process of a $(\mathbb{G}, \mathbb{P})$-Poisson process with intensity ρ^2.

PROOF.– We use similar arguments as those of proposition 1 of Corcuera *et al.* [COR 04] to generalize their result in the case of our mixed diffusive-jumps model.

Let $q \in \mathbb{N}^*$ and $s_1 \leq \cdots \leq s_q \leq s < t$. Let $C \in \mathcal{F}_s$ and h a bounded measurable function on $\mathbb{R}^q$. Set $H = h(L_{s_1}, \cdots, L_{s_q})$. Using lemma 2.1 for the second equality, we obtain

$$E_{\mathbb{P}} \left[(W_t - W_s) \mathbf{1}_C H | \mathcal{B}_{s_1} = b_1, \cdots, \mathcal{B}_{s_q} = b_q \right]$$
$$= E_{\mathbb{P}} \left[(W_t - W_s) \mathbf{1}_C h \left(\mathcal{L}(L, b_1), \cdots, \mathcal{L}(L, b_q) \right) \right]$$
$$= E_{\mathbb{P}} \left[\mathbf{1}_C h \left(\mathcal{L}(L, b_1), \cdots, \mathcal{L}(L, b_q) \right) \int_s^t \frac{\alpha_u(L)}{p_u(L)} du \right]$$
$$= E_{\mathbb{P}} \left[\mathbf{1}_C H \int_s^t \frac{\alpha_u(L)}{p_u(L)} du | \mathcal{B}_{s_1} = b_1, \cdots, \mathcal{B}_{s_q} = b_q \right].$$

Taking expectation with respect to $\left(\mathcal{B}_{s_1}, \cdots, \mathcal{B}_{s_q} \right)$ yields

$$E_{\mathbb{P}} \left[(W_t - W_s) \mathbf{1}_C H \right] = E_{\mathbb{P}} \left[\mathbf{1}_C H \int_s^t \frac{\alpha_u(L)}{p_u(L)} du \right].$$

Therefore, $W_. - \int_0^. \rho_s^1 ds$ is a continuous $(\mathbb{G}, \mathbb{P})$-local martingale. Lévy's characterization theorem implies that $W_. - \int_0^. \rho_s^1 ds$ is a $(\mathbb{G}, \mathbb{P})$-Brownian motion. The same procedure with N instead of W yields

$$E_{\mathbb{P}} \left[(N_t - N_s) \mathbf{1}_C H \right] = E_{\mathbb{P}} \left[\mathbf{1}_C H \int_s^t \lambda_u * \left(I_{m'} + \frac{\beta_u(L)}{p_{u-}(L)} \right) du \right].$$

Thus, $N_. - \int_0^. \rho_s^2 ds$ is a $(\mathbb{G}, \mathbb{P})$-local martingale and theorem 5 in [BRÉ 81, p. 25] implies that $N_. - \int_0^. \rho_s^2 ds$ is the compensated process of a $(\mathbb{G}, \mathbb{P})$-point process with intensity ρ^2. $\qquad\square$

2.3. Progressive enlargement of filtration

In this section, we consider a random time τ valued in $\mathbb{R}_+$ and we denote by D the process $(\mathbb{1}_{\{\tau \leq t\}})_{t \in [0,T]}$, i.e. $D_t := \mathbb{1}_{\{\tau \leq t\}}$, $t \in [0,T]$.

Let $\mathbb{G} = (\mathcal{G}_t)_{t \in [0,T]}$ be the progressive enlargement of the filtration $\mathbb{F}$ by the filtration $\mathbb{D} = (\mathcal{D}_t)_{t \in [0,T]}$ generated by the process D. Note that we have

$$\mathcal{D}_t = \sigma(\mathbb{1}_{\{\tau \leq s\}},\ 0 \leq s \leq t)$$

and

$$\mathcal{G}_t = \mathcal{F}_t \vee \mathcal{D}_t, \quad t \in [0,T].$$

By definition and according to [JEU 80], a $\mathcal{G}_t$-measurable random variable can be written in the form:

$$X_t \mathbb{1}_{\{\tau > t\}} + X_t(\tau) \mathbb{1}_{\{\tau \leq t\}},$$

where $X_t^{\mathbb{F}}$ is an $\mathcal{F}_t$-measurable random variable and $X_t(\cdot)$ is an $\mathcal{F}_t \otimes \mathcal{B}(\mathbb{R}_+)$-measurable random variable. Therefore, a $\mathbb{G}$-adapted process X can be written in the form:

$$X = (1 - D)X^{\mathbb{F}} + DX(\tau), \qquad [2.9]$$

where $X^{\mathbb{F}}$ is an $\mathbb{F}$-adapted process and $X(\cdot)$ is an $\mathbb{F} \otimes \mathcal{B}(\mathbb{R}_+)$-adapted process. Formula [2.9] is called a *decomposed form* of the $\mathbb{G}$-adapted process X.

PROPOSITION 2.10.– Let Z be a $\mathbb{G}$-adapted process. Then, it is $\mathbb{G}$-predictable if and only if it can be written in the form:

$$Z = (1 - D_-)Y^{\mathbb{F}} + D_- Y(\tau), \qquad [2.10]$$

where $Y^{\mathbb{F}}$ is an $\mathbb{F}$-predictable process and $Y(\cdot)$ is a $\mathcal{P}(\mathbb{F}) \otimes \mathcal{B}(\mathbb{R}_+)$-measurable function, $\mathcal{P}(\mathbb{F})$ being the predictable σ-algebra of $\mathbb{F}$.

PROOF.– We begin with the proof of the sufficient condition. Assume that the process Z can be written in the form [2.10] with $Y^{\mathbb{F}}$ being $\mathbb{F}$-predictable and $Y(\cdot)$ being $\mathcal{P}(\mathbb{F}) \otimes \mathcal{B}(\mathbb{R}_+)$-measurable. Since the process D_- is left continuous and $\mathbb{G}$-adapted, it is $\mathbb{G}$-predictable. Moreover, since the process

$Y^{\mathbb{F}}$ is $\mathbb{F}$-predictable, it is also $\mathbb{G}$-predictable. Therefore, the process $(1 - D_-)Y^{\mathbb{F}}$ is $\mathbb{G}$-predictable. It remains to show that the process $D_-Y(\tau)$ is also $\mathbb{G}$-predictable. By a monotone class argument (see, for example, [DEL 75] I.19-24), we may assume that $Y(\cdot)$ is of the form $Xf(\tau)$, where X is an $\mathbb{F}$-predictable process and f is a Borel function. Note that the process $D_-f(\tau)$ is left continuous and $\mathbb{G}$-adapted, hence is $\mathbb{G}$-predictable. Therefore, the process $D_-Y(\tau) = (D_-f(\tau))X$ is also $\mathbb{G}$-predictable.

We now proceed with the proof of the necessary condition. Recall that the $\mathbb{G}$-predictable σ-algebra $\mathcal{P}(\mathbb{G})$ is generated by the following processes: $\mathbb{1}_{\{0\}\times A}$ where $A \in \mathcal{F}_0 \cup \mathcal{D}_0$ and $\mathbb{1}_{(s,\infty)\times A}$ where $A \in \mathcal{F}_s \cup \mathcal{D}_s$. Still by a monotone class argument, it suffices to verify the assertion for such processes. For the first case, if $A \in \mathcal{F}_0$ then the process $Z = \mathbb{1}_{\{0\}\times A}$ is $\mathbb{F}$-predictable and hence the decomposition $Z = (1 - D_-)Z + D_-Z$ satisfies the required conditions; if $A = \{\tau = 0\}$, then we have

$$Z_t = \mathbb{1}_{\{\tau \leq t\}}\mathbb{1}_{\{0\}}(t), \quad t \in [0, T]$$

and the assertion is also true. It remains to treat the case where $Z = \mathbb{1}_{(s,\infty)\times A}$ with $A \in \mathcal{F}_s \cup \mathcal{D}_s$. If $A \in \mathcal{F}_s$, then Z is $\mathbb{F}$-predictable and the decomposition $Z = (1 - D_-)Z + D_-Z$ satisfies the required conditions; if A is of the form $\{\tau \leq u\}$ with $u \in (0, s]$, then we have

$$Z_t = \mathbb{1}_{\{\tau \leq t\}}\mathbb{1}_{(s,\infty)}(t)\mathbb{1}_{[0,u]}(\tau)$$

and the assertion also holds. The proposition is thus proved. $\qquad\square$

REMARK 2.5.– The optional analog of the above proposition is much more subtle. We refer the readers to the work of Song [SON 14] for a general discussion on the decomposition of $\mathbb{G}$-optional processes.

Similarly to the previous section, *we assume that the random variable τ satisfies the conditional density hypothesis with respect to the reference filtration* $\mathbb{F}$, and we denote by $(p_t(\cdot))_{t \in [0,T]}$ a càdlàg martingale version of the $\mathbb{F}$-conditional density process of τ (see remark 2.3). Let $\mathbb{Q}$ be the equivalent probability measure of $\mathbb{P}$ such that

$$\frac{d\mathbb{Q}}{d\mathbb{P}}\bigg|_{\mathcal{F}_t \vee \sigma(\tau)} = p_t(\tau)^{-1}. \tag{2.11}$$

Recall that (see proposition 2.2) the random variable τ is independent of $\mathbb{F}$ under the probability $\mathbb{Q}$, and $\mathbb{Q}$ identifies with $\mathbb{P}$ on $\mathcal{F}_T$ and on $\sigma(\tau)$.

EXAMPLE 2.2.– Assume that the $\mathcal{F}_T$-conditional law of the random variable τ is equivalent to the Lebesgue measure on $\mathbb{R}_+$, and admits $\alpha_T(\cdot)$ as its Radon–Nikodym density with respect to the Lebesgue measure. Then, the probability law of τ is also equivalent to the Lebesgue measure, and admits $\mathbb{E}^{\mathbb{P}}[\alpha_T(\cdot)]$ as its Radon–Nikodym density with respect to the Lebesgue measure. Therefore, in this case, the random time τ satisfies the conditional density hypothesis. Moreover, there exists an $\mathbb{F} \otimes \sigma(\mathbb{R}_+)$-adapted process $(\alpha_t(\cdot))_{t\in[0,T]}$ such that $\alpha_t(x) = \mathbb{E}^{\mathbb{P}}[\alpha_T(x) \,|\, \mathcal{F}_t]$ for any $x \in \mathbb{R}_+$. With this notation, a càdlàg martingale version of the $\mathbb{F}$-conditional density of τ is given by

$$p_t(x) = \frac{\alpha_t(x)}{\mathbb{E}^{\mathbb{P}}[\alpha_t(x)]}, \quad t \in [0, T].$$

2.3.1. Conditional expectation

Given a non-negative random variable, the following proposition by [JEU 80] computes its $\mathcal{G}_t$-conditional expectation of Z on $\{\tau > t\}$, where $t \in [0, T]$.

PROPOSITION 2.11.– Let Z be a non-negative random variable. For any $t \in [0, T]$, we have

$$\mathbb{1}_{\{\tau>t\}}\mathbb{E}^{\mathbb{P}}[Z \,|\, \mathcal{G}_t] = \mathbb{1}_{\{\tau>t\}}\frac{\mathbb{E}^{\mathbb{P}}[Z\mathbb{1}_{\{\tau>t\}} \,|\, \mathcal{F}_t]}{\mathbb{E}^{\mathbb{P}}[\mathbb{1}_{\{\tau>t\}} \,|\, \mathcal{F}_t]}. \qquad [2.12]$$

PROOF.– Let X_t be a non-negative $\mathcal{G}_t$-measurable random variable, which is written in the decomposition form as:

$$X_t = X_t^{\mathbb{F}}\mathbb{1}_{\{\tau>t\}} + X_t(\tau)\mathbb{1}_{\{\tau\leq t\}}.$$

We have

$$\mathbb{E}^{\mathbb{P}}[\mathbb{1}_{\{\tau>t\}}ZX_t] = \mathbb{E}^{\mathbb{P}}[\mathbb{1}_{\{\tau>t\}}ZX_t^{\mathbb{F}}].$$

Moreover,

$$\mathbb{E}^{\mathbb{P}}\left[\mathbb{1}_{\{\tau>t\}}\frac{\mathbb{E}^{\mathbb{P}}[Z\mathbb{1}_{\{\tau>t\}} \,|\, \mathcal{F}_t]}{\mathbb{E}^{\mathbb{P}}[\mathbb{1}_{\{\tau>t\}} \,|\, \mathcal{F}_t]}X_t\right] = \mathbb{E}^{\mathbb{P}}\left[\mathbb{1}_{\{\tau>t\}}\frac{\mathbb{E}^{\mathbb{P}}[Z\mathbb{1}_{\{\tau>t\}} \,|\, \mathcal{F}_t]}{\mathbb{E}^{\mathbb{P}}[\mathbb{1}_{\{\tau>t\}} \,|\, \mathcal{F}_t]}X_t^{\mathbb{F}}\right]$$
$$= \mathbb{E}^{\mathbb{P}}\left[\mathbb{E}^{\mathbb{P}}[Z\mathbb{1}_{\{\tau>t\}} \,|\, \mathcal{F}_t]X_t^{\mathbb{F}}\right] = \mathbb{E}^{\mathbb{P}}[\mathbb{1}_{\{\tau>t\}}ZX_t^{\mathbb{F}}].$$

Hence, the formula [2.12] holds. $\qquad\qquad\square$

REMARK 2.6.– Recall that the *Azéma supermartingale* of the random time τ is defined as:

$$G_t := \mathbb{P}(\tau > t \mid \mathcal{F}_t), \quad t \in [0, T].$$

Note that G_t figures in the denominator term of the right-hand side of [2.12]. In general, G_t needs not be positive almost everywhere (it is the case when the $\mathcal{F}_t$-conditional law of τ has a positive density with respect to the Lebesgue measure). However, G_t is $\mathbb{P}$-a.e. positive on the set $\{\tau > t\}$. Hence, the formula [2.12] is well-defined. Moreover, in the case where Z is of the form $X_T(\tau)$, where $X_T(\cdot)$ is an $\mathcal{F}_T \otimes \mathcal{B}(\mathbb{R}_+)$-measurable random variable, the formula [2.12] can be rewritten as:

$$\mathbb{1}_{\{\tau > t\}} \mathbb{E}^{\mathbb{P}}[X_T(\tau) \mid \mathcal{G}_t] = \mathbb{1}_{\{\tau > t\}} \frac{\int_t^\infty \mathbb{E}[X_T(s) p_T(s) \mid \mathcal{F}_t] \, \eta(ds)}{\int_t^\infty p_t(s) \, \eta(ds)}, \quad [2.13]$$

where η denotes the probability law of τ.

PROPOSITION 2.12.– Let $X_T(\cdot)$ be an $\mathcal{F}_T \otimes \mathcal{B}(\mathbb{R}_+)$-measurable random variable. We have

$$\mathbb{1}_{\{\tau \leq t\}} \mathbb{E}^{\mathbb{P}}[X_T(\tau) \mid \mathcal{G}_t] = \mathbb{1}_{\{\tau \leq t\}} \frac{\mathbb{E}^{\mathbb{P}}[X_T(\theta) p_T(\theta) \mid \mathcal{F}_t]}{p_t(\theta)} \bigg|_{\theta = \tau}. \quad [2.14]$$

PROOF.– Let Y_t be a non-negative $\mathcal{G}_t$-measurable random variable, which is written in the decomposition form as:

$$Y_t = Y_t^{\mathbb{F}} \mathbb{1}_{\{\tau > t\}} + Y_t(\tau) \mathbb{1}_{\{\tau \leq t\}}.$$

We have

$$
\begin{aligned}
\mathbb{E}^{\mathbb{P}}[\mathbb{1}_{\{\tau \leq t\}} X_T(\tau) Y_t] &= \mathbb{E}^{\mathbb{P}}[\mathbb{1}_{\{\tau \leq t\}} X_T(\tau) Y_t(\tau)] \\
&= \mathbb{E}^{\mathbb{P}}\left[\int_0^t X_T(\theta) Y_t(\theta) p_T(\theta) \eta(d\theta) \right].
\end{aligned}
$$

Moreover,

$$
\begin{aligned}
&\mathbb{E}^{\mathbb{P}}\left[\mathbb{1}_{\{\tau \leq t\}} \left.\frac{\mathbb{E}^{\mathbb{P}}[X_T(\theta)p_T(\theta) \mid \mathcal{F}_t]}{p_t(\theta)}\right|_{\theta=\tau} Y_t\right] \\
&= \mathbb{E}^{\mathbb{P}}\left[\mathbb{1}_{\{\tau \leq t\}} \left.\frac{\mathbb{E}^{\mathbb{P}}[X_T(\theta)p_T(\theta) \mid \mathcal{F}_t]}{p_t(\theta)}\right|_{\theta=\tau} Y_t(\tau)\right] \\
&= \mathbb{E}^{\mathbb{P}}\left[\int_0^t \frac{\mathbb{E}^{\mathbb{P}}[X_T(\theta)p_T(\theta) \mid \mathcal{F}_t]}{p_t(\theta)} Y_t(\theta)p_t(\theta)\, \eta(d\theta)\right] \\
&= \mathbb{E}^{\mathbb{P}}\left[\int_0^t X_T(\theta)Y_t(\theta)p_T(\theta)\eta(d\theta)\right].
\end{aligned}
$$

Therefore, the equality [2.14] holds. □

The following proposition computes the Radon–Nikodym density $d\mathbb{Q}/d\mathbb{P}$ on the σ-algebra $\mathcal{G}_t$, which is represented in the decomposed form.

PROPOSITION 2.13.– Let t be an element in $[0, T]$. The Radon–Nikodym density $d\mathbb{Q}/d\mathbb{P}$ on $\mathcal{G}_t$ is given by

$$
\left.\frac{d\mathbb{Q}}{d\mathbb{P}}\right|_{\mathcal{G}_t} = \mathbb{1}_{\{\tau>t\}}\frac{\mathbb{P}(\tau > t)}{G_t} + \mathbb{1}_{\{\tau \leq t\}}p_t(\tau)^{-1}, \quad \mathbb{P}\text{-a.s.} \qquad [2.15]
$$

PROOF.– By [2.11], we obtain that the Radon–Nikodym density $d\mathbb{Q}/d\mathbb{P}$ on $\mathcal{G}_t$ is

$$
\mathbb{E}^{\mathbb{P}}[p_t(\tau)^{-1} \mid \mathcal{G}_t].
$$

By [2.13] and [2.14], we have

$$
\mathbb{E}^{\mathbb{P}}[p_t(\tau)^{-1} \mid \mathcal{G}_t] = \mathbb{1}_{\{\tau>t\}}\frac{\mathbb{P}(\tau > t)}{G_t} + \mathbb{1}_{\{\tau \leq t\}}p_t(\tau)^{-1}.
$$

Therefore, the equality [2.15] holds. □

2.3.2. *Right-continuity of the enlarged filtration*

In order to study the stochastic analysis of the enlarged filtration $\mathbb{G}$, the right-continuity of the filtration $\mathbb{G}$ is a convenient property. Similarly to the result of Amendinger [AME 00, proposition 3.3], under the conditional density hypothesis, the progressive enlargement $\mathbb{G} = (\mathcal{G}_t \vee \mathcal{D}_t)_{t \in [0,T]}$ is right-continuous. This section is devoted to the proof of this result. Note that the change to an equivalent probability measure under which $\sigma(\tau)$ and $\mathbb{F}$ are independent plays an important role in the proof.

PROPOSITION 2.14.– Under the conditional density hypothesis on τ, the enlarged filtration $\mathbb{G}$ is right-continuous.

PROOF.– The assertion of the proposition is invariant under change of probability measure. We can thus assume that τ is independent of $\mathbb{F}$ under the probability measure $\mathbb{P}$. In this case, the $\mathbb{F}$-conditional density is constant 1. Let t be an element in $[0, T)$, $\varepsilon \in (0, T - t)$ and $X_{t+\varepsilon}$ be a bounded $\mathcal{G}_{t+\varepsilon}$-measurable random variable, which is written in the decomposed form as:

$$X_{t+\varepsilon} = Y_{t+\varepsilon}^{\mathbb{F}} \mathbb{1}_{\{\tau > t+\varepsilon\}} + Y_{t+\varepsilon}(\tau) \mathbb{1}_{\{\tau \leq t+\varepsilon\}},$$

where $Y_{t+\varepsilon}^{\mathbb{F}}$ and $Y_{t+\varepsilon}(\cdot)$ are, respectively, bounded $\mathcal{F}_{t+\varepsilon}$-measurable and $\mathcal{F}_{t+\varepsilon} \otimes \mathcal{B}(\mathbb{R}_+)$-measurable functions. Then, for any $\varepsilon' \in (0, \varepsilon)$, by [2.13] and [2.14], we have

$$\mathbb{E}^{\mathbb{P}}[X_{t+\varepsilon} \mid \mathcal{G}_{t+\varepsilon'}]$$
$$= \mathbb{1}_{\{\tau > t+\varepsilon'\}} \frac{\mathbb{E}^{\mathbb{P}}[Y_{t+\varepsilon}^{\mathbb{F}} \mathbb{1}_{\{\tau > t+\varepsilon\}} + Y_{t+\varepsilon}(\tau) \mathbb{1}_{\{t+\varepsilon' < \tau \leq t+\varepsilon\}} \mid \mathcal{F}_{t+\varepsilon'}]}{\mathbb{P}(\tau > t+\varepsilon \mid \mathcal{F}_{t+\varepsilon'})}$$
$$+ \mathbb{1}_{\{\tau \leq t+\varepsilon'\}} \mathbb{E}^{\mathbb{P}}[Y_{t+\varepsilon}(\theta) \mid \mathcal{F}_{t+\varepsilon'}]_{\theta=\tau},$$

where we have used the fact that the $\mathbb{F}$-conditional density is constant 1. By the independence between $\sigma(\tau)$ and $\mathbb{F}$, we obtain

$$\frac{\mathbb{E}^{\mathbb{P}}[Y_{t+\varepsilon}^{\mathbb{F}} \mathbb{1}_{\{\tau > t+\varepsilon\}} + Y_{t+\varepsilon}(\tau) \mathbb{1}_{\{t+\varepsilon' < \tau \leq t+\varepsilon\}} \mid \mathcal{F}_{t+\varepsilon'}]}{\mathbb{P}(\tau > t+\varepsilon \mid \mathcal{F}_{t+\varepsilon'})}$$
$$= \frac{\mathbb{P}(\tau > t+\varepsilon)\mathbb{E}^{\mathbb{P}}[Y_{t+\varepsilon}^{\mathbb{F}} \mid \mathcal{F}_{t+\varepsilon'}] + \int_{t+\varepsilon'}^{t+\varepsilon} \mathbb{E}[Y_{t+\varepsilon}(\theta) \mid \mathcal{F}_{t+\varepsilon'}]\eta(d\theta)}{\mathbb{P}(\tau > t+\varepsilon')}.$$

Note that the filtration $\mathbb{F}$ has assumed to be right-continuous and hence any $\mathbb{F}$-martingale has a right continuous version. Therefore, by taking suitable version of the process $(\mathbb{E}^{\mathbb{P}}[X_{t+\varepsilon} \mid \mathcal{G}_{t+\varepsilon'}], \varepsilon' \in (0, \varepsilon))$, we obtain,

$$\lim_{\varepsilon' \to 0+} \mathbb{E}^{\mathbb{P}}[X_{t+\varepsilon} \mid \mathcal{G}_{t+\varepsilon'}] = \mathbb{1}_{\{\tau > t\}} \mathbb{E}^{\mathbb{P}}[Y_{t+\varepsilon}^{\mathbb{F}} \mid \mathcal{F}_t] + \mathbb{1}_{\{\tau \leq t\}} \mathbb{E}^{\mathbb{P}}[Y_{t+\varepsilon}(\theta) \mid \mathcal{F}_t]_{\theta=\tau}.$$

Let $\mathcal{G}_{t+} = \bigcap_{s \in (t, T]} \mathcal{G}_s$. If Z is a bounded $\mathcal{G}_{t+}$-measurable random variable, then for any $\varepsilon' \in (0, \varepsilon)$ we have

$$\mathbb{E}^{\mathbb{P}}[X_{t+\varepsilon} Z] = \mathbb{E}^{\mathbb{P}}[\mathbb{E}^{\mathbb{P}}[X_{t+\varepsilon} \mid \mathcal{G}_{t+\varepsilon'}] Z]$$

since the random variable Z is $\mathcal{G}_{t+\varepsilon'}$-measurable. By taking $\varepsilon' \to 0+$, we obtain

$$\mathbb{E}^{\mathbb{P}}[X_{t+\varepsilon}Z] = \mathbb{E}^{\mathbb{P}}[(\mathbb{1}_{\{\tau>t\}}\mathbb{E}^{\mathbb{P}}[Y_{t+\varepsilon}^{\mathbb{F}} \mid \mathcal{F}_t] + \mathbb{1}_{\{\tau\leq t\}}\mathbb{E}^{\mathbb{P}}[Y_{t+\varepsilon}(\theta) \mid \mathcal{F}_t]_{\theta=\tau})Z].$$

Since Z is arbitrary, we have

$$\mathbb{E}^{\mathbb{P}}[X_{t+\varepsilon} \mid \mathcal{G}_{t+}] = \mathbb{1}_{\{\tau>t\}}\mathbb{E}^{\mathbb{P}}[Y_{t+\varepsilon}^{\mathbb{F}} \mid \mathcal{F}_t] + \mathbb{1}_{\{\tau\leq t\}}\mathbb{E}^{\mathbb{P}}[Y_{t+\varepsilon}(\theta) \mid \mathcal{F}_t]_{\theta=\tau},$$

which is actually $\mathcal{G}_t$-measurable. Therefore, we have $\mathcal{G}_{t+} = \mathcal{G}_t$ and the proposition is proved. $\qquad\square$

2.3.3. *Martingale characterization*

In this section, we consider the characterization of $\mathbb{G}$-martingales.

PROPOSITION 2.15.– Let X be a $\mathbb{G}$-adapted process, which is written in the decomposed form as:

$$X_t = \mathbb{1}_{\{\tau>t\}}X_t^{\mathbb{F}} + \mathbb{1}_{\{\tau\leq t\}}X_t(\tau), \quad t \in [0,T].$$

Suppose that the following conditions are satisfied:

1) for any $\theta \in [0,T]$, the process $(X_t(\theta)p_t(\theta))_{t\in[\theta,T]}$ is an $(\mathbb{F},\mathbb{P})$-martingale;

2) the process $(G_tX_t^{\mathbb{F}} + \int_0^t X_s(s)p_s(s)\eta(ds))_{t\in[0,T]}$ is an $(\mathbb{F},\mathbb{P})$-martingale.

Then, the process X is a $(\mathbb{G},\mathbb{P})$-martingale.

PROOF.– By [2.13] and [2.14], we have

$$\mathbb{E}^{\mathbb{P}}[X_T \mid \mathcal{G}_t]$$
$$= \frac{\mathbb{1}_{\{\tau>t\}}}{G_t}\left(\int_T^\infty \mathbb{E}^{\mathbb{P}}[X_T^{\mathbb{F}}p_T(s) \mid \mathcal{F}_t]\,\eta(ds) + \int_t^T \mathbb{E}^{\mathbb{P}}[X_T(s)p_T(s) \mid \mathcal{F}_t]\,\eta(ds)\right)$$
$$+\mathbb{1}_{\{\tau\leq t\}}\frac{\mathbb{E}^{\mathbb{P}}[X_T(\theta)p_T(\theta) \mid \mathcal{F}_t]}{p_t(\theta)}\bigg|_{\theta=\tau}.$$

The condition (1) implies that

$$\frac{\mathbb{E}^{\mathbb{P}}[X_T(\theta)p_T(\theta) \mid \mathcal{F}_t]}{p_t(\theta)} = X_t(\theta).$$

Moreover, for $s \in (t, T]$, we have

$$\mathbb{E}^{\mathbb{P}}[X_T(s)p_T(s) \mid \mathcal{F}_t] = \mathbb{E}^{\mathbb{P}}[X_s(s)p_s(s) \mid \mathcal{F}_t]$$

and hence

$$\frac{\int_T^\infty \mathbb{E}^{\mathbb{P}}[X_T^{\mathbb{F}} p_T(s) \mid \mathcal{F}_t] \, \eta(ds) + \int_t^T \mathbb{E}^{\mathbb{P}}[X_T(s)p_T(s) \mid \mathcal{F}_t] \, \eta(ds)}{G_t}$$
$$= \frac{\mathbb{E}^{\mathbb{P}}[X_T^{\mathbb{F}} G_T + \int_t^T X_s(s)p_s(s) \, \eta(ds) \mid \mathcal{F}_t]}{G_t} = X_t^{\mathbb{F}},$$

where the second equality comes from the condition (2). The proposition is thus proved. □

From the above proposition, we deduce the following analog of proposition 2.9 in the setting of progressive enlargement of filtration.

PROPOSITION 2.16.– Let X be a local $(\mathbb{F}, \mathbb{P})$-martingale on $[0, T]$. Then, it is a $\mathbb{G}$-semimartingale. Moreover, its decomposition in the filtration $\mathbb{G}$ is given by

$$X_t = \widetilde{X}_t + \int_0^{\tau \wedge t} \frac{d\langle X, M \rangle_s^{\mathbb{F}, \mathbb{P}}}{G_{s-}} + \int_{\tau \wedge t}^t \left. \frac{d\langle X, p(\theta) \rangle_s^{\mathbb{F}, \mathbb{P}}}{p_{s-}(\theta)} \right|_{\theta = \tau}, \quad t \in [0, T] \quad [2.16]$$

where $\widetilde{X}$ is a local $(\mathbb{G}, \mathbb{P})$-martingale and M is the $(\mathbb{F}, \mathbb{P})$-martingale defined as:

$$M_t = \mathbb{E}^{\mathbb{P}}\left[\int_0^T p_s(s) \, \eta(ds) + \int_T^\infty p_T(s) \, \eta(ds) \;\middle|\; \mathcal{F}_t \right], \quad t \in [0, T].$$

PROOF.– Let A be the process

$$A_t = \int_0^t p_s(s) \, \eta(ds).$$

Thus, we have

$$G_t + A_t = \int_t^\infty p_t(s) \, \eta(ds) + \int_0^t p_s(s) \, \eta(ds) = M_t, \quad t \in [0, T].$$

We let

$$K_t = \int_0^{\tau \wedge t} \frac{d\langle X, M \rangle_s^{\mathbb{F}, \mathbb{P}}}{G_{s-}}, \quad t \in [0, T]$$

and for $\theta \leq t$

$$K_t(\theta) = \int_{\tau \wedge t}^{t} \frac{d\langle X, p(\theta)\rangle_s^{\mathbb{F},\mathbb{P}}}{p_{s-}(\theta)}.$$

With this notation, we can rewrite $\widetilde{X}$ as:

$$\widetilde{X}_t = \mathbb{1}_{\{\tau > t\}}(X_t - K_t) + \mathbb{1}_{\{\tau \leq t\}}(X_t - K_\tau - K_t(\tau)).$$

We let

$$U_t = X_t - K_t \quad \text{and} \quad U_t(\theta) = X_t - K_\theta - K_t(\theta).$$

Note that

$$\begin{aligned}
d(U_t(\theta)p_t(\theta)) &= (X_{t-} - K_\theta - K_{t-}(\theta))dp_t(\theta) + p_{t-}(\theta)dX_t \\
&\quad + d[X, p(\theta)]_t - d\langle X, p(\theta)\rangle_t.
\end{aligned}$$

Hence, $(U_t(\theta)p_t(\theta))_{t \in [\theta, T]}$ is a local $(\mathbb{F}, \mathbb{P})$-martingale. Moreover, if we denote by

$$Z_t = U_t G_t + \int_0^t U_s(s)dA_s,$$

then, we have

$$\begin{aligned}
dZ_t &= d(U_t G_t) + U_t(t)dA_t = d(X_t G_t) - d(K_t G_t) + (X_t - K_t)dA_t \\
&= X_{t-}dG_t + G_{t-}dX_t + d[X, G]_t - K_t dG_t \\
&\quad - G_{t-}dK_t + X_{t-}dA_t - K_t dA_t + d[X, A]_t \\
&= (X_{t-} - K_t)dM_t + G_{t-}dX_t + d[X, M]_t - d\langle X, M\rangle_t^{\mathbb{F},\mathbb{P}},
\end{aligned}$$

which shows that Z is a local $(\mathbb{F}, \mathbb{P})$-martingale. By the local version of proposition 2.15, we obtain that the process is a local $(\mathbb{G}, \mathbb{P})$-martingale. The proposition is thus proved. $\square$

2.3.4. *Dynamic enlargement with a process*

Initial enlargement of filtrations, such as modeling a private piece of information received at time 0 that does not evolve nor become more accurate over time, seems to be a bit too strong a hypothesis, at least for its financial application. One relaxation of this hypothesis that we have presented in section 2.2.3 is the case in which the private information is affected by an independent noise process, vanishing as the revelation time approaches (see [COR 04]). This noisy initial enlargement framework still allows us to use tractable formulas.

Several papers have studied the issue of dynamic enlargement filtrations with more general filtrations or processes. We provide below a brief overview of some of them.

Blanchet-Scalliet *et al.* [BLA 16] consider the successive enlargement of a reference filtration $\mathbb{F}$ at time t_i by a random variable L_i. In this framework of successive initial enlargement, a generalization of Jacod's hypothesis is discussed and consistent expressions for conditional expectation with respect to the enlarged filtration are provided. Following the handwritten notes of Marc Yor, Aksamit and Jeanblanc in [AKS 16] give martingale decompositions in filtrations dynamically enlarged by the future maximum of specific continuous processes (such as a local martingale tending to 0 when time goes to ∞). Jeulin [JEU 80] studies the case of the future minimum of a three-dimensional Bessel process.

Song [SON 87, SON 13] uses the local solution method to study the semimartingales properties in a filtration enlarged by another filtration of countably generated sub-Borel σ-algebras, with very weak assumptions. The local method can be applied in a large setting of enlargement filtrations, and gives locally the decomposition of martingales in the small filtration as semimartingales in the enlarged filtration. It generalizes the results of standard formulas, such as initial enlargement under Jacod's criteria, or progressive enlargement up to a random time.

The more general framework is certainly the one studied by Kchia and Protter [KCH 15], which consists of the dynamic progressive filtration enlargement with a càdlàg process. The methodology is the following. First, they enlarge with marked point processes, then they consider càdlàg processes whose increments satisfy a generalized Jacod's criterion with respect to the reference filtration $\mathbb{F}$ along some sequence of subdivisions whose mesh tends to zero. To do this, they assume a density hypothesis for all the increments.

Then, using technical results from the theory of the weak convergence of σ-fields, they establish a semimartingale convergence theorem. They provide sufficient conditions for a semimartingale of the base filtration to remain a semimartingale in the enlarged filtration.

For the financial applications, the following chapters of the book use the two main types of enlargement of filtrations, as those two settings lead to tractable formulas.

3

Portfolio Optimization with Credit Risk

In this chapter, we study the portfolio optimization problem subject to credit risks, namely, the risks associated with a default event. The impact of the default event on the portfolio may have various nature. In the case where the portfolio contains credit derivatives or credit sensitive assets, the portfolio value may have an instantaneous loss at the default time. Moreover, the default event may also lead to a regime change of the price dynamics of the assets in the portfolio, in the form of a jump or a regime change of the drift and the volatility terms. We refer the readers to the pioneer paper of Jarrow and Yu [JAR 01] and the books of Brigo *et al.* [BRI 13] and Crepey *et al.* [CRE 14] for an overview of the counterparty default risks.

In the optimization of portfolio under credit risks, we need to deal with the jumps of portfolio value and the regime switching. Moreover, in the setting where the global market is described by the progressive enlargement of filtration, the market is usually not complete. Although incomplete market optimization has been studied in general by Kramkov and Schachermayer [KRA 99], the explicit optimization of portfolio under credit risk is a challenging problem when we are interested in the impact of the default event on the remaining market. There are two main approaches in the literature. The first one deals with the market filtration directly and works under some conditions on the portfolio such as no investment after the default event and the martingale representation hypothesis in the enlarged filtration. We refer the readers to the works [BLA 08, BOU 04, COL 07, LIM 11, LIM 15] in this direction. The second approach decomposes the optimization problem into two parts: the after-default part and the before-default one. Each one of the decomposed optimization problems is defined with respect to the reference filtration instead of the enlarged one, which is easier to handle. Note that the after-default problem should be solved in the first place, and its optimal value serves as an additive utility weight in the before-default optimization problem, which computes the optimal value of the initial optimization problem. This approach has been proposed in Jiao and Pham [JIA 11] and then has been generalized to multidefault case in [PHA 10, JIA 13, KHA 14]. We will explain both approaches in the context of progressive enlargement of filtration.

In this chapter, we also discuss the optimal investment problem for the insider possessing some extra information on the default risk of counterparty and hence who has access to a larger set of available trading strategies, leading to a higher expected utility from the terminal wealth. Note that similar problem has been considered by Amendinger, Becherer and Schweizer [AME 03], where the authors study the value of an initial information in the setting of a complete default-free market. We focus on the comparison between the standard investor and the insider. Both agents can invest in the same risk-free asset and risky one and they observe the same market price for each asset. However, the insider possesses more information on the risky asset since it is influenced by the counterparty default on which the insider has additional knowledge. Due to the extra information, the insider may gain larger profit. The insider's information is modeled by using an initial enlargement of filtration as in Amendiger et al. [AME 98] and in Grorud and Pontier [GRO 98]. More precisely, we model the default time as the first time that a stochastic process hits a random barrier. The insider knows the barrier from the initial time and the other investors only see its value at the default time but have knowledge on the conditional probability distribution of the default barrier with respect to the reference filtration. This total information is called the insider's information, or the full information in Hillairet and Jiao [HIL 11]. We will apply the decomposition method to the insider's optimization problem. Due to the extra knowledge on the default barrier, the insider's strategy depends on the barrier value before the counterparty default, which is not the case for the standard investor. If the default occurs, the insider's strategy will also depend on the default time. From the methodology point of view, the main difference here is that for the insider, the default time is modeled, as in the classical structural approach model, since the random barrier is known, so that the default time becomes a stopping time with respect to the insider's filtration. Therefore, the default density hypothesis fails to hold for the insider and we can no longer adopt the conditional density approach in this situation. We apply the theory of initial enlargement of filtration, assuming that the conditional law of the default time given the reference filtration is equivalent to its probability law. The corresponding Radon–Nikodym derivative process will play a key role in our methodology.

Following the practice of regulation on financial markets exposed to the counterparty risk, we assume that the short-selling is prohibited for all investors and we discuss the possibility and the impact of relaxing this short-selling constraint.

3.1. Model setup

We consider a portfolio consisting of the risk-free asset and one risky asset and suppose that the price S of the risky asset is influenced by a default event. We denote by τ the random variable indicating the time of the default event. Let D be the default process $(\mathbb{1}_{\{\tau \le t\}})_{t \in [0,T]}$, where T is the time horizon.

3.1.1. Preliminaries

We introduce a reference filtration $\mathbb{F} = (\mathcal{F}_t)_{t \ge 0}$ satisfying the usual conditions and assume that the market filtration $\mathbb{G}$ is the progressive enlargement of the filtration $\mathbb{F}$ by the default information. In other words, $\mathbb{G}$ is the smallest filtration satisfying the usual conditions such that τ is a $\mathbb{G}$-stopping time. We suppose that the following basic hypotheses are satisfied:

1) the filtration $\mathbb{F}$ is generated by a Brownian motion $W^{\mathbb{F}}$;

2) the $\mathcal{F}_T$-conditional probability law of τ admits a positive density $\alpha_T(\cdot)$ with respect to the Lebesgue measure.

We denote by $L^2_{\mathrm{loc}}(W^{\mathbb{F}})$ the set of all $\mathbb{F}$-adapted processes ϕ on $[0,T]$ such that

$$\int_0^T |\phi_t|^2 dt < +\infty \qquad \mathbb{P}\text{-a.s.}$$

For any $\phi \in L^2_{\mathrm{loc}}(W^{\mathbb{F}})$, the stochastic integral

$$\int_0^t \phi_s dW_s^{\mathbb{F}}, \quad t \in [0,T]$$

is well-defined, and defines a local $(\mathbb{F}, \mathbb{P})$-martingale.

The density condition (2) implies that, for any $t \in [0,T]$, the $\mathcal{F}_t$-conditional probability law of τ admits a positive density $\alpha_t(\cdot)$ with respect to the Lebesgue measure. We can also choose a suitable version of the $\mathbb{F}$-conditional density $\alpha(\cdot)$ which is $\mathbb{F} \otimes \mathcal{B}(\mathbb{R}_+)$ adapted and such that, for any $u \in \mathbb{R}_+$, the process $(\alpha_t(u))_{t \in [0,T]}$ is a càdlàg $\mathbb{F}$-martingale. By the martingale representation theorem under the Brownian filtration (applied to the stochastic logarithm of $\alpha(u)$), there exists an $\mathbb{F}$-predictable process $\beta(u) \in L^2_{\text{loc}}(W^{\mathbb{F}})$ such that

$$\alpha_t(u) = \alpha_0(u) \exp \left(\int_0^t \beta_s(u) dW_s^{\mathbb{F}} - \frac{1}{2} \int_0^t \beta_s(u)^2 ds \right). \qquad [3.1]$$

In other words, $\alpha(u)$ is the Doléans–Dade exponential of $\beta(u)$.

Let G be the Azéma supermartingale of the random time τ, defined as

$$G_t = \mathbb{P}(\tau > t \,|\, \mathcal{F}_t), \quad t \in [0, T].$$

Under the density hypothesis, G is a continuous $(\mathbb{F}, \mathbb{P})$-supermartingale which is positive. Its compensator process is given by

$$\int_0^t \alpha_s(s) ds, \quad t \in [0, T].$$

Then, there exists an $\mathbb{F}$-predictable process $(m_t, \, t \in [0, T])$ such that

$$\forall t \in [0, T], \quad G_t + \int_0^t \alpha_s(s) ds = \int_0^t G_s m_s dW_s^{\mathbb{F}}.$$

We note that the Brownian motion $W^{\mathbb{F}}$ admits a semimartingale decomposition in the enlarged filtration $\mathbb{G}$. By proposition 2.16, the process

$$W_t = W_t^{\mathbb{F}} - \int_0^{\tau \wedge t} m_s ds - \int_{\tau \wedge t}^t \beta_s(\tau) ds, \quad t \in [0, T] \qquad [3.2]$$

is a Brownian motion with respect to the filtration $\mathbb{G}$ under the probability $\mathbb{P}$. We can also write it in a decomposed form as

$$W_t = \mathbb{1}_{\{\tau > t\}} \left(W_t^{\mathbb{F}} - \int_0^t m_s ds \right)$$
$$+ \mathbb{1}_{\{\tau \le t\}} \left(W_t^{\mathbb{F}} - \int_0^t (\mathbb{1}_{\{\tau > s\}} m_s + \mathbb{1}_{\{\tau \le s\}} \beta_s(\tau)) ds \right), \qquad [3.3]$$

where we observe a phenomenon of regime switching upon the default event of the $(\mathbb{G}, \mathbb{P})$-compensator process of $W^{\mathbb{F}}$.

Let Λ be the $(\mathbb{G}, \mathbb{P})$-compensator process of τ, namely, $N := D - \Lambda$ is a $(\mathbb{G}, \mathbb{P})$-martingale. We note that the process Λ can be written (see [ELK 10, proposition 4.1]) as

$$\Lambda_t = \int_0^{\tau \wedge t} \frac{\alpha_s(s)}{G_s} ds.$$

Therefore, the random time τ admits an intensity, given by

$$\lambda_t = \mathbb{1}_{\{\tau > t\}} \frac{\alpha_t(t)}{G_t}.$$

We assume that the price S of the risky asset, which is a $\mathbb{G}$-adapted process, satisfies the following stochastic differential equation

$$dS_t = S_{t-}(\mu_t dt + \sigma_t dW_t^{\mathbb{F}} - \gamma_t dD_t), \quad t \in [0, T], \quad S_0 = 1, \qquad [3.4]$$

where the coefficients μ, σ and γ are $\mathbb{G}$-predictable processes, $\sigma_t > 0$ for any $t \in [0, T]$, and such that the following conditions are satisfied:

$$\int_0^T \left(\left| \frac{\mu_t}{\sigma_t} \right|^2 + |\sigma_t|^2 + |\mu_t|^2 \right) dt < +\infty, \quad \mathbb{P}\text{-a.s.,} \qquad [3.5]$$

$$\forall t \in [0, T], \quad \gamma_t < 1. \qquad [3.6]$$

Note that the above conditions ensure that the process S in equation [3.4] is well-defined and takes strictly positive values. It can actually be written as

$$S_t = \exp \left(\int_0^t \left(\mu_s - \frac{\sigma_s^2}{2} \right) ds + \int_0^t \sigma_s dW_s^{\mathbb{F}} \right) (1 - \gamma_\tau \mathbb{1}_{\{\tau \leq t\}}).$$

The value γ_τ represents the proportional jump of the asset price S when the default event occurs.

We assume that the Novikov's condition is satisfied:

$$\mathbb{E}^{\mathbb{P}} \left[\exp \left(\frac{1}{2} \int_0^T \left| \frac{\mu_t}{\sigma_t} \right|^2 dt \right) \right] < +\infty.$$

Since the price process S satisfies the stochastic differential equation [3.4]. We obtain that the no-arbitrage condition is satisfied, namely, the set

$$\mathcal{M}(\mathbb{G}) := \{\mathbb{Q} \sim \mathbb{P} \text{ on } (\Omega, \mathcal{G}_T) : S \text{ is a } (\mathbb{G}, \mathbb{Q})\text{-local martingale}\}$$

is not empty. However, the equivalent martingale measures $\mathbb{Q} \in \mathcal{M}(\mathbb{G})$ are not unique, due to the appearance of the two $(\mathbb{G}, \mathbb{P})$-martingales W and N.

Note that any $\mathbb{G}$-adapted process Y can be written in a decomposed form as

$$\forall t \in [0, T], \quad Y_t = \mathbb{1}_{\{\tau > t\}} Y_t^{\mathbb{F}} + \mathbb{1}_{\{\tau \le t\}} Y_t(\tau),$$

where $Y^{\mathbb{F}}$ and $Y(\cdot)$ are, respectively, $\mathbb{F}$-adapted and $\mathbb{F} \otimes \sigma(\mathbb{R}_+)$-adapted processes. In particular, the drift term and the volatility term of the price dynamics [3.4] can be written in the decomposed form as

$$\mu_t = \mathbb{1}_{\{\tau > t\}} \mu_t^{\mathbb{F}} + \mathbb{1}_{\{\tau \le t\}} \mu_t(\tau), \quad \sigma_t = \mathbb{1}_{\{\tau > t\}} \sigma_t^{\mathbb{F}} + \mathbb{1}_{\{\tau \le t\}} \sigma_t(\tau).$$

Therefore, we can write the price process S as

$$\forall t \in [0, T], \quad S_t = \mathbb{1}_{\{\tau > t\}} S_t^{\mathbb{F}} + \mathbb{1}_{\{\tau \le t\}} S_t(\tau),$$

where the processes $S^{\mathbb{F}}$ and $S(\cdot)$ are determined by the following stochastic differential equations, respectively,

$$\begin{cases} dS_t^{\mathbb{F}} = S_t^{\mathbb{F}} (\mu_t^{\mathbb{F}} dt + \sigma_t^{\mathbb{F}} dW_t^{\mathbb{F}}), & t \in [0, T] \\ S_0^{\mathbb{F}} = 1, \end{cases} \qquad [3.7]$$

and for any $\theta \in [0, T]$

$$\begin{cases} dS_t(\theta) = S_t(\theta) (\mu_t(\theta) dt + \sigma_t(\theta) dW_t^{\mathbb{F}}), & t \in [\theta, T] \\ S_\theta(\theta) = S_\theta^{\mathbb{F}} (1 - \gamma_\theta). \end{cases} \qquad [3.8]$$

Although the asset price S is a $\mathbb{G}$-adapted càdlàg process and may jump at the random time τ, the solutions of the above equations are continuous processes. Here, the jump of the process S is interpreted as the difference between the two $\mathbb{F}$-adapted processes: $(S_\theta(\theta), \ \theta \in [0, T])$ and $S^{\mathbb{F}}$. A similar remark also applies to the dynamics of the portfolio value process which we discuss below.

The jump in the asset price S corresponds to a contagion risk, if we consider τ as the default time of a counterparty. In fact, the process $S^{\mathbb{F}}$ represents the asset price before the default event, the stock price jumps at the default time τ of the counterparty, where the jump size is described by the process γ, which may take positive or negative values, corresponding to proportional loss or gain on the stock price. After the default event at time $\tau = \theta$, the asset price process is described by $S(\theta)$, which satisfies a different diffusion equation, and $S_\theta(\theta) = S_\theta^{\mathbb{F}}(1 - \gamma_\theta)$ denotes the initial value of the after-default price. We observe a change of regimes in the drift and volatility depending upon the default event.

One typical situation can be as follows: in case of downward (respectively, upward) jump in the asset price at default time $\tau = \theta$, the rate of return $\mu(\theta)$ should be smaller (respectively, greater) than the rate of return $\mu^{\mathbb{F}}$ before the default, and this gap should increase when the default occurs early, i.e. $\mu(\theta)$ is increasing (respectively, decreasing) in θ with $\mu(\theta) <$ (respectively, $>$) $\mu^{\mathbb{F}}$. For example, we may choose in the case of downward jump, i.e. $\gamma > 0$, a rate of return coefficient in the form: $\mu(\theta) = \mu^{\mathbb{F}}\theta/T$, for $\theta \in [0, T]$. However, we also expect that the volatility $\sigma(\theta)$ after default is greater than the volatility $\sigma^{\mathbb{F}}$ before default, and this gap should also increase when the default occurs early. An example of volatility coefficient is: $\sigma(\theta) = \sigma^{\mathbb{F}}(2 - \theta/T)$.

We make precise the investment strategies, respectively, in quantitative form and proportional form. Let ϕ be an investment strategy, which is a $\mathbb{G}$-predictable process integrable with respect to the semimartingale S. We can write it in the decomposed form as

$$\phi_t = \phi_t^{\mathbb{F}}\mathbb{1}_{\{\tau \geq t\}} + \phi_t(\tau)\mathbb{1}_{\{\tau < t\}}, \quad t \in [0, T] \tag{3.9}$$

where $\phi^{\mathbb{F}}$ is an $\mathbb{F}$-predictable process and $\phi(\cdot)$ is a $\mathcal{P}(\mathbb{F}) \otimes \mathcal{B}(\mathbb{R}_+)$-measurable function, $\mathcal{P}(\mathbb{F})$ being the predictable σ-algebra of the filtration $\mathbb{F}$. The corresponding value process X^ϕ, determined by the dynamics

$$\begin{cases} dX_t^\phi = \phi_t dS_t, & t \in [0, T], \\ X_0^\phi = X_0, \end{cases} \tag{3.10}$$

can be written in the decomposed form as

$$X_t^\phi = \mathbb{1}_{\{\tau > t\}} X_t^{\phi, \mathbb{F}} + \mathbb{1}_{\{\tau \leq t\}} X_t^\phi(\tau),$$

where the processes $X^{\phi, \mathbb{F}}$ and $X^\phi(\cdot)$ satisfy the following stochastic differential equations

$$\begin{cases} dX_t^{\phi, \mathbb{F}} = \phi_t^{\mathbb{F}} S_t^{\mathbb{F}} \left(\mu_t^{\mathbb{F}} dt + \sigma_t^{\mathbb{F}} dW_t^{\mathbb{F}} \right), \ t \in [0, T], \\ X_0^{\phi, \mathbb{F}} = X_0, \end{cases}$$ [3.11]

and for any $\theta \in [0, T]$

$$\begin{cases} dX_t^\phi(\theta) = \phi_t(\theta) S_t(\theta) \left(\mu_t(\theta) dt + \sigma_t(\theta) dW_t^{\mathbb{F}} \right), \ t \in [\theta, T], \\ X_\theta^\phi(\theta) = X_\theta^{\phi, \mathbb{F}} - \phi_\theta^{\mathbb{F}} S_\theta^{\mathbb{F}} \gamma_\theta. \end{cases}$$ [3.12]

Similarly, if π is an investment strategy in the proportional form, which is a $\mathbb{G}$-predictable process written in the decomposed form as

$$\pi_t = \pi_t^{\mathbb{F}} \mathbb{1}_{\{\tau \geq t\}} + \pi_t(\tau) \mathbb{1}_{\{\tau < t\}}, \quad t \in [0, T]$$

Then, the corresponding value process X^π, determined by the dynamics

$$\begin{cases} \dfrac{dX_t^\pi}{X_t^\pi} = \pi_t \dfrac{dS_t}{S_{t-}}, \quad t \in [0, T], \\ X_0^\pi = X_0, \end{cases}$$

can be written in the decomposed form

$$X_t^\pi = \mathbb{1}_{\{\tau > t\}} X_t^{\pi, \mathbb{F}} + \mathbb{1}_{\{\tau \leq t\}} X_t^\pi(\tau),$$ [3.13]

where the processes $X^{\pi, \mathbb{F}}$ and $X^\pi(\cdot)$ satisfy the following stochastic differential equations

$$\begin{cases} \dfrac{dX_t^{\pi, \mathbb{F}}}{X_t^{\pi, \mathbb{F}}} = \pi_t^{\mathbb{F}} \left(\mu_t^{\mathbb{F}} dt + \sigma_t^{\mathbb{F}} dW_t^{\mathbb{F}} \right), \quad t \in [0, T], \\ X_0^{\pi, \mathbb{F}} = X_0 \end{cases}$$ [3.14]

and

$$\begin{cases} \dfrac{dX_t^\pi(\theta)}{X_t^\pi(\theta)} = \pi_t(\theta)\Big(\mu_t(\theta)dt + \sigma_t(\theta)dW_t^{\mathbb{F}}\Big), \quad t \in [\theta, T], \\ X_\theta^\pi(\theta) = X_\theta^{\pi,\mathbb{F}}(1 - \pi_\theta^{\mathbb{F}}\gamma_\theta). \end{cases} \qquad [3.15]$$

3.1.2. *The optimization problem*

In this section, we present the portfolio optimization problem. We first consider the investment strategies in the proportional form. We denote by $\mathcal{A}$ a family of $\mathbb{G}$-predictable processes π satisfying the following conditions

$$\forall t \in [0, T], \quad \pi_{t-}\gamma_t < 1, \qquad [3.16]$$

$$\int_0^T |\pi_t\sigma_t|^2 dt < +\infty. \qquad [3.17]$$

Under these conditions, for any initial portfolio value $X_0 > 0$, the stochastic differential equation

$$\frac{X_t^\pi}{X_{t-}^\pi} = \pi_t\frac{dS_t}{S_{t-}} = \pi_t(\mu_t dt + \sigma_t dW_t^{\mathbb{F}} - \gamma_t dD_t) \qquad [3.18]$$

admits a unique strong solution, which is given by

$$X_t^\pi = X_0 \exp\left(\int_0^t \left(\pi_s\mu_s - \frac{|\pi_s\sigma_s|^2}{2}\right)ds + \int_0^t \pi_s\sigma_s dW_s^{\mathbb{F}}\right)$$
$$\cdot (1 - \pi_\tau\gamma_\tau \mathbb{1}_{\{\tau \le t\}}). \qquad [3.19]$$

We now consider the following portfolio optimization problem

$$V_0(X_0) = \sup_{\pi \in \mathcal{A}} \mathbb{E}^{\mathbb{P}}[U(X_T^\pi)], \qquad [3.20]$$

where $U(\cdot)$ is a utility function on $(0, +\infty)$ satisfying Inada conditions. Problem [3.20] is a maximization problem of expected utility from terminal wealth in an incomplete market due to the jump of the risky asset. This optimization problem can be studied by convex duality methods. In fact, under the condition that

$$V_0(X_0) < \infty, \tag{3.21}$$

which is satisfied once

$$\mathbb{E}^{\mathbb{P}}\left[\widetilde{U}\left(y\frac{d\mathbb{Q}}{d\mathbb{P}}\right)\right] < \infty, \quad \text{for some } y > 0,$$

where $\widetilde{U}(y) = \sup_{x>0}[U(x) - xy]$ is the Legendre transform of U, and under the so-called condition of reasonable asymptotic elasticity:

$$AE(U) := \limsup_{x\to\infty} \frac{xU'(x)}{U(x)} < 1,$$

we know from the general results of Kramkov and Schachermayer [KRA 99] that there exists a solution to [3.20]. We also have a dual characterization of the solution, but this does not lead to explicit results due to the incompleteness of the market, i.e. the infinite cardinality of $\mathcal{M}(\mathbb{G})$. We can also deal directly with problem [3.20] by dynamic programming methods in the $\mathbb{G}$-filtration, as done in Lim and Quenez [LIM 11], where the authors consider a similar model as in [3.4] by assuming that $W^{\mathbb{F}}$ is a $\mathbb{G}$-Brownian motion. This means implicitly that (H)-hypothesis is in fact satisfied. We also mention a recent related paper by Ankirchner, Blanchet-Scalliet and Eyraud-Loisel [ANK 10], who considered an indifference pricing problem for exponential utility function in a market with a risky asset subject to a single jump, and adopted as in Lim and Quenez [LIM 11] a BSDE approach for solving this stochastic control problem. In both papers, the authors studied the problem globally in the $\mathbb{G}$-filtration, which leads to a derivation of the solution in terms of BSDE with jumps. This method does not really use the particular feature of the single jump at the default, and the results obtained are rather similar to those derived in market model with jumps, as in Morlais [MOR 09], for which it is, in general, difficult to obtain explicit characterization of the solutions. In Jiao and Pham [JIA 11], a decomposition method has been proposed to solve the optimization problem.

We can also consider the quantitative version of the investment strategies. Let $\mathcal{A}'$ be a family of $\mathbb{G}$-predictable processes ϕ which are integrable with respect to S. We consider the following optimization problem

$$V_0(X_0) = \sup_{\phi\in\mathcal{A}'} \mathbb{E}^{\mathbb{P}}[U(X_T^\phi)], \tag{3.22}$$

where $U(\cdot) : \mathbb{R} \to \mathbb{R}$ is a utility function, X_0 denotes the initial value of the portfolio and the portfolio value process X^ϕ is given by the stochastic differential equation $dX_t^\phi = \phi_t dS_t$.

In the forthcoming section, we present different methods for the resolution of the optimization problem [3.20]. In section 3.2, we explain the direct approach with the logarithmic utility function. In section 3.3, we explain the decomposition approach with the power utility function.

3.2. Direct method with the logarithmic utility

In this section, we consider the optimization problem with the logarithmic utility function and the investment strategy in the proportional form. We let $\mathcal{A}$ be the set of $\mathbb{G}$-predictable processes π satisfying the following conditions

$$\forall t \in [0, T], \quad \pi_{t-}\gamma_t < 1, \tag{3.23}$$

$$\mathbb{E}^\mathbb{P}\left[\int_0^T \left(|\pi_t \sigma_t|^2 + |\log(1 - \pi_t \gamma_t)| \right) dt \right] < +\infty. \tag{3.24}$$

By [3.19], for any investment strategy, $\pi \in \mathcal{A}$ we have

$$\begin{aligned} \log(X_t^\pi) = \log(X_0) &+ \int_0^t \left(\pi_s \mu_s - \frac{|\pi_s \sigma_s|^2}{2} \right) ds \\ &+ \int_0^t \pi_s \sigma_s dW_s^\mathbb{F} + \int_0^t \log(1 - \pi_s \gamma_s) dD_s. \end{aligned} \tag{3.25}$$

Note that the difference $\log(X_t^\pi) - \log(X_0)$ does not depend on the initial portfolio value. Moreover, by [3.2], we can rewrite $\log(X_t^\pi) - \log(X_0)$ as

$$\begin{aligned} \int_0^t \left(\pi_s \mu_s - \frac{|\pi_s \sigma_s|}{2} + \pi_s \sigma_s \left(\mathbb{1}_{\{\tau > s\}} m_s + \mathbb{1}_{\{\tau \leq s\}} \beta_s(\tau) \right) \right) ds \\ + \int_0^t \pi_s \sigma_s dW_s + \int_0^t \log(1 - \pi_s \gamma_s) dD_s. \end{aligned}$$

We now consider the following portfolio optimization problem

$$V_0(X_0) = \sup_{\pi \in \mathcal{A}} \mathbb{E}^\mathbb{P}[\log(X_T^\pi)]. \tag{3.26}$$

The expression [3.25] then leads to

$$V_0(X_0) = \log(X_0) + V_0(1)$$

with

$$V_0(1) = \sup_{\pi \in \mathcal{A}} \mathbb{E}^{\mathbb{P}} \Big[\int_0^T \Big(\pi_t \mu_t - \frac{|\pi_t \sigma_t|^2}{2} + \pi_t \sigma_t q_t \Big) dt + \int_0^T \log(1 - \pi_t \gamma_t) d\Lambda_t \Big]$$ [3.27]

where Λ is the compensator of the default process D, and

$$q_t = \big(\mathbb{1}_{\{\tau > t\}} m_t + \mathbb{1}_{\{\tau \le t\}} \beta_t(\tau) \big).$$

Since the random time τ admits an intensity, namely, the random measure $d\Lambda_t$ admits a density $(\lambda_t)_{t \in [0,T]}$ with respect to the Lebesgues measure, the formula [3.27] can be written as

$$V_0(1) = \sup_{\pi \in \mathcal{A}} \int_0^T \mathbb{E}^{\mathbb{P}} \Big[\pi_t(\mu_t + \sigma_t q_t) - \frac{|\pi_t \sigma_t|^2}{2} + \lambda_t \log(1 - \pi_t \gamma_t) \Big] dt.$$

For fixed $t \in [0, T]$ (and also a trajectory in Ω), we consider the following function on $\pi \in \mathbb{R}$

$$F_t(\pi) = \pi(\mu_t + \sigma_t q_t) - \pi^2 \frac{\sigma_t^2}{2} + \lambda_t \log(1 - \pi \gamma_t).$$

We have

$$F_t'(\pi) = (\mu_t + \sigma_t q_t) - \sigma_t^2 \pi - \frac{\lambda_t \gamma_t}{1 - \gamma_t \pi}.$$

For any $t \in [0, T]$, let

$$\pi_t^* = \begin{cases} \dfrac{\gamma_t \widetilde{\mu}_t + \sigma_t^2 - \sqrt{(\gamma_t \widetilde{\mu}_t - \sigma_t^2)^2 + 4\lambda_t \gamma_t^2 \sigma_t^2}}{2\sigma_t^2 \gamma_t}, & 0 < \gamma_t < 1, \\[4mm] \dfrac{\widetilde{\mu}_t}{\sigma_t^2}, & \gamma_t = 0, \\[4mm] \dfrac{\gamma_t \widetilde{\mu}_t + \sigma_t^2 + \sqrt{(\gamma_t \widetilde{\mu}_t - \sigma_t^2)^2 + 4\lambda_t \gamma_t^2 \sigma_t^2}}{2\sigma_t^2 \gamma_t}, & \gamma_t < 0, \end{cases}$$ [3.28]

where

$$\widetilde{\mu}_t = \mu_t + \sigma_t q_t = \mu_t + \sigma_t \big(\mathbb{1}_{\{\tau > t\}} m_t + \mathbb{1}_{\{\tau \le t\}} \beta_t(\tau) \big).$$

We observe that π_t^* verifies the equation $F_t'(\pi) = 0$ which is equivalent to

$$(\widetilde{\mu}_t - \lambda_t\gamma_t) - (\gamma_t\widetilde{\mu}_t + \sigma_t^2)\pi + \sigma_t^2\gamma_t\pi^2 = 0.$$

Moreover, it maximizes the function $F_t(\cdot)$. Thus, we obtain the following result.

PROPOSITION 3.1.– Assume that the compensator process of the default process D admits a density λ with respect to the Lebesgue measure. Then, the optimal investment strategy is given by the formula [3.28], and the optimal utility value is

$$V_0(X_0) = \log(X_0) + \int_0^T \mathbb{E}^{\mathbb{P}}\left[\pi_t^*\widetilde{\mu}_t - \frac{|\pi_t^*\sigma_t|^2}{2} + \lambda_t\log(1 - \pi_t^*\gamma_t)\right]dt.$$

REMARK 3.1.– We observe that, for the logarithmic utility optimization problem, it is not necessary to assume the density hypothesis for the default time τ. It suffices to assume that, first the default time τ admits an intensity process λ, second the diffusion equation of X^π can be written in terms of integrals with a $(\mathbb{G}, \mathbb{P})$-Brownian motion W and the default process D. However, it turns out that the $\mathbb{F}$-density condition is a natural condition which guarantees the semimartingale decomposition of $\mathbb{F}$-martingales in $\mathbb{G}$ and hence is adequate here.

3.3. Optimization for standard investor: power utility

In this section, we study the optimization problem with the power utility function $U(x) = x^p/p$, where $p < 1$, $p \neq 0$. As in the previous section, we consider investment strategies in the proportional form and we denote by $\mathcal{A}$ the set of $\mathbb{G}$-predictable processes π satisfying the conditions

$$\forall t \in [0, T], \quad \pi_{t-}\gamma_t < 1 \text{ and } \int_0^T |\pi_t\sigma_t|^2 dt < +\infty.$$

For any investment strategy $\pi \in \mathcal{A}$, the portfolio value process X^π is given by

$$X_t^\pi = X_0 \exp\left(\int_0^t \left(\pi_s\mu_s - \frac{|\pi_s\sigma_s|^2}{2}\right)ds + \int_0^t \pi_s\sigma_s dW_s^{\mathbb{F}}\right)(1 - \pi_\tau\gamma_\tau \mathbb{1}_{\{\tau \leq t\}}).$$

However, in the case of power utility functions, it is no longer possible to write the process $U(X_t^\pi)$ in a similar form of [3.25] as a sum of simple integrals with respect to the Brownian motion W and the default process D. In this section, we use the decomposition formulae [3.14] and [3.15] to study this problem. We decompose an optimization strategy π into two pieces according to the default time. More precisely, we let $\mathcal{A}^{\mathbb{F}}$ be the set of $\mathbb{F}$-predictable processes $\pi^{\mathbb{F}}$ such that

$$\pi_t^{\mathbb{F}} \gamma_t < 1 \text{ a.s. for any } t \in [0, T]$$

and

$$\int_0^T |\pi_t^{\mathbb{F}} \sigma_t^{\mathbb{F}}|^2 dt + \int_0^T |\log(1 - \pi_t^{\mathbb{F}} \gamma_t)| \lambda_t dt < +\infty.$$

Similarly for any $\theta \in [0, T]$, let $\mathcal{A}(\theta)$ be the set of $\mathbb{F}$-predictable processes $\pi(\theta)$ on $[\theta, T]$ such that

$$\int_\theta^T |\pi_t(\theta) \sigma_t(\theta)|^2 dt < +\infty.$$

Note that, if $\pi^{\mathbb{F}}$ is an element in $\mathcal{A}^{\mathbb{F}}$ and if for any $\theta \in \mathcal{A}(\theta)$, $\pi(\theta)$ is an element in $\mathcal{A}(\theta)$, then the process

$$\pi_t^{\mathbb{F}} \mathbb{1}_{\{\tau > t\}} + \pi_t(\tau) \mathbb{1}_{\{\tau < t\}}, \quad t \in [0, T]$$

belongs to the investment strategy set $\mathcal{A}$. Conversely, any investment strategy $\pi \in \mathcal{A}$ can be decomposed into the form

$$\pi_t = \pi_t^{\mathbb{F}} \mathbb{1}_{\{\tau \geq t\}} + \pi_t(\tau) \mathbb{1}_{\{\tau < t\}}$$

with $\pi^{\mathbb{F}} \in \mathcal{A}^{\mathbb{F}}$ and $\pi(\theta) \in \mathcal{A}(\theta)$ for any $\theta \in [0, T]$ (the decomposition does not need to be unique).

3.3.1. *Decomposition of the optimization problem*

We separate the optimization problem [3.20] into after- and before-default optimization problems. The key point of this approach is to reduce the initial incomplete market problem formulated in the $\mathbb{G}$-filtration into two portfolio optimization problems with respect to the reference filtration $\mathbb{F}$. Notice that the (H)-hypothesis, which is usually assumed in the direct method with respect to the $\mathbb{G}$-filtration, is not needed here. Moreover, this gives a better understanding of the optimal strategy and allows us to derive explicit results in some particular cases of interest. We introduce a conditional expectation according to the default time, which leads to the introduction of an "after-default" and a global "before-default" optimization problem, the latter involving the optimal value of the former. Each of these optimization problems is performed in market models driven by the Brownian motion and with coefficients adapted with respect to the Brownian reference filtration. The main advantage of this approach is then to reduce the problem to the resolution of two optimization problems in complete default-free markets, which are simpler to deal with, and give more explicit results than the incomplete market framework studied by the dynamic programming approach or the convex duality method.

We now consider the following portfolio optimization problem

$$V_0(X_0) = \sup_{\pi \in \mathcal{A}} \mathbb{E}^{\mathbb{P}}[U(X_T^\pi)]. \tag{3.29}$$

We introduce a family of auxiliary dynamical portfolio optimization problems with respect to the filtration $\mathbb{F}$. For any $\mathcal{F}_\theta$-measurable random variable X_θ, we let

$$V_\theta^{\mathrm{a}}(X_\theta) := \operatorname*{ess\,sup}_{\pi(\theta) \in \mathcal{A}(\theta)} \mathbb{E}^{\mathbb{P}}[U(X_T^{\pi(\theta)})\alpha_T(\theta) \mid \mathcal{F}_\theta], \tag{3.30}$$

where the process $X^{\pi(\theta)}$ on $[\theta, T]$ is determined by the stochastic differential equation

$$\frac{dX_t^{\pi(\theta)}}{X_t^{\pi(\theta)}} = \pi_t(\theta)\Big(\mu_t(\theta)dt + \sigma_t(\theta)dW_t^{\mathbb{F}}\Big), \quad X_\theta^{\pi(\theta)} = X_\theta. \tag{3.31}$$

The superscript symbol "a" in the expression $V_\theta^{\mathrm{a}}(X_\theta)$ stands for "after default". By using a dynamical programming principle, we can transform the optimization problem [3.29] into a "before default optimization" as shown in the theorem below. This theorem can be viewed as a dynamic programming-type relation. Indeed, compared to the dynamic programming principle (see theorem 1.3) where we look for a relation on the value function by varying the initial states and consider deterministic consecutive dates, here we consider the value function between the initial time and a random default time (which is not even an $\mathbb{F}$-stopping time). The key point is to take a conditional expectation of the terminal information.

THEOREM 3.1.– For any $X_0 > 0$, we have

$$V_0(X_0) = \sup_{\pi^{\mathbb{F}} \in \mathcal{A}^{\mathbb{F}}} \mathbb{E}^{\mathbb{P}} \left[U(X_T^{\pi^{\mathbb{F}}}) G_T + \int_0^T V_\theta^{\mathrm{a}}(X_\theta^{\pi^{\mathbb{F}}}(1 - \pi_\theta^{\mathbb{F}} \gamma_\theta)) d\theta \right], \qquad [3.32]$$

where the process $X^{\pi^{\mathbb{F}}}$ is determined by the following stochastic differential equation

$$\begin{cases} \dfrac{dX_t^{\pi^{\mathbb{F}}}}{X_t^{\pi^{\mathbb{F}}}} = \pi_t^{\mathbb{F}} \left(\mu_t^{\mathbb{F}} dt + \sigma_t^{\mathbb{F}} dW_t^{\mathbb{F}} \right), \quad t \in [0, T], \\ X_0^{\pi^{\mathbb{F}}} = X_0, \end{cases}$$

and $G_T = \mathbb{P}(\tau > T \,|\, \mathcal{F}_T)$.

PROOF.– Let π be an element of $\mathcal{A}$, which is written in the decomposed form

$$\pi_t = \mathbb{1}_{\{\tau \geq t\}} \pi_t^{\mathbb{F}} + \mathbb{1}_{\{\tau < t\}} \pi_t(\theta),$$

where $\pi^{\mathbb{F}} \in \mathcal{A}^{\mathbb{F}}$, and $\pi(\theta) \in \mathcal{A}(\theta)$ for any $\theta \in [0, T]$. We also write the random variable X_T^π in the decomposed form

$$X_T^\pi = \mathbb{1}_{\{\tau > T\}} X_T^{\pi,\mathbb{F}} + \mathbb{1}_{\{\tau \leq T\}} X_T^\pi(\tau)$$

so that

$$\begin{aligned} &\mathbb{E}^{\mathbb{P}}[U(X_T^\pi)] \\ &= \mathbb{E}^{\mathbb{P}}[U(X_T^{\pi,\mathbb{F}}) G_T] + \int_0^T \mathbb{E}^{\mathbb{P}}[U(X_T^\pi(\theta)) \alpha_T(\theta)] d\theta \qquad [3.33] \\ &= \mathbb{E}^{\mathbb{P}}[U(X_T^{\pi,\mathbb{F}}) G_T] + \mathbb{E}^{\mathbb{P}} \left[\int_0^T \mathbb{E}^{\mathbb{P}}[U(X_T^\pi(\theta)) \alpha_T(\theta) \,|\, \mathcal{F}_\theta] d\theta \right]. \end{aligned}$$

By definition of the "after default optimization problem" [3.30], we obtain

$$\mathbb{E}^{\mathbb{P}}[U(X_T^\pi)] \leq \mathbb{E}^{\mathbb{P}}[U(X_T^{\pi,\mathbb{F}}) G_T] + \mathbb{E}^{\mathbb{P}} \left[\int_0^T V_\theta^{\mathrm{a}}(X_\theta^{\pi,\mathbb{F}}(1 - \pi_\theta^{\mathbb{F}} \gamma_\theta)) d\theta \right].$$

Note that $X_t^{\pi^F} = X_t^{\pi,F}$ for any $t \in [0, T]$, we thus obtain

$$\mathbb{E}^{\mathbb{P}}[U(X_T^{\pi})] \leq \sup_{\pi^F \in \mathcal{A}^F} \mathbb{E}^{\mathbb{P}}\left[U(X_T^{\pi^F})G_T + \int_0^T V_\theta^a(X_\theta^{\pi^F}(1 - \pi_\theta^F \gamma_\theta))d\theta\right].$$

Since $\pi \in \mathcal{A}$ is arbitrary, we obtain

$$V_0(X_0) \leq \sup_{\pi^F \in \mathcal{A}^F} \mathbb{E}^{\mathbb{P}}\left[U(X_T^{\pi^F})G_T + \int_0^T V_\theta^a(X_\theta^{\pi^F}(1 - \pi_\theta^F \gamma_\theta))d\theta\right]. \qquad [3.34]$$

Conversely, let π^F be an element of $\mathcal{A}_{\mathbb{F}}$. By the definition of V^a, for any $\theta \in [0, T]$, and $\varepsilon > 0$, there exists $\pi^\varepsilon(\theta) \in \mathcal{A}(\theta)$ such that

$$V_\theta^a(X_\theta^{\pi^F}(1 - \pi_\theta^F \gamma_\theta)) \leq \mathbb{E}^{\mathbb{P}}[U(X_T^{\pi^\varepsilon(\theta)})\alpha_T(\theta) \mid \mathcal{F}_\theta] + \varepsilon \quad d\mathbb{P} \otimes d\theta \ a.e.,$$

where the process $X^{\pi^\varepsilon(\theta)}$ on $[\theta, T]$ is determined by the stochastic differential equation

$$\frac{dX_t^{\pi^\varepsilon(\theta)}}{X_t^{\pi^\varepsilon(\theta)}} = \pi_t(\theta)\left(\mu_t(\theta)dt + \sigma_t(\theta)dW_t^{\mathbb{F}}\right), \quad X_\theta^{\pi^\varepsilon(\theta)} = X_\theta^{\pi^F}(1 - \pi_\theta^F \gamma_\theta).$$

We can use a measurable selection result (see, e.g. [WAG 80]) to ensure the measurability of $\pi^\varepsilon(\theta)$ with respect to θ. Let π^ε be the investment strategy in $\mathcal{A}$ such that

$$\pi_t^\varepsilon = \pi_t^F \mathbb{1}_{\{\tau \geq t\}} + \pi_t^\varepsilon(\tau)\mathbb{1}_{\{\tau < t\}}.$$

By [3.33] again, we obtain

$$\begin{aligned}
V_0(X_0) &\geq \mathbb{E}^{\mathbb{P}}[U(X_T^{\pi^\varepsilon})] \\
&= \mathbb{E}\left[U(X_T^{\pi^F})G_T + \int_0^T \mathbb{E}^{\mathbb{P}}[U(Y_T^{\pi^\varepsilon(\theta)})\alpha_T(\theta) \mid \mathcal{F}_\theta]d\theta\right] \\
&\geq \mathbb{E}\left[U(X_T^{\pi^F})G_T + \int_0^T V_\theta^a(X_\theta^{\pi^F}(1 - \pi_\theta^F \gamma_\theta))d\theta\right] - \varepsilon T.
\end{aligned}$$

Since $\pi^F \in \mathcal{A}_{\mathbb{F}}$ and $\varepsilon > 0$ are arbitrary, we obtain converse inequality of [3.34]. The theorem is thus proved. $\qquad \square$

REMARK 3.2.– Theorem 3.1 also provides a method to find the global optimal investment strategy in terms of the optimal strategies of the decomposed optimization problems. More precisely, if $\widehat{\pi}^{\mathbb{F}}$ is an optimal strategy of the optimization problem [3.32] and if $\widehat{\pi}(\theta)$ is an optimal strategy of [3.30] with

$$X_\theta = X_\theta^{\widehat{\pi}_\theta^{\mathbb{F}}}\left(1 - \widehat{\pi}_\theta^{\mathbb{F}}\gamma_\theta\right).$$

Then, the global optimal investment strategy is given by

$$\widehat{\pi}_t = \widehat{\pi}_t^{\mathbb{F}}\mathbb{1}_{\{\tau \geq t\}} + \widehat{\pi}_t(\tau)\mathbb{1}_{\{\tau < t\}}, \quad 0 \leq t \leq T. \tag{3.35}$$

Observe that the optimal trading strategy follows the trading strategy $\widehat{\pi}^{\mathbb{F}}$ before default time τ, and then switches to the after-default trading strategy $\widehat{\pi}(\tau)$, which depends on the default time.

We now discuss the resolution of the two optimization problems arising from the decomposition of the initial optimization problem. We first explain the resolution of the after-default optimal investment problem by the duality method, and then the before-default optimization problem by using the dynamic programming principle.

3.3.2. *Solution to the after-default optimization problem*

In this section, we solve the after-default optimal investment problem. Note that [3.30] is an optimal investment problem in a complete market model after default. However, the coefficients $\mu(\theta)$ and $\sigma(\theta)$ of the diffusion equation [3.31] depend on the initial time θ of the optimization problem. Therefore, the optimization problem is not time-consistent. Moreover, in the optimization problem [3.30], there appears the density term $\alpha_T(\theta)$ as a multiplicative utility weight to the utility function U. We will use the duality method (see theorem 1.1) to solve the problem. We first determine the equivalent martingale measure for the semimartingale

$$\int_\theta^t \mu_s(\theta)ds + \int_\theta^t \sigma_s(\theta)dW_s^{\mathbb{F}}, \quad t \in [\theta, T]. \tag{3.36}$$

We assume that the Novikov's condition

$$\mathbb{E}^{\mathbb{P}}\left[\exp\left(\frac{1}{2}\int_\theta^T \left|\frac{\mu_s(\theta)}{\sigma_s(\theta)}\right|^2 ds\right)\right] < +\infty$$

is satisfied and define

$$Z_t(\theta) = \exp\left(-\int_\theta^t \frac{\mu_s(\theta)}{\sigma_s(\theta)} dW_s^{\mathbb{F}} - \frac{1}{2}\int_\theta^t \left|\frac{\mu_s(\theta)}{\sigma_s(\theta)}\right|^2 ds\right), \quad t \in [\theta, T]. \quad [3.37]$$

Let $\mathbb{Q}^\theta$ be the equivalent probability measure of $\mathbb{P}$ such that

$$\frac{d\mathbb{Q}^\theta}{d\mathbb{P}} = Z_t(\theta) \quad \text{on } \mathcal{F}_t.$$

Then, the $(\mathbb{F}, \mathbb{P})$-semimartingale [3.36] becomes a $(\mathbb{F}, \mathbb{Q}^\theta)$-martingale. Hence, theorem 1.1 leads to the following result. Recall that I is the inverse function of U'.

THEOREM 3.2.– Assume that, for any $y > 0$, the random variable $I(yZ_T(\theta)/\alpha_T(\theta))$ is integrable with respect to the probability measure $\mathbb{Q}^\theta$, or equivalently $Z_T(\theta)I(yZ_T(\theta)/\alpha_T(\theta))$ is integrable with respect to $\mathbb{P}$. Then, the following equality holds

$$V_\theta^{\mathrm{a}}(X_\theta) = \mathbb{E}^{\mathbb{P}}\left[\alpha_T(\theta)U\left(I\left(\frac{\widehat{Y}_\theta Z_T(\theta)}{\alpha_T(\theta)}\right)\right)\Big|\, \mathcal{F}_\theta\right], \quad \mathbb{P}\text{-a.s}, \quad [3.38]$$

where the $\mathcal{F}_\theta$-measurable random variable $\widehat{Y}_\theta$ is determined by the following equation

$$\mathbb{E}^{\mathbb{P}}\left[Z_T(\theta)I\left(\widehat{Y}_\theta \frac{Z_T(\theta)}{\alpha_T(\theta)}\right)\Big|\, \mathcal{F}_\theta\right] = X_\theta. \quad [3.39]$$

Moreover, the optimal investment strategy $\widehat{\pi}(\theta)$ after default is determined by the relation

$$X_\theta \exp\left(\int_\theta^T \left(\widehat{\pi}_s(\theta)\mu_s(\theta) - \frac{1}{2}\widehat{\pi}_s(\theta)^2\sigma_s(\theta)^2\right)ds + \int_\theta^T \sigma_s(\theta)dW_s^{\mathbb{F}}\right)$$

$$= I\left(\frac{\widehat{Y}_\theta Z_T(\theta)}{\alpha_T(\theta)}\right).$$

PROOF.– The main point is to show that the random variable $I(\widehat{Y}_\theta Z_T(\theta)/\alpha_T(\theta))$ can be realized by some investment strategy, namely, there exists an element $\widehat{\pi}(\theta) \in \mathcal{A}(\theta)$ such that $X_T^{\pi(\theta)} = I(\widehat{Y}_\theta Z_T(\theta)/\alpha_T(\theta))$. This follows from equation [3.39], which can be written as

$$
\mathbb{E}^{\mathbb{Q}^\theta}\left[I\left(\widehat{Y}_\theta \frac{Z_T(\theta)}{\alpha_T(\theta)}\right) \Big| \mathcal{F}_\theta\right] = X_\theta
$$

and the martingale representation theorem for the Brownian filtration.   □

REMARK 3.3.– Under the (H)-hypothesis, we have $\alpha_T(\theta) = \alpha_\theta(\theta)$, which is $\mathcal{F}_\theta$-measurable. In this case, the above theorem takes a simpler form as follows. Let $\widehat{y}_\theta$ be the $\mathcal{F}_\theta$-measurable random variable determined by the equation

$$
\mathbb{E}^{\mathbb{P}}\left[Z_T(\theta)I(\widehat{y}_\theta Z_T(\theta)) \Big| \mathcal{F}_\theta\right] = X_\theta.
$$

Then, we have

$$
V_\theta^{\mathrm{a}}(X_\theta) = \alpha_\theta(\theta)\mathbb{E}^{\mathbb{P}}\left[U(I(\widehat{y}_\theta Z_T(\theta))) \Big| \mathcal{F}_\theta\right].
$$

The parameters $\widehat{y}_\theta$ and $\widehat{Y}_\theta$ are related by the relation $\widehat{y}_\theta = \widehat{Y}_\theta \alpha_\theta(\theta)$. We observe that $\widehat{y}_\theta$ does not depend on the conditional density process $\alpha(\cdot)$. In particular, the optimal investment strategy $\widehat{\pi}(\theta)$ does not depend on the conditional density process either.

We now apply theorem 3.2 to the power utility function $U(x) = x^p/p$, where $p < 1$, $p \neq 0$. Recall that the function $I = (U')^{-1}$ can be written as $I(y) = y^{1/(p-1)}$. Hence, equation [3.39] becomes

$$
\widehat{Y}_\theta^{1/(p-1)}\mathbb{E}^{\mathbb{P}}\left[Z_T(\theta)\left(\frac{Z_T(\theta)}{\alpha_T(\theta)}\right)^{1/(p-1)} \Big| \mathcal{F}_\theta\right] = X_\theta.
$$

Hence, we have

$$
\widehat{Y}_\theta = X_\theta^{p-1}\mathbb{E}^{\mathbb{P}}\left[Z_T(\theta)\left(\frac{Z_T(\theta)}{\alpha_T(\theta)}\right)^{1/(p-1)} \Big| \mathcal{F}_\theta\right]^{1-p},
$$

which leads to

$$
I\left(\widehat{Y}_\theta \frac{Z_T(\theta)}{\alpha_T(\theta)}\right) = X_\theta\mathbb{E}^{\mathbb{P}}\left[Z_T(\theta)\left(\frac{Z_T(\theta)}{\alpha_T(\theta)}\right)^{1/(p-1)} \Big| \mathcal{F}_\theta\right]^{-1}\left(\frac{Z_T(\theta)}{\alpha_T(\theta)}\right)^{1/(p-1)}.
$$

Thus, the formula [3.38] leads to

$$
\begin{aligned}
&V_\theta^{\mathrm{a}}(X_\theta)/\left(\tfrac{X_\theta^p}{p}\right)\\
&= \mathbb{E}^{\mathbb{P}}\left[Z_T(\theta)\left(\tfrac{Z_T(\theta)}{\alpha_T(\theta)}\right)^{1/(p-1)}\Big|\mathcal{F}_\theta\right]^{-p}\mathbb{E}^{\mathbb{P}}\left[\alpha_T(\theta)\left(\tfrac{Z_T(\theta)}{\alpha_T(\theta)}\right)^{p/(p-1)}\Big|\mathcal{F}_\theta\right]\\
&= \mathbb{E}^{\mathbb{P}}\left[\alpha_T(\theta)\left(\tfrac{Z_T(\theta)}{\alpha_T(\theta)}\right)^{p/(p-1)}\Big|\mathcal{F}_\theta\right]^{1-p}.
\end{aligned}
$$

Note that the quotient $V_\theta^{\mathrm{a}}(X_\theta)/U(X_\theta)$ does not depend on the value of X_θ.

3.3.3. *Resolution of the before-default optimization problem*

The purpose of this section is to explain the resolution of the before-default optimization problem

$$
V_0(X_0) = \sup_{\pi^{\mathbb{F}}\in\mathcal{A}^{\mathbb{F}}} \mathbb{E}^{\mathbb{P}}\left[U(X_T^{\pi^{\mathbb{F}}})G_T + \int_0^T V_\theta^{\mathrm{a}}(X_\theta^{\pi^{\mathbb{F}}}(1-\pi_\theta^{\mathbb{F}}\gamma_\theta))d\theta\right], \qquad [3.40]
$$

with $V_\theta^{\mathrm{a}}(\cdot)$ being the solution of the after-default optimization problem [3.38]. We aim to provide an explicit characterization of the optimal strategy $\widehat{\pi}^{\mathbb{F}}$, by using the dynamic programming approach. For any $t \in [0,T]$ and $\nu \in \mathcal{A}^{\mathbb{F}}$, let $\mathcal{A}^{\mathbb{F}}(t,\nu)$ be the set of strategies in $\mathcal{A}^{\mathbb{F}}$ which coincide with ν until time t:

$$
\mathcal{A}^{\mathbb{F}}(t,\nu) := \{\pi^{\mathbb{F}} \in \mathcal{A}^{\mathbb{F}} \mid \pi_s^{\mathbb{F}} = \nu_s \text{ for any } s \in [0,t]\}.
$$

We introduce the dynamic version of the optimization problem [3.32] as follows:

$$
V_t(X_0,\nu) := \operatorname*{ess\,sup}_{\pi^{\mathbb{F}}\in\mathcal{A}^{\mathbb{F}}(t,\nu)} \mathbb{E}\left[U(X_T^{\pi^{\mathbb{F}}})G_T + \int_t^T V_\theta^{d}(X_\theta^{\pi^{\mathbb{F}}}(1-\pi_\theta^{\mathbb{F}}\gamma_\theta))d\theta\Big|\mathcal{F}_t\right],
$$

$$
0 \le t \le T.
$$

In the above expression, $X^{\pi^{\mathbb{F}}}$ is the wealth process of the dynamics

$$
\begin{cases}
\dfrac{dX_t^{\pi^{\mathbb{F}}}}{X_t^{\pi^{\mathbb{F}}}} = \pi_t^{\mathbb{F}}\left(\mu_t^{\mathbb{F}}dt + \sigma_t^{\mathbb{F}}dW_t^{\mathbb{F}}\right), & t \in [0,T],\\
X_0^{\pi^{\mathbb{F}}} = X_0,
\end{cases}
$$

which coincides with X^ν on $[0, t]$. Note that $V_0(X_0) = V_0(X_0, \nu)$ for any $\nu \in \mathcal{A}^{\mathbb{F}}$. Moreover, by the dynamic programming principle (see theorem 1.3), we obtain that for any $\nu \in \mathcal{A}_{\mathbb{F}}$, the process

$$V_t(X_0, \nu) + \int_0^t V_\theta^{\mathrm{a}}(X_\theta^\nu(1 - \nu_\theta \gamma_\theta)) d\theta, \quad 0 \le t \le T \qquad [3.41]$$

is a $(\mathbb{P}, \mathbb{F})$-supermartingale. Moreover, the optimal strategy ν^* to the optimization problem [3.40] is characterized by the $(\mathbb{P}, \mathbb{F})$-martingale property of the process

$$V_t(\nu^*) + \int_0^t V_\theta^{\mathrm{a}}(X_\theta^{\nu^*}(1 - \nu_\theta^* \gamma_\theta)) d\theta, \quad 0 \le t \le T. \qquad [3.42]$$

In the following, we apply the above martingale property characterization to the case of power utility function

$$U(x) = \frac{x^p}{p}, \quad p < 1, \, p \ne 0, \, x > 0.$$

In this case, we have

$$V_\theta^{\mathrm{a}}(x) = U(x)K_\theta^p = \frac{x^p}{p} K_\theta^p,$$

where

$$K_\theta = \left(\mathbb{E}\left[\alpha_T(\theta) \left(\frac{Z_T(\theta)}{\alpha_T(\theta)} \right)^{-q} \Big| \mathcal{F}_\theta \right] \right)^{\frac{1}{q}},$$

with $q = p/(1 - p)$. We assume that K_θ is $\mathbb{P}$-a.s. finite for any $\theta \in [0, T]$. The optimization problem [3.32] is written as

$$V_0(X_0) = \sup_{\nu \in \mathcal{A}^{\mathbb{F}}} \mathbb{E}^{\mathbb{P}}\left[U(X_T^\nu)G_T + \int_0^T U(X_\theta^\nu)(1 - \nu_\theta \gamma_\theta)^p K_\theta^p d\theta \right]. \qquad [3.43]$$

Therefore, the càdlàg $\mathbb{F}$-adapted process Y defined by $Y_t := V_t(\nu)/U(X_t^{\nu,\mathbb{F}})$ satisfies

$$Y_t = p \operatorname*{ess\,sup}_{\pi^{\mathbb{F}} \in \mathcal{A}^{\mathbb{F}}(t,\nu)} \mathbb{E}\left[U\left(\frac{X_T^{\pi^{\mathbb{F}}}}{X_t^\nu} \right) G_T + \int_t^T U\left(\frac{X_\theta^{\pi^{\mathbb{F}}}}{X_t^\nu} \right)(1 - \pi_\theta^{\mathbb{F}} \gamma_\theta)^p K_\theta^p d\theta \Big| \mathcal{F}_t \right]. \qquad [3.44]$$

In particular, it does not depend on the choice of $\nu \in \mathcal{A}^{\mathbb{F}}$, and lies in the set $L_+(\mathbb{F})$ of non-negative càdlàg $\mathbb{F}$-adapted processes. For any $\nu \in \mathcal{A}^{\mathbb{F}}$, we define

$$\xi_t^\nu(Y) := U(X_t^\nu)Y_t + \int_0^t U(X_\theta^\nu)(1 - \nu_\theta\gamma_\theta)^p K_\theta^p d\theta, \quad 0 \le t \le T, \qquad [3.45]$$

From [3.41], we obtain that the process $\xi^\nu(Y)$ is a $(\mathbb{P}, \mathbb{F})$-supermartingale. In particular, by taking $\nu = 0$, we see that the process

$$Y_t + \int_0^t K_\theta^p d\theta, \qquad t \in [0, t]$$

is a $(\mathbb{P}, \mathbb{F})$-supermartingale. By Doob–Meyer decomposition, and the martingale representation theorem for the Brownian filtration, we get the existence of $\phi \in L_{\text{loc}}^2(W)$, and a finite variation increasing $\mathbb{F}$-adapted process A such that

$$dY_t = \phi_t dW_t - dA_t, \quad 0 \le t \le T. \qquad [3.46]$$

Recall that $L_{\text{loc}}^2(W^{\mathbb{F}})$ denotes the the set of $\mathbb{F}$-adapted process Z such that

$$\int_0^T |Z_t|^2 dt < \infty \qquad \text{a.s.}$$

We have the following BSDE interpretation of the process Y.

THEOREM 3.3.– The stochastic process Y satisfies the following backward stochastic differential equation

$$Y_t = G_T + \int_t^T f(s, Y_s, Z_s)ds - \int_t^T Z_s dW_s^{\mathbb{F}}, \quad t \in [0, T] \qquad [3.47]$$

for some $Z \in L_{\text{loc}}^2(W^{\mathbb{F}})$, where

$$f(s, Y_s, Z_s)$$

$$= p \operatorname*{ess\,sup}_{\nu \in \mathcal{A}^{\mathbb{F}}} \left[(\mu_s^{\mathbb{F}} Y_s + \sigma_s^{\mathbb{F}} Z_s)\nu_s - \frac{1-p}{2} Y_s |\nu_s \sigma_s^{\mathbb{F}}|^2 + K_s^p \frac{(1 - \nu_s\gamma_s)^p}{p} \right],$$

while the optimal strategy ν^* attains the essential supremum in the above formula.

PROOF.– Let ν be an element in $\mathcal{A}^{\mathbb{F}}$. By Itô's formula, we have

$$
\begin{aligned}
dU(X_t^\nu) &= (X_t^\nu)^{p-1}dX_t^\nu + \tfrac{p-1}{2}(X_t^\nu)^{p-2}d\langle X_t^\nu\rangle\\
&= (X_t^\nu)^p\nu_t(\mu_t^{\mathbb{F}}dt + \sigma_t^{\mathbb{F}}dW_t^{\mathbb{F}}) + \tfrac{p-1}{2}(X_t^\nu)^p|\nu_t\sigma_t^{\mathbb{F}}|^2dt\\
&= pU(X_t^\nu)\left[\left(\nu_t\mu_t^{\mathbb{F}}dt + \tfrac{p-1}{2}|\nu_t\sigma_t^{\mathbb{F}}|^2\right)dt + \nu_t\sigma_t^{\mathbb{F}}dW_t^{\mathbb{F}}\right].
\end{aligned}
$$

Therefore, we obtain

$$
\begin{aligned}
d(Y_tU(X_t^\nu)) &= U(X_t^\nu)(\phi_tdW_t - dA_t) + \phi_tpU(X_t^\nu)\nu_t\sigma_t^{\mathbb{F}}dt\\
&\quad + Y_tpU(X_t^\nu)\left[\left(\nu_t\mu_t^{\mathbb{F}}dt + \tfrac{p-1}{2}|\nu_t\sigma_t^{\mathbb{F}}|^2\right)dt + \nu_t\sigma_t^{\mathbb{F}}dW_t^{\mathbb{F}}\right].
\end{aligned}
$$

Hence, the finite variation process in the decomposition of the $(\mathbb{P},\mathbb{F})$-supermartingale $\xi^\nu(Y)$, is given by $-A^\nu$ with

$$
\begin{aligned}
dA_t^\nu &= (X_t^\nu)^p\left\{\frac{1}{p}dA_t - \left[(\mu_t^{\mathbb{F}}Y_t + \sigma_t^{\mathbb{F}}\phi_t)\nu_t - \frac{1-p}{2}Y_t|\nu_t\sigma_t^{\mathbb{F}}|^2\right.\right.\\
&\quad\left.\left. + K_t^p\frac{(1-\nu_t\gamma_t)^p}{p}\right]dt\right\}.
\end{aligned}
$$

By the supermartingale property of $\xi^\nu(Y)$, $\nu \in \mathcal{A}_{\mathbb{F}}$, we obtain that the process A^ν is non-decreasing. Moreover, if ν^* is the optimal investment strategy, then by the martingale property of $\xi^{\nu^*}(Y)$, we obtain that $A^{\nu^*} = 0$, which implies

$$
\begin{aligned}
dA_t &= p\left[(\mu_t^{\mathbb{F}}Y_t + \sigma_t^{\mathbb{F}}\phi_t)\nu_t^* - \tfrac{1-p}{2}Y_t|\nu_t^*\sigma_t^{\mathbb{F}}|^2 + K_t^p\frac{(1-\nu_t^*\gamma_t)^p}{p}\right]dt\\
&= p\operatorname*{ess\,sup}_{\nu\in\mathcal{A}_{\mathbb{F}}}\left[(\mu_t^{\mathbb{F}}Y_t + \sigma_t^{\mathbb{F}}\phi_t)\nu_t - \tfrac{1-p}{2}Y_t|\nu_t\sigma_t^{\mathbb{F}}|^2 + K_t^p\frac{(1-\nu_t\gamma_t)^p}{p}\right]dt.
\end{aligned}
$$

Observe from [3.44] that $Y_T = G_T$. This proves that (Y,ϕ) solves the backward stochastic differential equation [3.47]. $\qquad\square$

REMARK 3.4.– The driver $f(t, Y_t, Z_t)$ of the backward stochastic differential equation [3.47] is in general not Lipschitz in (Y_t, Z_t), and it is not known by standard arguments that there exists a unique solution to this BSDE. In fact, when $\gamma = 0$, the driver is equal to:

$$
f(t, Y_t, \phi_t) = \frac{1}{2}\frac{(\mu_t^{\mathbb{F}}Y_t + \sigma_t^{\mathbb{F}}Z_t)^2}{(1-p)\sigma_t^{\mathbb{F}}Y_t},
$$

and so is even not quadratic in (Y_t, Z_t).

The following lemma provides some basic properties of the process Y. Note that we also deal with the case $p < 0$, namely, the degree of risk aversion $1 - p$ is strictly larger than 1. In this case, we have some additional technical difficulties.

LEMMA 3.1.– The process Y in [3.44] is strictly positive, namely, we have

$$\mathbb{P}(Y_t > 0,\ 0 \leq t \leq T) = 1.$$

Moreover, for any $\nu \in \mathcal{A}^{\mathbb{F}}$, the process is bounded from below by an $(\mathbb{F}, \mathbb{P})$-martingale.

PROOF.–

1) We first consider the case $p > 0$. Then,

$$\begin{aligned} Y_t &= \operatorname*{ess\,sup}_{\pi^{\mathbb{F}} \in \mathcal{A}^{\mathbb{F}}(t,\nu)} \mathbb{E}^{\mathbb{P}}\left[\left(\frac{X_T^{\pi^{\mathbb{F}}}}{X_t^{\nu}}\right)^p G_T + \int_t^T \left(\frac{X_\theta^{\pi^{\mathbb{F}}}}{X_t^{\nu}}\right)^p (1 - \pi_\theta^{\mathbb{F}} \gamma_\theta)^p K_\theta^p d\theta \,\Big|\, \mathcal{F}_t \right] \\ &\geq \mathbb{E}^{\mathbb{P}}\left[G_T + \int_t^T K_\theta^p d\theta \,\Big|\, \mathcal{F}_t \right] > 0, \quad \forall\, t \in [0, T], \end{aligned}$$

[3.48]

by taking in [3.48] the element $\pi^{\mathbb{F}} \in \mathcal{A}^{\mathbb{F}}(t, \nu)$ with $\pi_s^{\mathbb{F}} = \nu_s \mathbb{1}_{s \leq t}$. Moreover, since $U(x)$ is non-negative, the process $\xi^{\nu}(Y)$ is non-negative, hence trivially bounded from below by the zero martingale.

2) We next consider the case $p < 0$. In this case, for any $t \in [0, T]$, we have

$$\begin{aligned} Y_t &= \operatorname*{ess\,inf}_{\pi^{\mathbb{F}} \in \mathcal{A}^{\mathbb{F}}(t,\nu)} \mathbb{E}\left[\left(\frac{X_T^{\pi^{\mathbb{F}}}}{X_t^{\nu}}\right)^p G_T + \int_t^T \left(\frac{X_\theta^{\pi^{\mathbb{F}}}}{X_t^{\nu}}\right)^p (1 - \pi_\theta^{\mathbb{F}} \gamma_\theta)^p K_\theta^p d\theta \,\Big|\, \mathcal{F}_t \right] \\ &\geq J_t := \operatorname*{ess\,inf}_{\pi^{\mathbb{F}} \in \mathcal{A}^{\mathbb{F}}(t,\nu)} \mathbb{E}\left[\left(\frac{X_T^{\pi^{\mathbb{F}}}}{X_t^{\nu,\mathbb{F}}}\right)^p G_T \,\Big|\, \mathcal{F}_t \right]. \end{aligned}$$

[3.49]

Note that we choose a càdlàg version of the process J. By definition, it is obvious that $J \geq 0$. We show that, for any $t \in [0, T]$, J_t is strictly positive and the essential infimum in J_t is attained. By a measurable selection argument, we can choose a sequence $(\pi^n)_{n \geq 1}$ in $\mathcal{A}^{\mathbb{F}}(t, \nu)$ such that

$$\lim_{n \to \infty} \mathbb{E}\left[\left(\frac{X_T^{\pi^n}}{X_t^{\nu}}\right)^p G_T \,\Big|\, \mathcal{F}_t \right] = J_t, \qquad \mathbb{P}\text{-a.s.}$$

[3.50]

Consider the density process

$$Z_s^t = \exp\left(-\int_t^s \frac{\mu_u^{\mathbb{F}}}{\sigma_u^{\mathbb{F}}} dW_u^{\mathbb{F}} - \frac{1}{2}\int_t^s \left|\frac{\mu_u^{\mathbb{F}}}{\sigma_u^{\mathbb{F}}}\right|^2 du\right), \quad s \in [t, T],$$

which is an $(\mathbb{F}, \mathbb{P})$-local martingale. By Itô's formula, the process $Z^t X^{\pi^n}$ is a non-negative $(\mathbb{F}, \mathbb{P})$-local martingale, hence a supermartingale on $[t, T]$. In particular, we have

$$\mathbb{E}^{\mathbb{P}}[X_T^{\pi^n} Z_T^t | \mathcal{F}_t] \leq X_t^{\pi^n} Z_t^t = X_t^{\nu}.$$

By Komlós lemma applied to the sequence of non-negative $\mathcal{F}_T$-measurable random variable $(X_T^{\pi^n})_{n\geq 1}$, there exists a convex combination $\widetilde{X}_T^n \in \text{conv}(X_T^{\pi^k}, k \geq n\}$ such that $(\widetilde{X}_T^n)_{n\geq 1}$ converges a.s. to some non-negative $\mathcal{F}_T$-measurable random variable $\widetilde{X}_T$. By Fatou's lemma, we have

$$\widetilde{X}_t := \mathbb{E}[\widetilde{X}_T Z_T^t \mid \mathcal{F}_t] \leq X_t^{\nu}.$$

Moreover, by the convexity of the function $x \mapsto x^p$, and by Fatou's lemma, it follows from [3.50] that

$$J_t \geq \mathbb{E}^{\mathbb{P}}\left[\left(\frac{\widetilde{X}_T}{X_t^{\nu}}\right)^p G_T \,\middle|\, \mathcal{F}_t\right], \quad a.s. \tag{3.51}$$

Since $p < 0$, we have $J_t < \infty$, and $G_T > 0$ a.s. We deduce that $\widetilde{X}_T > 0$, and $\widetilde{X}_t > 0$ a.s. Let $\overline{X}^t$ be the process

$$\overline{X}_s^t = \frac{X_t^{\nu}}{\widetilde{X}_t} \mathbb{E}^{\mathbb{P}}\left[\frac{Z_T^t}{Z_s^t} \widetilde{X}_T \,\middle|\, \mathcal{F}_s\right], \quad s \in [t, T].$$

By definition, $Z^t \overline{X}^t$ is a strictly positive $(\mathbb{F}, \mathbb{P})$-martingale on $[t, T]$. By the martingale representation theorem for Brownian filtration, we obtain the existence of an $\mathbb{F}$-adapted process $\overline{\pi}^t = (\overline{\pi}_s^t)_{s\in[t,T]}$ satisfying

$$\int_t^T |\overline{\pi}_s^t \sigma_s^{\mathbb{F}}|^2 ds < \infty,$$

such that

$$\begin{cases} \dfrac{d\overline{X}_s^t}{\overline{X}_s^t} = \overline{\pi}_s^t(\mu_s^{\mathbb{F}} ds + \sigma_s^{\mathbb{F}} dW_s^{\mathbb{F}}), \quad s \in [t,T] \\ \overline{X}_t^t = X_t^{\nu}. \end{cases}$$

Let $\overline{\pi}$ be the investment strategy in $\mathcal{A}^{\mathbb{F}}(t,\nu)$ defined as

$$\overline{\pi}_s = \nu_s \mathbb{1}_{s \le t} + \overline{\pi}_s^t \mathbb{1}_{s > t}, \quad s \in [0,T].$$

Then, we have $X_s^{\overline{\pi}} = \overline{X}_s^t$ for $s \in [t,T]$, and in particular

$$X_T^{\overline{\pi}} = \overline{X}_T^t = \frac{X_t^{\nu}}{\widetilde{X}_t} \widetilde{X}_T \ge \widetilde{X}_T \qquad \text{a.s.}$$

From [3.51], the non-increasing property of $x \to x^p$, and definition of J_t, we deduce that

$$J_t = \mathbb{E}^{\mathbb{P}}\left[\left(\frac{X_T^{\overline{\pi}}}{X_t^{\nu}}\right)^p G_T \,\Big|\, \mathcal{F}_t\right], \quad a.s. \qquad [3.52]$$

and hence $X_T^{\overline{\pi}} = \widetilde{X}_T$. Therefore, the process J, and consequently Y are strictly positive. From [3.49], we obtain that, for any $\nu \in \mathcal{A}^{\mathbb{F}}$ and any $t \in [0,T]$,

$$\xi_t^{\nu}(Y) = \operatorname*{ess\,sup}_{\pi^{\mathbb{F}} \in \mathcal{A}^{\mathbb{F}}(t,\nu)} \mathbb{E}^{\mathbb{P}}\left[U(X_T^{\pi^{\mathbb{F}}})G_T + \int_0^T U(X_\theta^{\pi^{\mathbb{F}}})(1 - \pi_\theta^{\mathbb{F}}\gamma_\theta)^p K_\theta^p d\theta \,\Big|\, \mathcal{F}_t\right]$$

$$\ge M_t^{\nu} := \mathbb{E}^{\mathbb{P}}\left[U(X_T^{\nu})G_T + \int_0^T U(X_\theta^{\nu})(1 - \nu_\theta\gamma_\theta)^p K_\theta^p d\theta \,\Big|\, \mathcal{F}_t\right],$$

$$[3.53]$$

by taking in [3.53] the investment strategy $\pi^{\mathbb{F}} = \nu \in \mathcal{A}^{\mathbb{F}}(t,\nu)$. The negative process $(M_t^{\nu})_{t \in [0,T]}$ is an integrable martingale, and the assertions of the lemma are proved. $\qquad \square$

In the sequel, we denote by $L_+^b(\mathbb{F})$ the set of processes $\widetilde{Y}$ in $L_+(\mathbb{F})$, such that for all $\nu \in \mathcal{A}^{\mathbb{F}}$, the process

$$\xi^{\nu}(\widetilde{Y}) := U(X_t^{\nu,\mathbb{F}})\widetilde{Y}_t + \int_0^t U(X_\theta^{\nu})(1 - \nu_\theta\gamma_\theta)^p K_\theta^p d\theta, \quad 0 \le t \le T, \quad [3.54]$$

is bounded from below by an $(\mathbb{F}, \mathbb{P})$-martingale. The following theorem gives a refinement of theorem 3.3. We refer the readers to [JIA 11, S4.2] for the detailed proof.

THEOREM 3.4.– When $p > 0$ (respectively, $p < 0$), the process Y in [3.44] is the smallest (respectively, largest) solution in $L_+^b(\mathbb{F})$ to the BSDE:

$$Y_t = G_T + \int_t^T f(s, Y_s, Z_s)ds - \int_t^T Z_s dW_s, \quad 0 \le t \le T, \quad [3.55]$$

where $f(s, Y_s, Z_s)$ is defined as in theorem 3.3. Moreover, under the integrability condition:

$$\int_0^T \left| \frac{K_t}{\sigma_t^{\mathbb{F}}} \right|^{2p/(2-p)} dt < \infty \quad \mathbb{P}\text{-a.s.,} \quad [3.56]$$

the optimal investment strategy can be computed pointwise, namely for all $t \in [0, T]$

$$\nu_t^* = \underset{x \in \mathbb{R}, \, x\gamma_t < 1}{\arg\max} \left[(\mu_t^{\mathbb{F}} Y_t + \sigma_t^{\mathbb{F}} \phi_t)x - \frac{1-p}{2} Y_t |x\sigma_t^{\mathbb{F}}|^2 + K_t^p \frac{(1 - x\gamma_t)^p}{p} \right]$$

It satisfies the estimates

$$-\rho_t \mathbb{1}_{\{\gamma_t \ge 0\}} \le \nu_t^* - \widehat{\nu}_t \le \rho_t \mathbb{1}_{\{\gamma_t < 0\}} \quad [3.57]$$

where

$$\widehat{\nu}_t = \min(\pi_t^M, \gamma_t^{-1}) \mathbb{1}_{\{\gamma_t \ge 0\}} + \max(\pi_t^M, \gamma_t^{-1}) \mathbb{1}_{\{\gamma_t < 0\}} \quad [3.58]$$

and

$$\pi_t^M = \frac{\mu_t^{\mathbb{F}}}{(1-p)|\sigma_t^{\mathbb{F}}|^2} + \frac{Z_t}{(1-p)Y_t \sigma_t^{\mathbb{F}}},$$

and

$$\rho_t = \left(\frac{|\gamma_t|^p K_t^p}{(1-p)Y_t|\sigma_t^{\mathbb{F}}|^2} \right)^{\frac{1}{2-p}}. \qquad [3.59]$$

REMARK 3.5.– In the case $p < 0$, and under the integrability condition [3.56], we can show the uniqueness of a solution in $L_+^b(\mathbb{F})$ to the BSDE [3.47]. Let us consider another solution $(\tilde{Y}, \tilde{Z}) \in L_+^b(\mathbb{F}) \times L_{\mathrm{loc}}^2(W)$ to [3.47], and take a pointwise maximizer of $f(t, \tilde{Y}_t, \tilde{Z}_t)$, which defines a control $\nu^* \in \mathcal{A}^{\mathbb{F}}$. By definition of the backward stochastic differential equation, the process $\xi^{\nu^*}(\tilde{Y})$ as defined in [3.54] is a local martingale. Since $p < 0$, the process $\xi^{\nu^*}(\tilde{Y})$ is non-positive, and hence is a submartingale. This implies that $\tilde{Y} \geq Y$, i.e. Y is also the smallest solution of the BSDE [3.47]. Since we already know from theorem 3.4 that it is the largest solution, we obtain that Y is the unique solution in $L_+^b(\mathbb{F})$.

We comment on, and interpret, the form of the optimal before-default strategy. We consider a default-free stock market model with drift and volatility coefficients $\mu^{\mathbb{F}}$ and $\sigma^{\mathbb{F}}$, respectively, and an investor with the power utility function $U(x) = x^p/p$ looking for the optimal investment problem:

$$V_0^M(X_0) = \sup_{\pi^{\mathbb{F}} \in \mathcal{A}^{\mathbb{F}}} \mathbb{E}[U(X_T^{\pi^{\mathbb{F}}})], \qquad [3.60]$$

where the wealth process $X^{\pi^{\mathbb{F}}}$ is determined by the stochastic differential equation

$$\begin{cases} \dfrac{dX_t^{\pi^{\mathbb{F}}}}{X_{t_-}^{\pi^{\mathbb{F}}}} = \pi_t^{\mathbb{F}}(\mu^{\mathbb{F}} dt + \sigma^{\mathbb{F}} dW_t^{\mathbb{F}}), \\ X_0^{\pi^{\mathbb{F}}} = X_0, \end{cases}$$

and $\mathcal{A}^{\mathbb{F}}$ is the set of $\mathbb{F}$-adapted processes $\pi^{\mathbb{F}}$ satisfying

$$\int_0^T |\pi_t^{\mathbb{F}} \sigma_t^{\mathbb{F}}|^2 dt < \infty$$

and

$$\forall t \in [0, T], \quad \pi_t \gamma_t < 1, \qquad \mathbb{P}\text{-a.s.}$$

In other words, $V_0^M(X_0)$ is the optimal value of Merton's optimal investment problem with strategies constrained to be upper-bounded (respectively, lower-bounded) in proportion by $1/\gamma_t$ when $\gamma_t \geq 0$ (respectively, < 0). By considering, similarly as in [3.44], the process (which does not depend on $\nu \in \mathcal{A}^{\mathbb{F}}$)

$$Y_t^M = p \operatorname*{ess\,sup}_{\pi^{\mathbb{F}} \in \mathcal{A}^{\mathbb{F}}(t,\nu)} \mathbb{E}\left[U\left(\frac{X_T^{\pi^{\mathbb{F}}}}{X_t^{\nu}}\right)\Big|\mathcal{F}_t\right], \quad 0 \leq t \leq T,$$

and arguing similarly as in theorem 3.4, we can prove that, when $p > 0$ (respectively, $p < 0$), Y^M is the smallest (respectively, largest) solution to the BSDE

$$Y_t^M = 1 + \int_t^T f^M(s, Y_s^M, Z_s^M)ds - \int_t^T Z_s^M dW_s^{\mathbb{F}}, \quad 0 \leq t \leq T,$$

for some $Z^M \in L_{\mathrm{loc}}^2(W^{\mathbb{F}})$, where

$$f^M(t, Y_t^M, Z_t^M) = p \operatorname*{ess\,sup}_{x \in \mathbb{R}\; x\gamma_t < 1}\left[(\mu_t^{\mathbb{F}} Y_t^M + \sigma_t^{\mathbb{F}} Z_t^M)x - \frac{1-p}{2}Y_t^M|x\sigma_t^{\mathbb{F}}|^2\right],$$

while the optimal strategy for Merton's optimization problem [3.60] is given by

$$\widehat{\pi}_t^{M,\gamma} = \min\left(\frac{\mu_t^{\mathbb{F}}}{(1-p)|\sigma_t^{\mathbb{F}}|^2} + \frac{\phi_t^M}{(1-p)Y_t^M\sigma_t^{\mathbb{F}}}, \frac{1}{\gamma_t}\right)\mathbb{1}_{\{\gamma_t \geq 0\}}$$
$$+ \max\left(\frac{\mu_t^{\mathbb{F}}}{(1-p)|\sigma_t^{\mathbb{F}}|^2} + \frac{\phi_t^M}{(1-p)Y_t^M\sigma_t^{\mathbb{F}}}, \frac{1}{\gamma_t}\right)\mathbb{1}_{\{\gamma_t < 0\}}.$$
[3.61]

Notice that when the processes $\mu^{\mathbb{F}}, \sigma^{\mathbb{F}}$ and γ are deterministic, then Y^M is also deterministic. In this case, we have $Z^M = 0$, and Y^M is the positive solution to the following ordinary differential equation

$$Y_t^M = 1 + \int_t^T f^M(s, Y_s^M)ds, \quad 0 \leq t \leq T,$$

where

$$f^M(t, y) = py \sup_{x \in \mathbb{R},\; x\gamma_t < 1}\left\{\mu_t^{\mathbb{F}} x - \frac{1-p}{2}|x\sigma_t^{\mathbb{F}}|^2\right\}.$$

With the notation

$$c(t) = \sup_{x \in \mathbb{R},\, x\gamma_t < 1} \left\{ \mu_t^{\mathbb{F}} x - \frac{1-p}{2} |x\sigma_t^{\mathbb{F}}|^2 \right\},$$

we can write Y^M as

$$Y_t^M = \exp\left(p \int_t^T c(s)ds \right).$$

We also recover in particular, when there is no constraint on trading strategies, i.e. $\gamma = 0$, the usual expression of the optimal Merton trading strategy:

$$\widehat{\pi}_t^{M,0} = \frac{\mu_t^{\mathbb{F}}}{(1-p)|\sigma_t^{\mathbb{F}}|^2}.$$

Note that in our default stock market model, the optimal before-default strategy ν^* satisfies the estimates (see equation [3.57])

$$-\rho_t \mathbb{1}_{\{\gamma_t \geq 0\}} \leq \nu_t^* - \widehat{\pi}_t^{M,\gamma} \leq \rho_t \mathbb{1}_{\{\gamma_t < 0\}},$$

which have the following interpretation. The process $\widehat{\pi}^{M,\gamma}$ has a similar form to the optimal Merton trading strategy described above, but includes further through the processes Y and K, the eventuality of a default of the stock price, inducing a jump of size γ, and then a switch of the coefficients of the stock price from $(\mu^{\mathbb{F}}, \sigma^{\mathbb{F}})$ to (μ^d, σ^d). In the case of a loss at default, i.e. positive jump γ, the optimal trading strategy ν^* is upper-bounded by $\widehat{\pi}^{M,\gamma}$, with a spread measured by the term ρ varying increasingly with the loss size γ, and converging to zero when the loss goes to zero, as expected since, in this case, the model behaves as a no-default market. Symmetrically, in the case of gain at default, i.e. negative jump γ, the optimal trading strategy ν^* is lower-bounded by $\widehat{\pi}^{M,\gamma}$, with a spread also measured by the term ρ.

3.3.4. *Example and numerical illustrations*

In this section, we present a simple illustrative example to show quantitatively the impact of counterparty default probability and the loss/gain given default on optimal investment. We consider a special case where $\mu^{\mathbb{F}}$, $\sigma^{\mathbb{F}}$, γ are constants, $\mu^d(\theta)$ $\sigma^d(\theta)$ are only deterministic functions of θ and the default time τ is independent of $\mathbb{F}$, so that $\alpha_t(\theta)$ is simply a known deterministic function $\alpha(\theta)$ of $\theta \in \mathbb{R}_+$, and the survival probability $G(t) = \mathbb{P}(\tau > t | \mathcal{F}_t) = \mathbb{P}(\tau > t) = \int_t^\infty \alpha(\theta) d\theta$ is a deterministic function. We also choose a CRRA utility function $U(x) = \frac{x^p}{p}$, $p < 1$, $p \neq 0$, $x > 0$. Notice that $V_\theta^d(x) = v^d(\theta, x) = U(x) k(\theta)^p$ with

$$k(\theta) = \left(\mathbb{E} \left[\alpha_T(\theta) \left(\frac{Z_T(\theta)}{\alpha_T(\theta)} \right)^{-q} \right] \right)^{\frac{1}{q}} = \alpha(\theta)^{\frac{1}{p}} \exp \left(\frac{1}{2} \left| \frac{\mu^d(\theta)}{\sigma^d(\theta)} \right|^2 \frac{1}{1-p} (T - \theta) \right)$$

Moreover, the optimal wealth process after-default does not depend on the default density, and the optimal strategy after-default is given, similarly as in the (unconstrained) Merton case, by:

$$\hat{\pi}^d(\theta) = \frac{\mu^d(\theta)}{(1-p)|\sigma^d(\theta)|^2}.$$

However, from the above results and discussion, we know that in this Markovian case, the value function of the global before-default optimization problem is in the form $V_0 = v(0, X_0)$ with:

$$v(t, x) = U(x) Y(t),$$

where Y is a deterministic function of time, solution to the first-order ordinary differential equation (ODE):

$$Y(t) = G(T) + \int_t^T f(\theta, Y(\theta)) d\theta, \quad t \in [0, T], \qquad [3.62]$$

with

$$f(t, y) = p \sup_{\pi\gamma < 1} \left[\left(\mu^F \pi - \frac{1-p}{2} |\pi\sigma^F|^2 \right) y + k(t)^p \frac{(1 - \pi\gamma)^p}{p} \right]. \qquad [3.63]$$

In general, there are no explicit solutions to this ODE, and we will give some numerical illustrations.

The following numerical results are based on the model parameters described below. We suppose that the survival probability follows the exponential distribution with constant default intensity, i.e. $G(t) = e^{-\lambda t}$ where $\lambda > 0$, and thus the density function is $\alpha(\theta) = \lambda e^{-\lambda \theta}$. In the case where $\gamma > 0$ (loss at default), we consider functions $\mu^d(\theta)$ and $\sigma^d(\theta)$ in the form

$$\mu^d(\theta) = \mu^{\mathbb{F}}\frac{\theta}{T}, \qquad \sigma^d(\theta) = \sigma^{\mathbb{F}}(2 - \frac{\theta}{T}), \qquad \theta \in [0, T],$$

which have the following economic interpretation. The ratio between the after- and before-default rate of return is smaller than 1, meaning that the asset is less competitive after the loss at default. Moreover, this ratio increases linearly with the default time: the after-default rate of return drops to zero, when the default time occurs near the initial date, and converges to the before-default rate of return, when the default time occurs near the finite investment horizon. We have a similar interpretation for the volatility but with symmetric relation: the ratio between the after- and before-default volatility is larger than 1, meaning that the market is more volatile after default. Moreover, this ratio decreases linearly with the default time, converging to the double (respectively, initial) value of the before-default volatility, when the default time goes to the initial (respectively, terminal horizon) time. When $\gamma < 0$, we choose the reciprocal model for μ^d, that is $\mu^d(\theta) = \mu^{\mathbb{F}}(2 - \frac{\theta}{T})$, $\theta \in [0, T]$ which means that the asset is more competitive in this case, and we suppose that σ^d is still defined as above.

Notice that in this example, $k(t)/\sigma^{\mathbb{F}}$ is a deterministic continuous function on $[0, T]$. To solve numerically the ODE [3.62], we apply the Howard algorithm, which consists of iterating in [3.63] the control value π at each step of the ODE resolution. We initialize the algorithm by choosing the constrained Merton strategy

$$\hat{\pi}^{M,\gamma} = \min\left(\frac{\mu^{\mathbb{F}}}{(1-p)|\sigma^{\mathbb{F}}|^2}, \frac{1}{\gamma}\right)1_{\gamma \geq 0} + \max\left(\frac{\mu^{\mathbb{F}}}{(1-p)|\sigma^{\mathbb{F}}|^2}, \frac{1}{\gamma}\right)1_{\gamma < 0}.$$

We perform numerical results with $\mu^{\mathbb{F}} = 0.03$, $\sigma^{\mathbb{F}} = 0.2$, $T = 1$, for various degrees of risk aversion $1 - p$: smaller, close to and larger than 1, and by varying both the intensity of default λ and the jump size γ. The numerical tests show that except in some extreme cases where both the default probability and the loss or gain given default are large, the optimal strategy is quite invariant with respect to time in most considered cases. So, we give below the optimal strategy as its expected value on time.

Figure 3.1 plots the graph of the optimal proportion $\hat{\pi}^{\mathbb{F}}$ (which thus takes into account the counterparty risk) invested in stock before default as a function of the jump size γ. When γ equals to zero, it is clear that the optimal strategy coincides with the Merton one. When there is a loss at default, i.e. $\gamma > 0$, this optimal strategy is always smaller than the Merton one, and the situation is inverted when there is a gain at default, i.e. $\gamma < 0$. Moreover, the strategy is decreasing with respect to γ, which means that we should reduce the stock investment when the loss given default is increasing, while we should increase investment when the gain at default increases. This behavior of the optimal trading strategy is consistent with the estimation [3.57]. These observations are more manifest when λ, that is when the default probability is large. Moreover, we see that when λ is small, $\hat{\pi}^{\mathbb{F}}$ approaches to the Merton strategy.

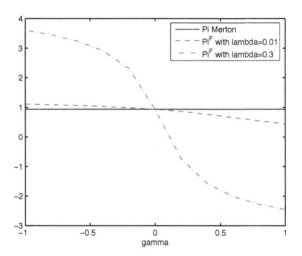

Figure 3.1. *Optimal strategy $\hat{\pi}^{\mathbb{F}}$ versus Merton $\hat{\pi}^{M,\gamma}$:*
$p = 0.2$, $\lambda = 0.01$ *and* 0.3, *respectively*

In the following numerical tests, we compare the value function, i.e. the performance of the optimal investment strategy, in our counterparty risk model, to that in the classical Merton model. This is equivalent here to compare the solution $Y(t)$ of the ODE [3.62] with the function $Y^M(t)$ deduced with $k(t) = 0$ and $G(T) = 1$. Figure 3.2 represents the curves of Y for different values of loss at default $\gamma > 0$ and for a given small intensity of default $\lambda = 0.01$. It appears that the value function $Y(t)$ obtained with counterparty risk is always below the Merton one Y^M, and Y is decreasing w.r.t. the proportional loss γ, which is *a priori* in accordance with the economic intuition. We also observe that Y is decreasing in time (as the Merton value Y^M) and converges at $T = 1$ to $G(T) = e^{-\lambda T} \approx 0.99$, the survival probability. Figure 3.3 provides similar tests but for different values of gain at default $\gamma < 0$, and with a given small intensity of default. In contrast with the loss situation at default in Figure 3.2, we observe here that the value function is larger than the Merton one in the beginning, and becomes smaller when one approaches the final horizon T since it converges to $G(T) < 1$. This confirms the intuition that the investor improves her optimal performance in the beginning by making profit from the rise of the asset value after default. In fact, as shown by Figure 3.4, we can also outperform the Merton strategy in the case of loss at default under extreme situations when the intensity of default is large, e.g. $\lambda = 0.5$ (corresponding approximately to a default probability of PD $= 40\%$ per year) by taking short positions on the asset, and this benefit is increasing with the size of the loss γ. For example, with a proportional loss of 80%, we find a relative ratio of overperformance in the beginning equal to $(Y - Y^M)(0)/Y^M(0) = 6.9\%$. This may be interpreted as follows: the investor knows that there is a high probability of default, and she takes advantage of this information, to shortsell in the beginning her positions on the asset, and then to buy off the asset after default at low price, improving consequently her optimal performance, at least far from the final horizon. The comparison of Figures 3.2 and 3.4 reveals an interesting feature in the case of loss at default, i.e. $\gamma > 0$: by doing more numerical tests, we observed that there is a critical level of default intensity λ (around 0.1 corresponding approximately to a default probability of 10%) from which the optimal performance Y exceeds the Merton one in the beginning. Furthermore, the monotonicity of Y with respect to γ switches from a decreasing to an increasing property.

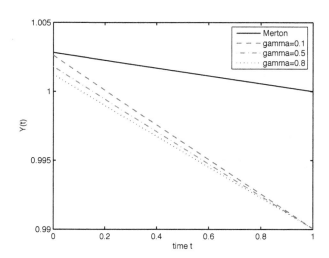

Figure 3.2. *Value function Y for loss at default versus Merton Y^M:*
$p = 0.2$, $\lambda = 0.01$ and γ positive

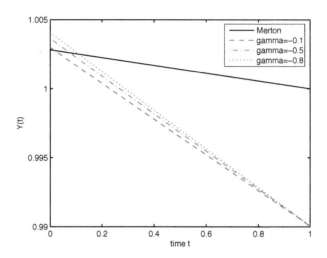

Figure 3.3. *Value function Y for gain at default versus Merton Y^M: $p = 0.2$, $\lambda = 0.01$ and γ negative*

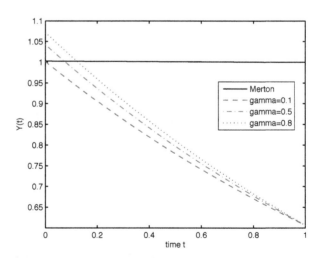

Figure 3.4. *Value function Y for loss at default versus Merton Y^M: $p = 0.2$, $\lambda = 0.5$ and γ positive*

3.4. Decomposition method with the exponential utility

The purpose of this section is to show that the decomposition method can also be applied to the optimization problem with other types of utility functions such as the exponential utility function $U(x) = -\mathrm{e}^{-px}$ with $x \in \mathbb{R}$, where $p > 0$ is a parameter describing the risk aversion. Here, we consider the investment strategies in the quantitative form as in [3.9]. We denote by $\mathcal{A}$ the set of $\mathbb{G}$-predictable processes

$$\phi_t = \mathbb{1}_{\{\tau \geq t\}} \phi_t^{\mathbb{F}} + \mathbb{1}_{\{\tau < t\}} \phi_t(\tau), \quad t \in [0, T]$$

satisfying the following condition

$$\forall \theta \in [0, T], \quad \int_0^T |\phi_t^{\mathbb{F}} S_t^{\mathbb{F}} \sigma_t^{\mathbb{F}}|^2 dt + \int_\theta^T |\phi_t(\theta) S_t(\theta) \sigma_t(\theta)^2| dt < +\infty,$$

where $S^{\mathbb{F}}$ and $S(\cdot)$ are determined by the following stochastic differential equations, respectively

$$\begin{cases} dS_t^{\mathbb{F}} = S_t^{\mathbb{F}} \left(\mu_t^{\mathbb{F}} dt + \sigma_t^{\mathbb{F}} dW_t^{\mathbb{F}} \right), \quad t \in [0, T] \\ S_0^{\mathbb{F}} = 1. \end{cases}$$

and for any $\theta \in [0, T]$,

$$\begin{cases} dS_t(\theta) = S_t(\theta) \left(\mu_t(\theta) dt + \sigma_t(\theta) dW_t^{\mathbb{F}} \right), \quad t \in [\theta, T] \\ S_\theta(\theta) = S_\theta^{\mathbb{F}} (1 - \gamma_\theta). \end{cases}$$

Our purpose is to solve the following optimization problem for the initial portfolio value $X_0 \in \mathbb{R}$

$$V_0(X_0) = \sup_{\phi \in \mathcal{A}} \mathbb{E}^{\mathbb{P}}[U(X_T^\phi)] = - \inf_{\phi \in \mathcal{A}} \mathbb{E}^{\mathbb{P}}[e^{-pX_T^\phi}], \qquad [3.64]$$

where the value process X^ϕ verifies the following stochastic differential equation

$$\begin{cases} dX_t^\phi = \phi_t dS_t, \quad t \in [0, T], \\ X_0^\phi = X_0, \end{cases}$$

with

$$S_t = \mathbb{1}_{\{\tau > t\}} S_t^{\mathbb{F}} + \mathbb{1}_{\{\tau \leq t\}} S_t(\tau).$$

As in the previous section, we introduce a family of auxiliary optimization problems as follows. For any $\theta \in [0, T]$, denote by $\mathcal{A}(\theta)$ the set of $\mathbb{F}$-predictable processes $\phi(\theta)$ on $[\theta, T]$ such that

$$\int_\theta^T |\phi(\theta)S_t(\theta)\sigma_t(\theta)|^2 dt < +\infty.$$

For any integrable $\mathcal{F}_\theta$-measurable random variable X_θ, we let $V_\theta^a(X_\theta)$ be the essential supremum

$$V_\theta^a(X_\theta) := \operatorname*{ess\,sup}_{\phi(\theta) \in \mathcal{A}_\theta} \mathbb{E}^{\mathbb{P}}[U(X_T^{\phi(\theta)})\alpha_T(\theta) \mid \mathcal{F}_\theta],$$

where $X_T^{\phi(\theta)}$ is determined by the following stochastic differential equation

$$\begin{cases} dX_t^{\phi(\theta)} = \phi_t(\theta)S_t(\theta)(\mu_t(\theta)dt + \sigma_t(\theta)dW_t^{\mathbb{F}}), \\ X_\theta^{\phi(\theta)} = X_\theta. \end{cases}$$

As in the previous section, we assume the Novikov's condition

$$\mathbb{E}^{\mathbb{P}}\left[\left(\frac{1}{2}\int_\theta^T \left|\frac{\mu_s(\theta)}{\sigma_s(\theta)}\right|^2 ds\right)\right] < +\infty$$

and introduce the Radon–Nikodym derivative of the auxiliary martingale measure $\mathbb{Q}^\theta$ with respect to $\mathbb{P}$ as follows:

$$Z_t(\theta) = \exp\left(-\int_\theta^t \frac{\mu_s(\theta)}{\sigma_s(\theta)}dW_s^{\mathbb{F}} - \frac{1}{2}\int_\theta^t \left|\frac{\mu_s(\theta)}{\sigma_s(\theta)}\right|^2 ds\right), \quad t \in [\theta, T].$$

Note that the after-default price process $S(\theta)$ becomes an $(\mathbb{F}, \mathbb{Q}^\theta)$-martingale.

Let I be the inverse function of U'. We recall that

$$I(y) = -\frac{1}{p}\log\left(\frac{y}{p}\right)$$

in the exponential utility case. Then, we have the following result.

PROPOSITION 3.2.– We assume that, for any positive number y, the random variable $Z_T(\theta)I(yZ_T(\theta)/\alpha_T(\theta))$ is integrable with respect to the probability measure $\mathbb{P}$. Then, we have

$$V_\theta^a(X_\theta) = \mathbb{E}^{\mathbb{P}}\left[\alpha_T(\theta)U\left(I\left(\frac{\widehat{Y}_\theta Z_T(\theta)}{\alpha_T(\theta)}\right)\right)\bigg|\mathcal{F}_\theta\right],$$

where the $\mathcal{F}_\theta$-measurable random variable $\widehat{Y}_\theta$ is determined by the following equation

$$\mathbb{E}^{\mathbb{P}}\left[Z_T(\theta)I(\widehat{Y}_\theta Z_T(\theta)/\alpha_T(\theta))\bigg|\mathcal{F}_\theta\right] = X_\theta. \qquad [3.65]$$

We can write equation [3.65] in a more explicit way as

$$\log(\widehat{Y}_\theta/p) + \mathbb{E}^{\mathbb{P}}\left[Z_T(\theta)\log(Z_T(\theta)/\alpha_T(\theta))\bigg|\mathcal{F}_\theta\right] = -pX_\theta.$$

Moreover, since $U(I(y)) = -y/p$ for any $y > 0$, we obtain that

$$\begin{aligned}V_\theta^a(X_\theta) &= -e^{-pX_\theta}\exp\left(-\mathbb{E}^{\mathbb{P}}\left[Z_T(\theta)\log(Z_T(\theta)/\alpha_T(\theta))\bigg|\mathcal{F}_\theta\right]\right)\\ &= U(X_\theta)\exp\left(-\mathbb{E}^{\mathbb{P}}\left[Z_T(\theta)\log(Z_T(\theta)/\alpha_T(\theta))\bigg|\mathcal{F}_\theta\right]\right).\end{aligned} \qquad [3.66]$$

In the following, we denote by K the process

$$K_\theta = \exp\left(-\mathbb{E}^{\mathbb{P}}\left[Z_T(\theta)\log(Z_T(\theta)/\alpha_T(\theta))\bigg|\mathcal{F}_\theta\right]\right), \quad \theta \in [0, T].$$

Note that this process does not depend on the risk aversion parameter p.

If the (H)-hypothesis is satisfied, namely, any $\mathbb{F}$-martingale is a $\mathbb{G}$-martingale, then the random variable $\alpha_T(\theta)$ is actually $\mathcal{F}_\theta$-measurable and we have $\alpha_T(\theta) = \alpha_\theta(\theta)$. In this case, we can rewrite K_θ as

$$K_\theta = \alpha_\theta(\theta)\exp\left(-\mathbb{E}^{\mathbb{P}}[Z_T(\theta)\log(Z_T(\theta))\,|\,\mathcal{F}_\theta]\right).$$

We observe in the above formula a term of the exponential conditional entropy of the auxiliary martingale measure $\mathbb{Q}^\theta$ with respect to $\mathbb{P}$.

In order to solve the global optimization problem [3.64], we let $\mathcal{A}^{\mathbb{F}}$ be the set of $\mathbb{F}$-predictable processes $\phi^{\mathbb{F}}$ such that

$$\forall t \in [0,T], \quad \int_0^T |\phi_t^{\mathbb{F}} S_t^{\mathbb{F}} \sigma_t^{\mathbb{F}}|^2 dt < +\infty.$$

Then, similarly to theorem 3.1, we have that, for any $X_0 \in \mathbb{R}$

$$V_0(X_0) = \sup_{\phi^{\mathbb{F}} \in \mathcal{A}^{\mathbb{F}}} \mathbb{E}^{\mathbb{P}} \left[U(X_T^{\phi^{\mathbb{F}}}) G_T + \int_0^T V_\theta^{\mathrm{a}}(X_\theta^{\phi^{\mathbb{F}}} - \phi_\theta^{\mathbb{F}} S_\theta^{\mathbb{F}} \gamma_\theta) d\theta \right], \qquad [3.67]$$

where the process $X^{\phi^{\mathbb{F}}}$ is determined by the following stochastic differential equation

$$\begin{cases} dX_t^{\phi^{\mathbb{F}}} = \phi_t^{\mathbb{F}} S_t^{\mathbb{F}} \left(\mu_t^{\mathbb{F}} dt + \sigma_t^{\mathbb{F}} dW_t^{\mathbb{F}} \right), & t \in [0,T], \\ X_0^{\phi^{\mathbb{F}}} = X_0. \end{cases}$$

We will use the dynamic programming principle to solve this optimization problem. For any $\varphi \in \mathcal{A}^{\mathbb{F}}$ and any $t \in [0,T]$, let $\mathcal{A}^{\mathbb{F}}(t,\varphi)$ be the set of investment strategies in $\mathcal{A}^{\mathbb{F}}$ which coincides with φ until time t, namely,

$$\mathcal{A}^{\mathbb{F}}(t,\varphi) = \{\phi^{\mathbb{F}} \in \mathcal{A}^{\mathbb{F}} \mid \phi_s^{\mathbb{F}} = \varphi_s \text{ on } [0,t]\}.$$

We introduce the dynamical version of the optimization problem [3.67] as follows.

$$V_t(X_0,\varphi) := \operatorname*{ess\,sup}_{\phi^{\mathbb{F}} \in \mathcal{A}^{\mathbb{F}}(t,\varphi)} \mathbb{E}^{\mathbb{P}} \left[U(X_T^{\phi^{\mathbb{F}}}) G_T + \int_t^T V_\theta^{\mathrm{a}}(X_\theta^{\phi^{\mathbb{F}}} - \phi_\theta^{\mathbb{F}} S_\theta^{\mathbb{F}} \gamma_\theta) d\theta \,\Big|\, \mathcal{F}_t \right].$$

By [3.66], we can rewrite $V_t(X_0,\varphi)$ as

$$V_t(X_0,\varphi) = \operatorname*{ess\,sup}_{\phi^{\mathbb{F}} \in \mathcal{A}^{\mathbb{F}}(t,\varphi)} \mathbb{E}^{\mathbb{P}} \left[U(X_T^{\phi^{\mathbb{F}}}) G_T + \int_t^T U(X_\theta^{\phi^{\mathbb{F}}} - \phi_\theta^{\mathbb{F}} S_\theta^{\mathbb{F}} \gamma_\theta) K_\theta d\theta \,\Big|\, \mathcal{F}_t \right]$$

In particular, the process

$$Y_t := \frac{V_t(X_0,\varphi)}{U(X_t^{\varphi})}, \quad t \in [0,T]$$

satisfies

$$Y_t = \underset{\phi^{\mathbb{F}} \in \mathcal{A}^{\mathbb{F}}(t,\varphi)}{\text{ess sup}} \ \mathbb{E}^{\mathbb{P}}\left[U(X_T^{\phi^{\mathbb{F}}} - X_t^{\varphi})G_T \right.$$

$$\left. + \int_t^T U(X_\theta^{\phi^{\mathbb{F}}} - X_t^{\varphi})\exp(-p\phi_\theta^{\mathbb{F}}S_\theta^{\mathbb{F}}\gamma_\theta)K_\theta d\theta \Big| \mathcal{F}_t \right],$$

which does not depend on the choice of $\varphi \in \mathcal{A}^{\mathbb{F}}$.

By the dynamic programming principle, for any $\varphi \in \mathcal{A}^{\mathbb{F}}$, the process

$$V_t(X_0,\varphi) + \int_0^t V_\theta^{\mathrm{a}}(X_\theta^{\varphi} - \varphi_\theta S_\theta^{\mathbb{F}}\gamma_\theta)d\theta, \ t \in [0,T] \qquad [3.68]$$

is an $(\mathbb{F},\mathbb{P})$-supermartingale. We can rewrite it as

$$\xi_t^{\varphi}(Y) := U(X_t^{\varphi})Y_t + \int_0^t U(X_\theta^{\varphi})\exp(-p\varphi_\theta S_\theta^{\mathbb{F}}\gamma_\theta)K_\theta d\theta, \ t \in [0,T]. \quad [3.69]$$

Moreover, if $\varphi^* \in \mathcal{A}^{\mathbb{F}}$ is the optimal investment strategy of the problem [3.67], then the process

$$\xi_t^{\varphi^*}(Y) := U(X_t^{\varphi^*})Y_t + \int_0^t U(X_\theta^{\varphi^*})\exp(-p\varphi_\theta^* S_\theta^{\mathbb{F}}\gamma_\theta)K_\theta d\theta, \ t \in [0,T][3.70]$$

is an $(\mathbb{F},\mathbb{P})$-martingale.

THEOREM 3.5.– The process Y is a solution to the following backward stochastic differential equation

$$Y_t = -G_T - \int_t^T f(s,Y_s,Z_s)ds - \int_t^T Z_s dW_s^{\mathbb{F}} \qquad [3.71]$$

for some $Z \in L_{\mathrm{loc}}^2(W)$, where for any $t \in [0,T]$

$$f(t,Y_t,Z_t) = \sup_{x\in\mathbb{R}} \left(pxS_t^{\mathbb{F}}(\mu_t^{\mathbb{F}}Y_t + \sigma_t^{\mathbb{F}}Z_t) - \frac{1}{2}(pxS_t^{\mathbb{F}}\sigma_t^{\mathbb{F}})^2 Y_t - \mathrm{e}^{-pxS_t^{\mathbb{F}}\gamma_t}K_t \right).$$

Moreover, the optimal investment strategy φ^* is given by

$$\varphi_t^* = \arg\max_{x \in \mathbb{R}} \left(px S_t^{\mathbb{F}} (\mu_t^{\mathbb{F}} Y_t + \sigma_t^{\mathbb{F}} Z_t) - \frac{1}{2} (px S_t^{\mathbb{F}} \sigma_t^{\mathbb{F}})^2 Y_t - e^{-px S_t^{\mathbb{F}} \gamma_t} K_t \right). \qquad [3.72]$$

PROOF.– By taking φ as the zero investment strategy in the formula [3.69], we obtain that the process

$$Y_t + \int_0^t \exp(-p\varphi_\theta S_\theta^{\mathbb{F}} \gamma_\theta) K_\theta d\theta, \quad t \in [0, T]$$

is an $(\mathbb{F}, \mathbb{P})$-submartingale. By Doob–Meyer decomposition theorem, there exists $\varphi \in L_{\text{loc}}^2$ and a non-decreasing $\mathbb{F}$-predictable A which is of finite variation, such that

$$dY_t = Z_t dW_t^{\mathbb{F}} + dA_t. \qquad [3.73]$$

By Itô's formula, we obtain

$$\begin{aligned} d\xi_t^\varphi(Y) &= U(X_t^\varphi) dY_t + Y_t dU(X_t^\varphi) + d\langle U(X^\varphi), Y \rangle \\ &\quad + U(X_t^\varphi) \exp(-p\varphi_t S_t^{\mathbb{F}} \gamma_t) K_t dt. \end{aligned}$$

Note that

$$\begin{aligned} dU(X_t^\varphi) &= -pU(X_t^\varphi) dX_t^\varphi + \tfrac{1}{2} p^2 U(X_t^\varphi) d\langle X^\varphi \rangle_t \\ &= U(X_t^\varphi) \left[\left(-p\varphi_t S_t^{\mathbb{F}} \mu_t^{\mathbb{F}} + \tfrac{1}{2} p^2 (\varphi_t S_t^{\mathbb{F}} \sigma_t^{\mathbb{F}})^2 \right) dt - p\varphi_t S_t^{\mathbb{F}} \sigma_t^{\mathbb{F}} dW_t^{\mathbb{F}} \right]. \end{aligned}$$

Therefore, we have

$$\begin{aligned} d\xi_t^\varphi(Y) &= U(X_t^\varphi)(Z_t dW_t^{\mathbb{F}} + dA_t) \\ &\quad + Y_t U(X_t^\varphi) \left[\left(-p\varphi_t S_t^{\mathbb{F}} \mu_t^{\mathbb{F}} + \tfrac{1}{2} p^2 (\varphi_t S_t^{\mathbb{F}} \sigma_t^{\mathbb{F}})^2 \right) dt - p\varphi_t S_t^{\mathbb{F}} \sigma_t^{\mathbb{F}} dW_t^{\mathbb{F}} \right] \\ &\quad - U(X_t^\varphi) p\varphi_t S_t^{\mathbb{F}} \sigma_t^{\mathbb{F}} Z_t dt + U(X_t^\varphi) \exp\left(-p\varphi_t S_t^{\mathbb{F}} \gamma_t \right) K_t dt \\ &= U(X_t^\varphi) \left(Z_t dW_t^{\mathbb{F}} - pY_t \varphi_t S_t^{\mathbb{F}} \sigma_t^{\mathbb{F}} \right) dW_t^{\mathbb{F}} - dA_t^\varphi, \end{aligned}$$

with

$$\begin{aligned} dA_t^\varphi &= U(X_t^\varphi) \bigg(-dA_t + \left(p\varphi_t S_t^{\mathbb{F}} \mu_t^{\mathbb{F}} Y_t - \frac{1}{2} p^2 (\varphi_t S_t^{\mathbb{F}} \sigma_t^{\mathbb{F}})^2 Y_t \right. \\ &\qquad + p\varphi_t S_t^{\mathbb{F}} \sigma_t^{\mathbb{F}} Z_t - e^{-p\varphi_t S_t^{\mathbb{F}} \gamma_t} K_t \bigg) dt \bigg). \end{aligned}$$

Thus, we obtain

$$A_t = \operatorname*{ess\,sup}_{\varphi \in \mathcal{A}^{\mathbb{F}}} \left(p\varphi_t S_t^{\mathbb{F}} \mu_t^{\mathbb{F}} Y_t - \frac{1}{2} p^2 (\varphi_t S_t^{\mathbb{F}} \sigma_t^{\mathbb{F}})^2 Y_t \right.$$
$$\left. + p\varphi_t S_t^{\mathbb{F}} \sigma_t^{\mathbb{F}} Z_t - e^{-p\varphi_t S_t^{\mathbb{F}} \gamma_t} K_t \right).$$

Moreover, for fixed $t \in [0, T]$ and $\omega \in \Omega$, the function

$$F_{t,\omega}(x) = p S_t^{\mathbb{F}} (\mu_t^{\mathbb{F}} Y_t + \sigma_t^{\mathbb{F}} Z_t) x - \frac{1}{2} (p S_t^{\mathbb{F}} \sigma_t^{\mathbb{F}}) Y_t x^2 - e^{-p S_t^{\mathbb{F}} \gamma_t x} K_t$$

on $x \in \mathbb{R}$ is concave, and tends to $-\infty$ when $x \to \pm\infty$. Therefore, the essential supremum in the above formula can be computed pointwise. Namely, we have

$$A_t = \sup_{x \in \mathbb{R}} \left(p x S_t^{\mathbb{F}} (\mu_t^{\mathbb{F}} Y_t + \sigma_t^{\mathbb{F}} Z_t) - \frac{1}{2} (p x S_t^{\mathbb{F}} \sigma_t^{\mathbb{F}})^2 Y_t - e^{-p x S_t^{\mathbb{F}} \gamma_t} K_t \right). \qquad [3.74]$$

By definition, we have $Y_T = -G_T$. Hence, we obtain from [3.73] and [3.74] that the process Y verifies the backward stochastic differential equation [3.71], and that the optimal investment strategy is given by [3.72].   □

3.5. Optimization with insider's information

In this section, we consider the optimization problem for an insider who has private information on the counterparty default event. The objective is to compare the results with those obtained with the standard investor's information in section 3.3, and study the gain obtained from the corresponding extra information. For the purpose of comparison, we consider in this section the power utility function as in section 3.3. We suppose that the default of the counterparty is described in a general barrier model. Let $(\lambda_t, \ t \geq 0)$ be a positive $\mathbb{F}$-adapted process and $\Lambda_t = \int_0^t \lambda_s ds$ which is an increasing process. We model the default time as the first passage time of the process Λ to a positive random barrier L, i.e.

$$\tau = \inf\{t \geq 0 : \Lambda_t \geq L\}. \qquad [3.75]$$

In the widely used Cox process model, λ is the intensity of the default and Λ is the compensator process of the default, L is independent of $\mathcal{F}_\infty$ and follows the uni-exponential law. In the classical structural default models, Λ can represent the cumulated losses of the counterparty and L is constant or deterministic, thus τ is an $\mathbb{F}$-stopping time. In our model, the default threshold L is a positive $\mathcal{A}$-measurable random variable which can be correlated with the reference filtration $\mathbb{F}$. The information of the insider is modeled as the initial enlargement of the filtration $\mathbb{F}$ by L and is denoted by

$$\mathbb{G}^I = (\mathcal{G}_t^I)_{t\in[0,T]}, \qquad \mathcal{G}_t^I = \mathcal{F}_t \vee \sigma(L).$$

As in previous sections, a standard investor on the market observes the information contained in the filtration $\mathbb{F}$, and whether the default has occurred or not and if so, the default time τ. This information is represented by the progressive enlargement $\mathbb{G} = (\mathcal{G}_t)_{t\in[0,T]}$ of the filtration $\mathbb{F}$ by τ. The standard investor will estimate the default event through the conditional density of τ with respect to the filtration $\mathbb{F}$ and thus establishes a link with the conditional law of L.

Note that the standard investor's information is included in the insider's information flow: we have $\mathcal{G}_t \subseteq \mathcal{G}_t^I$ for any $t \in [0,T]$. Moreover, before the default τ, the insider has additional information on L, and whose information σ-algebra $\mathcal{G}_t^I$ is in general strictly larger than $\mathcal{G}_t$. After the default occurs, both of them observe the default event and subsequently the value of L so that they have equal information flow.

3.5.1. *Insider's optimization problem*

We consider the trading strategy of the insider, whose investment strategy process is given by a $\mathbb{G}^M$-predictable process π which represents the proportion of wealth invested in the risky asset. We can write an investment strategy π in a decomposed form (see Jeulin [JEU 80] lemmas 3.13 and 4.4)

$$\pi_t = \mathbb{1}_{\{\tau \geq t\}}\pi_t^0(L) + \mathbb{1}_{\{\tau < t\}}\pi_t^1(\tau),$$

where $\pi^0(\cdot)$ and $\pi^1(\cdot)$ are $\mathcal{P}(\mathbb{F}) \otimes \mathcal{B}(\mathbb{R}_+)$-measurable processes. Starting from an initial wealth X_0, the total wealth of the insider's portfolio is then a $\mathbb{G}^I$-adapted process $X^\pi(L)$ given by

$$X_t^\pi(L) = \mathbb{1}_{\{\tau > t\}}X_t^{\pi,0}(L) + \mathbb{1}_{\{\tau \leq t\}}X_t^{\pi,1}(\tau), \qquad [3.76]$$

where the before-default wealth process satisfies the stochastic differential equation for any $\ell \in \mathbb{R}_+$

$$\begin{cases} \dfrac{dX_t^{\pi,0}(\ell)}{X_t^0(\ell)} = \pi_t^0(\ell)\dfrac{dS_t^{\mathbb{F}}}{S_t^{\mathbb{F}}} = \pi_t^0(\ell)(\mu_t^{\mathbb{F}}dt + \sigma_t^{\mathbb{F}}dW_t^{\mathbb{F}}), \quad t \in [0, T], \\ X_0^{\pi,0} = X_0, \end{cases}$$

and after-default wealth process satisfies the following stochastic differential equation for any $\theta \subset [0, T]$

$$\begin{cases} \dfrac{dX_t^{\pi,1}(\theta)}{X_t^{\pi,1}(\theta)} = \pi_t^1(\theta)\dfrac{dS_t(\theta)}{S_t(\theta)} = \pi_t^1(\theta)(\mu_t(\theta)dt + \sigma_t(\theta)dW_t^{\mathbb{F}}), \quad t \in [\theta, T], \\ X_\theta^{\pi,1}(\theta) = X_\theta^{\pi,0}(\Lambda_\theta)(1 - \pi_\theta^0(\Lambda_\theta)\gamma_\theta). \end{cases}$$

Note that the portfolio value jumps upon the default, and its diffusion has a regime changing after the default time, as in the case of a standard investor. We suppose that $\pi_\tau^0(\Lambda_\theta)\gamma_\theta < 1$, so that the wealth remains strictly positive after the jump due to the counterparty default.

We discuss first the constraints on the investment in the risky assets. On the one hand, in practice, there are buying constraints: for diversification and regulation reasons, investors are limited to invest in a given asset below a certain level. Otherwise, they must report and explain their strategy to the authorities. On the other hand, after the financial crisis in 2008, regulators prohibited short-selling on several equity markets. Nowadays, these restrictions have been relaxed for liquidity reason. Based on these observations, in our framework, the regulators are concerned about the default risk of the counterparty and its impact on the risky asset. Thus, they impose a buying constraint and they forbid short-selling as long as the default has not occurred yet. After the counterparty default, those restrictions will be relaxed.

This motivates us to propose the following admissible trading strategy family $\mathcal{A}_L$ as the set of pairs $(\pi^0(\cdot), \pi^1(\cdot))$, where $\pi^0(\cdot)$ and $\pi^1(\cdot)$ are $\mathcal{P}(\mathbb{F}) \otimes \mathcal{B}(\mathbb{R}_+)$-measurable processes such that, for any $\ell > 0$,

$$\int_0^{\tau_\ell \wedge T} |\pi_t^0(\ell)\sigma_t^{\mathbb{F}}|^2 dt + \int_{\tau_\ell \wedge T}^T |\pi_t^1(\tau_\ell)\sigma_t(\tau_\ell)|^2 dt < \infty, \quad a.s. \qquad [3.77]$$

$$0 \leq \pi^0(\ell) \leq b \quad \text{and} \quad \pi_{\tau_\ell}^0(\ell)\gamma_{\tau_\ell} < 1, \qquad [3.78]$$

where τ_ℓ is the $\mathbb{F}$-stopping time defined by $\tau_\ell := \inf\{t : \Lambda_t \geq \ell\}$, and b is a constant, representing the level of the buying constraint.

Let U be a utility function defined on $(0, +\infty)$, which satisfies the Inada conditions. The insider aims to maximize the expected value of the utility function U valued on the terminal portfolio value $X_T^\pi(L)$. Note that the initial σ-field is non-trivial and this initial information has to be taken into consideration for the formulation of the optimization problem:

$$\operatorname*{ess\,sup}_{\pi \in \mathcal{A}_L} \mathbb{E}^{\mathbb{P}}[U(X_T^\pi) \mid \mathcal{G}_0^I], \qquad\qquad [3.79]$$

where $\mathcal{G}_0^I = \sigma(L)$. The link between the optimization problem (3.79) and the classical optimization problem

$$V_0(X_0) = \sup_{\pi \in \mathcal{A}_L} \mathbb{E}^{\mathbb{P}}[U(X_T^\pi)] \qquad\qquad [3.80]$$

is given by [AME 03]. If the supremum in [3.79] is attained by some strategy in $\mathcal{A}_L$, then the same strategy also gives a solution to [3.80]. Note that the essential supremum in [3.79] is not necessarily attained. Nevertheless, there exists a sequence of admissible strategies $(\pi_n \in \mathcal{A}_L, \ n \in \mathbb{N})$ such that $\mathbb{E}^{\mathbb{P}}[U(X_T^{\pi_n}) \mid \mathcal{G}_0^I]$ converges in L^1 to [3.79] and we can prove that for the same sequence, $\mathbb{E}^{\mathbb{P}}[U(X_T^{\pi_n})]$ converges to $V_0(X_0)$.

The method to solve the initial optimization problem [3.79], similar as in the previous two sections, is to reduce the problem in an incomplete market into two problems, the after-default and before-default ones, in a complete market. Nevertheless, the approach we adopt here is different since the random time τ is not a totally inaccessible random time for the insider filtration $\mathbb{G}^I$ and we can no longer use the conditional default density approach. We will use the theory of initial enlargement of filtration instead. More precisely, we introduce a family of $\mathbb{F}$-stopping times $\tau_\ell = \inf\{t : \Lambda_t \geq \ell\}$ for all $\ell > 0$ which are possible realizations of the random barrier L and we work under an equivalent probability measure $\mathbb{P}^L$ under which L is independent of $\mathcal{F}_T$. Thus, in our framework, we will need the Radon–Nikodym derivative process $p_t(L)$ which is the density of the historical probability measure $\mathbb{P}$ with respect to this equivalent probability measure $\mathbb{P}^L$ and it will play a similar role as the default density process.

We assume that L is a $\mathcal{G}$-measurable random variable with values in $(0, +\infty)$, which satisfies the assumption (as in definition 2.1):

$$\mathbb{P}(L \in d\ell \mid \mathcal{F}_t)(\omega) \sim \mathbb{P}(L \in d\ell), \quad \forall\, t \in [0, T], \ \mathbb{P}\text{-a.s..} \qquad [3.81]$$

We denote by $\eta_t^L(d\ell)$ a regular version of the conditional law of L given $\mathcal{F}_t$ and by $\eta^L(d\ell)$ the probability law of L under the probability measure $\mathbb{P}$. According to [JAC 85], there exists a measurable version of the conditional density

$$p_t(x)(\omega) = \frac{d\eta_t^L}{d\eta^L}(\omega, x) \qquad [3.82]$$

which is a positive $(\mathbb{F}, \mathbb{P})$-martingale. It is proved in [GRO 98] that hypothesis 2.1 is satisfied if and only if there exists a probability measure equivalent to $\mathbb{P}$ and under which $\mathcal{F}_T$ and $\sigma(L)$ are independent. Among such equivalent probability measures, the probability $\mathbb{P}^L$ defined by the Radon–Nikodym derivative process

$$\mathbb{E}^{\mathbb{P}^L}\left[\frac{d\mathbb{P}}{d\mathbb{P}^L} \,\Big|\, \mathcal{G}_t^I \right] = p_t(L)$$

is the only one that is identical to $\mathbb{P}$ on $\mathcal{F}_T$. In the particular case of L independent of $\mathbb{F}$ (that is the counterparty firm's manager fixes an arbitrary threshold without taking into account the economic perspectives), the process $p_t(L)$ is identically equal to 1 and the insider's optimization problem only depends on the value of the threshold but not on its conditional distribution. Otherwise, if L depends on $\mathbb{F}$, the process $p_t(L)$ reflects the anticipation of the insider on the economic situation and naturally appears in the resolution of the insider's optimization problem.

PROPOSITION 3.3.– Under the hypothesis [3.81], we have

$$\mathbb{E}^{\mathbb{P}}[U(X_T^\pi)|\mathcal{G}_0^I]$$

$$= \mathbb{E}^{\mathbb{P}}\left[p_T(\ell) \left(\mathbb{1}_{\{\tau_\ell > T\}} U(X_T^{\pi,0}(\ell)) + \mathbb{1}_{\{\tau_\ell \leq T\}} U(X_T^{\pi,1}(\tau_\ell)) \right) \right]_{\ell = L}$$

for any $\pi \in \mathcal{A}_L$.

PROOF.– We will use the change of probability to $\mathbb{P}^L$ in order to reduce to the case where L and $\mathcal{F}_T$ are independent. First,

$$\begin{aligned}
\mathbb{E}^{\mathbb{P}}[U(X_T^\pi)|\mathcal{G}_0^I] &= \mathbb{E}^{\mathbb{P}}\left[\mathbb{1}_{\{\tau>T\}}U(X_T^{\pi,0}(L)) + \mathbb{1}_{\{\tau\leq T\}}U(X_T^{\pi,1}(\tau))\,|L\right] \\
&= \mathbb{E}^{\mathbb{P}^L}\left[p_T(\ell)\left(\mathbb{1}_{\{\tau_\ell>T\}}U(X_T^{\pi,0}(\ell)) + \mathbb{1}_{\{\tau_\ell\leq T\}}U(X_T^{\pi,1}(\tau_\ell))\right)\right]_{\ell=L} \\
&= \mathbb{E}^{\mathbb{P}}\left[p_T(\ell)\left(\mathbb{1}_{\{\tau_\ell>T\}}U(X_T^{\pi,0}(\ell)) + \mathbb{1}_{\{\tau_\ell\leq T\}}U(X_T^{\pi,1}(\tau_\ell))\right)\right]_{\ell=L}
\end{aligned}$$

where the last two equalities follow, respectively, from the facts that $\mathcal{F}_T$ and $\sigma(L)$ are independent under $\mathbb{P}^L$ and that $\mathbb{P}^L$ is identical to $\mathbb{P}$ on $\mathcal{F}_T$.   □

This motivates us to introduce, for any $\ell > 0$, the set $\mathcal{A}_\ell$ of pairs $\pi = (\pi^0, \pi^1(\cdot))$, where π^0 and $\pi^1(\cdot)$ are, respectively, $\mathbb{F}$-predictable and $\mathcal{P}(\mathbb{F}) \otimes \mathcal{B}(\mathbb{R}_+)$-measurable processes, such that

$$\int_0^{\tau_\ell\wedge T} |\pi_t^0\sigma_t^{\mathbb{F}}|^2 dt + \int_{\tau_\ell\wedge T}^T |\pi_t^1(\tau_\ell)\sigma_t(\tau_\ell)|^2 dt < \infty, \quad a.s. \qquad [3.83]$$

$$0 \leq \pi^0 \leq b \quad \text{and} \quad \pi_{\tau_\ell}^0\gamma_{\tau_\ell} < 1, \qquad\qquad [3.84]$$

and consider the following optimization problem

$$\begin{aligned}
&V_0^\ell(X_0) \\
&= \sup_{\pi\in\mathcal{A}_\ell} \mathbb{E}^{\mathbb{P}}\left[p_T(\ell)\left(\mathbb{1}_{\{\tau_\ell>T\}}U(X_T^{\pi,0}) + \mathbb{1}_{\{\tau_\ell\leq T\}}U(X_T^{\pi,1}(\tau_\ell))\right)\right],
\end{aligned} \qquad [3.85]$$

where $\tau_\ell = \inf\{t \geq 0 : \Lambda_t \geq \ell\}$ is an $\mathbb{F}$-stopping time.

The following theorem shows that the optimal value of the optimization problem [3.79] is actually equal to $V_0(X_0, L)$.

THEOREM 3.6.– With the above notation, we have

$$V_0^L(X_0) = \operatorname*{ess\,sup}_{\pi\in\mathcal{A}_L} \mathbb{E}[U(X_T)\,|\,\mathcal{G}_0^I] \qquad a.s.$$

PROOF.– Assume that $(\pi^0(\cdot), \pi^1(\cdot))$ is an element in $\mathcal{A}_L$, then $(\pi^0(\ell), \pi^1(\cdot)) \in \mathcal{A}_l$. By proposition 3.3 we obtain that

$$\operatorname*{ess\,sup}_{\pi \in \mathcal{A}_L} \mathbb{E}[U(X_T) \mid \mathcal{G}_0^I] \leq V_0(X_0, L).$$

For the converse inequality, we will use a measurable selection theorem. For any $\varepsilon > 0$ and any $l \in (0, +\infty)$, let $F_\varepsilon(\ell)$ be the set of strategies $(\pi^0, \pi^1(\cdot)) \in \mathcal{A}_\ell$ which are ε-optimal with respect to the problem [3.85], namely, such that

$$\mathbb{E}^{\mathbb{P}}\left[p_T(\ell)\left(\mathbb{1}_{\{\tau_\ell > t\}} U(X_T^{\pi,0}(\ell)) + \mathbb{1}_{\{\tau_\ell \leq T\}} U(X_T^{\pi,1}(\tau_\ell))\right)\right]$$

is bounded from below by $V_0(X_0, \ell) - \varepsilon$ if $V_0(X_0, \ell) < +\infty$, and by $1/\varepsilon$ if $V_0(X_0, \ell) = +\infty$. By a measurable selection theorem (see Benes [BEN 70, lemma 1]), there exists a measurable (with respect to ℓ) family $\{(\pi^0(\ell), \pi^1(\cdot, \ell))\}_{\ell \in \mathbb{R}_+}$ with value in $F_\varepsilon(\ell)$ for any $\ell > 0$. Finally, let

$$\widetilde{\pi}^0(\cdot) := \pi^0(\cdot), \quad \widetilde{\pi}_t^1(x) := \mathbb{1}_{t > x} \pi_t^1(x, \Lambda_x).$$

We have $\widetilde{\pi} = (\widetilde{\pi}^0(\cdot), \widetilde{\pi}^1(\cdot)) \in \mathcal{A}_L$ and $\widetilde{\pi}_t^1(\tau_\ell) = \pi_t^1(\tau_\ell, \ell)$ on $\{\tau_\ell < t\}$ for any $\ell > 0$. Therefore, by proposition 3.3,

$$\begin{aligned}
&\mathbb{E}^{\mathbb{P}}[U(X_T^{\widetilde{\pi}}) \mid \mathcal{G}_0^I] \\
&= \mathbb{E}^{\mathbb{P}}\left[p_T(\ell)\left(\mathbb{1}_{\{\tau_\ell > T\}} U(X_T^0(\ell)) + \mathbb{1}_{\{\tau_\ell \leq T\}} U(X_T^1(\tau_\ell))\right)\right]_{\ell = L} \\
&\geq \begin{cases} V_0(X_0, L) - \varepsilon, & \text{if } V_0(X_0, L) < +\infty, \\ 1/\varepsilon, & \text{if } V_0(X_0, L) = +\infty. \end{cases}
\end{aligned}$$

Since ε is arbitrary, we obtain $\mathbb{E}^{\mathbb{P}}[U(\widetilde{X}_T^\pi) \mid \mathcal{G}_0^M] \geq V_0(X_0, L)$. $\qquad\square$

3.5.2. Decomposition of the optimization problem

In the following section, we discuss the resolution of the optimization problem [3.85] for any fixed $\ell > 0$. We introduce a family of auxiliary optimization problems as follows

$$V_{\tau_\ell}^{\ell,\mathrm{a}}(X_{\tau_\ell}) := \operatorname*{ess\,sup}_{\pi^1(\cdot) \in \mathcal{A}_\ell^1} \mathbb{E}^{\mathbb{P}}[p_T(\ell) U(X_T^{\pi^1}(\tau_\ell)) \mid \mathcal{F}_{\tau_\ell}], \qquad [3.86]$$

where X_{τ_ℓ} is an integrable $\mathcal{F}_{\tau_\ell}$-measurable random variable, $\mathcal{A}_\ell^1$ denotes the set of $\mathcal{P}(\mathbb{F}) \otimes \mathcal{B}(\mathbb{R}_+)$-measurable processes $\pi^1(\cdot)$ such that

$$\int_{\tau_\ell}^{\tau_\ell \vee T} |\pi_t(\tau_\ell) \sigma_t(\tau_\ell)|^2 dt < \infty, \qquad \mathbb{P}\text{-a.s.,}$$

and the process X^{π^1} on the stochastic interval $[\![\tau_\ell, T]\!]$ is determined by the following equation

$$\begin{cases} \dfrac{dX_t^{\pi^1}}{X_t^{\pi^1}} = \pi_t^1(\tau_\ell) \dfrac{dS_t(\tau_\ell)}{S_t(\tau_\ell)}, & \tau_\ell \le t \le T, \\ X_{\tau_\ell}^{\pi^1} = X_{\tau_\ell}. \end{cases}$$

To solve this problem, we introduce the following process

$$Z_t(\tau_\ell) = \exp\left(-\int_{\tau_\ell}^{\tau_\ell \vee t} \frac{\mu_s(\tau_\ell)}{\sigma_s(\tau_\ell)} dW_s - \frac{1}{2} \int_{\tau_\ell}^{\tau_\ell \vee t} \left| \frac{\mu_s(\tau_\ell)}{\sigma_s(\tau_\ell)} \right|^2 ds \right), \quad t \in [0, T].$$

Under the following Novikov condition

$$\mathbb{E}^{\mathbb{P}}\left[\exp\left(\frac{1}{2} \int_{\tau_\ell}^{\tau_\ell \vee T} \left| \frac{\mu_s(\tau_\ell)}{\sigma_s(\tau_\ell)} \right|^2 ds \right) \right] < \infty, \tag{3.87}$$

the process $Z(\tau_\ell)$ is an $\mathbb{F}^1$-martingale, where $\mathbb{F}^1 = (\mathcal{F}_{\tau_\ell \vee t})_{t \in [0,T]}$ (see [KAR 91b, page 20]). Moreover, if we introduce a new probability measure $\mathbb{Q}^\ell$ such that $d\mathbb{Q}^\ell / d\mathbb{P} = Z_t(\tau_\ell)$ on $\mathcal{F}_{\tau_\ell \vee t}$, then the process $(S_t(\tau_\ell), t \in [0, T])$ becomes an $(\mathbb{F}, \mathbb{Q}^\ell)$-martingale on $[\![\tau_\ell, T]\!]$. From theorem 1.1, we obtain the following result.

THEOREM 3.7.– We assume that the condition [3.87] is satisfied. Then, the value function process to problem [3.86] is a.s. finite and is given by

$$V_{\tau_\ell}^{\ell,\mathrm{a}}(X_{\tau_\ell}) = \mathbb{E}^{\mathbb{P}}\left[p_T(\ell) U\left(I\left(\widehat{Y}_{\tau_\ell} \frac{Z_T(\tau_\ell)}{p_T(\ell)} \right) \right) \middle| \mathcal{F}_{\tau_\ell} \right] \tag{3.88}$$

where I is the inverse function of U' and $\widehat{Y}_{\tau_\ell}$ is the solution of the equation

$$\mathbb{E}^{\mathbb{P}}\left[Z_T(\tau_\ell) I\left(\widehat{Y}_{\tau_\ell} \frac{Z_T(\tau_\ell)}{p_T(\ell)} \right) \middle| \mathcal{F}_{\tau_\ell} \right] = X_{\tau_\ell}. \tag{3.89}$$

Moreover, the essential supremum in [3.86] is attained by an optimal strategy $\widehat{\pi}^1(\cdot) \in \mathcal{A}_\ell^1$ such that

$$\int_{\tau_\ell}^T \widehat{\pi}_t^1(\tau_\ell) \frac{dS_t(\tau_\ell)}{S_t(\tau_\ell)} = I\left(\widehat{Y}_{\tau_\ell} \frac{Z_T(\tau_\ell)}{p_T(\ell)}\right).$$

EXAMPLE 3.1.– Consider the case where $U(\cdot)$ is the logarithmic utility function. In this case, we have $I(y) = 1/y$ for any $y \in (0, +\infty)$. Therefore, equation [3.89] becomes

$$\mathbb{E}^\mathbb{P}\left[Z_T(\tau_\ell)\widehat{Y}_{\tau_\ell}^{-1} \frac{p_T(\ell)}{Z_T(\tau_\ell)} \,\middle|\, \mathcal{F}_{\tau_\ell}\right] = \widehat{Y}_{\tau_\ell}^{-1} p_{\tau_\ell}(\ell) = X_{\tau_\ell},$$

which leads to

$$\widehat{Y}_{\tau_\ell} = \frac{p_{\tau_\ell}(\ell)}{X_{\tau_\ell}}.$$

Moreover, we have $U(I(y)) = -\log(y)$. Therefore, the optimal value $V_{\tau_\ell}^\ell(X_{\tau_\ell})$ is given by

$$V_{\tau_\ell}^{\ell,\mathrm{a}}(X_{\tau_\ell}) = -\mathbb{E}^\mathbb{P}\left[p_T(\ell) \log\left(\widehat{Y}_{\tau_\ell} \frac{Z_T(\tau_\ell)}{p_T(\ell)}\right) \,\middle|\, \mathcal{F}_{\tau_\ell}\right]$$

$$= p_{\tau_\ell}(\ell)U(X_{\tau_\ell}) + \mathbb{E}^\mathbb{P}\left[p_T(\ell) \log\left(\frac{p_T(\ell)}{Z_T(\tau_\ell)}\right) \,\middle|\, \mathcal{F}_{\tau_\ell}\right] - p_{\tau_\ell}(\ell) \log(p_{\tau_\ell}(\ell)).$$

With the notation

$$J_{\tau_\ell} := \mathbb{E}^\mathbb{P}\left[p_T(\ell) \log\left(\frac{p_T(\ell)}{Z_T(\tau_\ell)}\right) \,\middle|\, \mathcal{F}_{\tau_\ell}\right] - p_{\tau_\ell}(\ell) \log(p_{\tau_\ell}(\ell)), \qquad [3.90]$$

we can write the above formula as

$$V_{\tau_\ell}^{\ell,\mathrm{a}}(X_{\tau_\ell}) = p_{\tau_\ell}(\ell)U(X_{\tau_\ell}) + J_{\tau_\ell}. \qquad [3.91]$$

EXAMPLE 3.2.– Consider the case where $U(x) = x^p/p$ is the power utility function, where $p < 1$ and $p \neq 0$. In this case, we have $I(y) = y^{1/(p-1)}$. Therefore, equation [3.89] becomes

$$\mathbb{E}^\mathbb{P}\left[\widehat{Y}_{\tau_\ell}^{1/(p-1)} \frac{Z_T(\tau_\ell)^{p/(p-1)}}{p_T(\ell)^{1/(p-1)}} \,\middle|\, \mathcal{F}_{\tau_\ell}\right] = X_{\tau_\ell},$$

which leads to

$$\widehat{Y}_{\tau_\ell} = X_{\tau_\ell}^{p-1} \mathbb{E}^{\mathbb{P}} \left[\frac{Z_T(\tau_\ell)^{p/(p-1)}}{p_T(\ell)^{1/(p-1)}} \Bigg| \mathcal{F}_{\tau_\ell} \right]^{1-p}.$$

Moreover, since $U(I(y)) = p^{-1} y^{p/(p-1)}$, we have

$$V_{\tau_\ell}^{\ell,\mathrm{a}}(X_{\tau_\ell}) = \frac{1}{p} \mathbb{E}^{\mathbb{P}} \left[p_T(\ell) \left(\widehat{Y}_{\tau_\ell} \frac{Z_T(\tau_\ell)}{p_T(\ell)} \right)^{p/(p-1)} \Bigg| \mathcal{F}_{\tau_\ell} \right]$$

$$= \frac{X_{\tau_\ell}^p}{p} \mathbb{E}^{\mathbb{P}} \left[\frac{Z_T(\tau_\ell)^{p/(p-1)}}{p_T(\ell)^{1/(p-1)}} \Bigg| \mathcal{F}_{\tau_\ell} \right]^{1-p}.$$

With the notation

$$K_{\tau_\ell} := \mathbb{E}^{\mathbb{P}} \left[\frac{Z_T(\tau_\ell)^{p/(p-1)}}{p_T(\ell)^{1/(p-1)}} \Bigg| \mathcal{F}_{\tau_\ell} \right]^{1-p}, \qquad [3.92]$$

we have

$$V_{\tau_\ell}^{\ell,\mathrm{a}}(X_{\tau_\ell}) = U(X_{\tau_\ell}) K_{\tau_\ell}. \qquad [3.93]$$

The following theorem relates the solution of [3.85] to a "before default" optimization problem.

THEOREM 3.8.– Let $\ell > 0$ and $\mathcal{A}_\ell^0$ be the set of $\mathbb{F}$-predictable processes π^0 on $[0, T]$ such that

$$\int_0^{\tau_\ell \wedge T} |\pi_t^0 \sigma_t^{\mathbb{F}}|^2 dt < \infty \qquad \mathbb{P}\text{-a.s.}$$

Then, for any $X_0 \in \mathbb{R}$, the optimal value $V_0^\ell(X_0)$ of [3.85] is equal to

$$\sup_{\pi^0 \in \mathcal{A}_\ell^0} \mathbb{E}^{\mathbb{P}} \left[\mathbb{1}_{\{\tau_\ell > T\}} p_T(\ell) U(X_T^{\pi^0}) + \mathbb{1}_{\{\tau_\ell \leq T\}} V_{\tau_\ell}^{\ell,\mathrm{a}} \left(X_{\tau_\ell}^{\pi^0} (1 - \pi_{\tau_\ell}^0 \gamma_{\tau_\ell}) \right) \right] \quad [3.94]$$

where the process X^{π^0} is determined by the following stochastic differential equation

$$\begin{cases} \dfrac{dX_t^{\pi^0}}{X_t^{\pi^0}} = \pi_t^0 \dfrac{dS_t^{\mathbb{F}}}{S_t^{\mathbb{F}}}, \\ X_0^{\pi^0} = X_0. \end{cases} \qquad [3.95]$$

PROOF.– The proof is very similar to that of theorem 1.3, except that here we consider an intermediate stopping time rather than a deterministic time. If $\pi = (\pi^0, \pi^1(\cdot))$ is an element of $\mathcal{A}_\ell$, then we have $\pi^0 \in \mathcal{A}_\ell^0$ and $\pi^1(\cdot) \in \mathcal{A}_\ell^1$. Taking the conditional expectation with respect to $\mathcal{F}_{\tau_\ell}$, we obtain

$$\mathbb{E}^{\mathbb{P}}\big[p_T(\ell)\big(\mathbb{1}_{\{\tau_\ell > T\}} U(X_T^{\pi,0}(\ell)) + \mathbb{1}_{\{\tau_\ell \le T\}} U(X_T^{\pi,1}(\tau_\ell)))\big)\big]$$
$$= \mathbb{E}^{\mathbb{P}}\big[\mathbb{1}_{\{\tau_\ell > T\}} p_T(\ell) U(X_T^{\pi,0}(\ell)) + \mathbb{1}_{\{\tau_\ell \le T\}} \mathbb{E}^{\mathbb{P}}\big[p_T(\ell) U(X_T^{\pi,1}(\tau_\ell)) \mid \mathcal{F}_{\tau_\ell}\big]\big]$$
$$\le \mathbb{E}^{\mathbb{P}}\big[\mathbb{1}_{\{\tau_\ell > T\}} p_T(\ell) U(X_T^{\pi,0}(\ell)) + \mathbb{1}_{\{\tau_\ell \le T\}} V_{\tau_\ell}^{\ell,\mathrm{a}}(X_{\tau_\ell}^{\pi,0}(\ell)(1 - \pi_{\tau_\ell}^0 \gamma_{\tau_\ell}))\big]$$
$$\le \widetilde{V}_0^\ell(X_0, \ell),$$

where $\widetilde{V}_0^\ell(X_0)$ is the supremum defined in [3.94]. Since π is arbitrary, we obtain $V_0^\ell(X_0) \le \widetilde{V}_0^\ell(X_0)$.

Conversely, let $\pi^1(\cdot)$ be an element in $\mathcal{A}_\ell^1$. For any $\pi^0 \in \mathcal{A}_\ell^0$, the couple $\pi = (\pi^0, \pi^1(\cdot))$ belongs to $\mathcal{A}_\ell$. Since $\pi^1(\cdot)$ is arbitrary, we have

$$V_0^\ell(X_0) \ge \mathbb{E}^{\mathbb{P}}\big[\mathbb{1}_{\{\tau_\ell > T\}} p_T(\ell) U(X_T^{\pi,0}(\ell)) \\ + \mathbb{1}_{\{\tau_\ell \le T\}} V_{\tau_\ell}^{\ell,\mathrm{a}}(X_{\tau_l}^{\pi,0}(\ell)(1 - \pi_{\tau_\ell}^0 \gamma_{\tau_\ell}))\big]$$

By taking the supremum with respect to π^0, we obtain $V_0^\ell(X_0) \ge \widetilde{V}_0^\ell(X_0)$. The theorem is thus proved. □

The following result shows that the strategy constraints play a crucial role in the optimization: the optimal strategy at the default time is the short-selling (respectively, buying) constraint bound if γ_{τ_ℓ} is positive (respectively, negative). For any $\nu \in \mathcal{A}_\ell^0$, we let

$$\mathcal{X}_0(\nu) = \mathbb{E}^{\mathbb{P}}\big[\mathbb{1}_{\{\tau_\ell > T\}} p_T(\ell) U(X_T^\nu) + \mathbb{1}_{\{\tau_\ell \le T\}} V_{\tau_\ell}^{\ell,\mathrm{a}}\big(X_{\tau_\ell}^\nu(1 - \nu_{\tau_\ell} \gamma_{\tau_\ell}))\big].$$

We recall that b is the buying constraint (see 3.78).

PROPOSITION 3.4.– For any $\nu \in \mathcal{A}_\ell^0$, there exists a sequence of strategies $(\nu_n \in \mathcal{A}_\ell^0)_{n \in \mathbb{N}}$ such that $\nu_{n,\tau_\ell} = b\mathbb{1}_{\{\gamma_{\tau_\ell}<0\}}$ and

$$\lim_{n \to +\infty} \mathcal{X}_0(\nu_n) \geq \mathcal{X}_0(\nu).$$

PROOF.– Let $(\tau_n)_{n \in \mathbb{N}}$, with $\tau_n < \tau_\ell$, be an increasing sequence of $\mathbb{F}$-stopping times that converges to τ_ℓ. For any $n \in \mathbb{N}$, we define

$$\nu_n = \mathbb{1}_{[\![0,\tau_n]\!]}\nu + \mathbb{1}_{]\!]\tau_n,\tau_\ell]\!]}b\mathbb{1}_{\{\gamma_{\tau_\ell}<0\}}$$

which belongs to $\mathcal{A}_\ell^0$. On the one hand, by dominated convergence theorem, we have

$$\lim_{n \to +\infty} \mathbb{E}^{\mathbb{P}}\left[\mathbb{1}_{\{\tau_\ell>T\}}p_T(l)|U(X_T^{\nu_n}) - U(X_T^{\nu})|\right] = 0.$$

On the other hand, on the event $\{\tau_\ell \leq T\}$, we have

$$\frac{X_{\tau_\ell}^{\nu_n}(1 - \nu_{n,\tau_\ell}\gamma_{\tau_\ell})}{X_{\tau_\ell}^{\nu}(1 - \nu_{\tau_\ell}\gamma_{\tau_\ell})}$$
$$= \frac{(1 - b\mathbb{1}_{\{\gamma_{\tau_\ell}<0\}}\gamma_{\tau_\ell})}{(1 - \nu_{\tau_\ell}\gamma_{\tau_\ell})} \cdot \exp\left(\int_{\tau_n}^{\tau_l}\left(-(\pi_s^{\mathrm{F}} - b\mathbb{1}_{\{\gamma_{\tau_\ell}<0\}})\mu_s^{\mathrm{F}}\right.\right.$$
$$\left.\left. + \frac{1}{2}(\sigma_s^{\mathrm{F}})^2((\pi_s^{\mathrm{F}})^2 - \mathbb{1}_{\{\gamma_{\tau_\ell}<0\}}b^2))ds - \int_{\tau_n}^{\tau_\ell}(\pi_s^{\mathrm{F}} - b\mathbb{1}_{\{\gamma_{\tau_\ell}<0\}})\sigma_s^{\mathrm{F}}dW_s\right)$$

By the definition of $\mathcal{A}_\ell^0$, we have

$$0 \leq \nu_{\tau_\ell} \leq b, \quad \text{and} \quad \frac{(1 - b\mathbb{1}_{\{\gamma_{\tau_\ell}<0\}}\gamma_{\tau_\ell})}{(1 - \nu_{\tau_\ell}\gamma_{\tau_\ell})} \geq 1.$$

Moreover, $\tau_n \to \tau_\ell$ implies that the exponential term tends to 1 almost surely. Thus,

$$\lim_{n \to +\infty} \frac{X_{\tau_\ell}^{\nu_n}(1 - \nu_{n,\tau_\ell}\gamma_{\tau_\ell})}{X_{\tau_\ell}^{\nu}(1 - \nu_{\tau_\ell}\gamma_{\tau_\ell})} \geq 1$$

and hence

$$\lim_{n \to +\infty} \mathbb{E}^{\mathbb{P}}\left[\mathbb{1}_{\{\tau_\ell \leq T\}}V_{\tau_\ell}^{\ell,\mathrm{a}}(X_{\tau_\ell}^{\nu_n}(1 - \nu_{n,\tau_\ell}\gamma_{\tau_\ell}))\right]$$
$$\geq \mathbb{E}^{\mathbb{P}}\left[\mathbb{1}_{\{\tau_\ell \leq T\}}V_{\tau_\ell}^{\ell,\mathrm{a}}(X_{\tau_\ell}^{\nu}(1 - \nu_{\tau_\ell}\gamma_{\tau_\ell}))\right].$$

Consequently,

$$\lim_{n \to +\infty} \mathcal{X}_0(\nu_n) \geq \mathcal{X}_0(\nu).$$

$\square$

We introduce the dynamic version of the optimization problem [3.94]. Let ν be an element in $\mathcal{A}_\ell^0$. For any $t \in [0, T]$, we denote by $\mathcal{A}_\ell^0(t, \nu)$ the set of investment strategies $\pi^0 \in \mathcal{A}_\ell^0$ which coincides with ν on $[0, t]$ and define $V_t^\ell(X_0, \nu)$ as

$$\operatorname*{ess\,sup}_{\pi^0 \in \mathcal{A}_\ell^0(t,\nu)} \mathbb{E}^{\mathbb{P}} \left[\mathbb{1}_{\{\tau_\ell > T\}} p_T(\ell) U(X_T^{\pi^0}) \right.$$
$$\left. + \mathbb{1}_{\{t < \tau_\ell \leq T\}} V_{\tau_\ell}^{\ell,\mathrm{a}} \big(X_{\tau_\ell}^{\pi^0} (1 - \pi_{\tau_\ell}^0 \gamma_{\tau_\ell}) \big) \,\Big|\, \mathcal{F}_{\tau_\ell \wedge t} \right].$$

By the dynamic programming principle (see theorem 1.3), we obtain the following result.

PROPOSITION 3.5.– Let ν be an element of $\mathcal{A}_\ell^0$. The process

$$\xi_t^\nu := V_t^\ell(X_0, \nu) + \mathbb{1}_{\{\tau_\ell \leq t\}} V_{\tau_\ell}^{\ell,\mathrm{a}}(X_{\tau_\ell}^\nu(1 - \nu_{\tau_\ell} \gamma_{\tau_\ell})), \quad t \in [0, T]$$

is an $(\mathbb{F}^0, \mathbb{P})$-supermartingale, where $\mathbb{F}^0 = (\mathcal{F}_{\tau_\ell \wedge t}, \ t \in [0, T])$. Moreover, ν^* is an optimal investment strategy for the problem [3.94] if and only if the process ξ^{ν^*} is an $(\mathbb{F}^0, \mathbb{P})$-martingale.

PROOF.– Let s, t two times such that $s \leq t \leq T$.

$$\mathbb{E}^{\mathbb{P}} \left[V_t^\ell(X_0, \nu) + \mathbb{1}_{\{\tau_\ell \leq t\}} V_{\tau_\ell}^{\ell,\mathrm{a}}(X_{\tau_\ell}^\nu(1 - \nu_{\tau_\ell} \gamma_{\tau_\ell})) \,\Big|\, \mathcal{F}_{\tau_\ell \wedge s} \right]$$
$$= \mathbb{E}^{\mathbb{P}} \left[V_t^\ell(X_0, \nu) + \mathbb{1}_{\{s < \tau_l \leq t\}} V_{\tau_\ell}^{\ell,\mathrm{a}}(X_{\tau_\ell}^\nu(1 - \nu_{\tau_\ell} \gamma_{\tau_l})) \,\Big|\, \mathcal{F}_{\tau_\ell \wedge s} \right]$$
$$+ \mathbb{1}_{\{\tau_\ell \leq s\}} V_{\tau_\ell}^{\ell,\mathrm{a}}(1 - \nu_{\tau_\ell} \gamma_{\tau_\ell})$$

By the definition of $V_t^\ell(X_0, \nu)$, we obtain that

$$\mathbb{E}^{\mathbb{P}}\left[V_t^\ell(X_0, \nu) + \mathbb{1}_{\{s < \tau_l \leq t\}} V_{\tau_\ell}^{\ell,\mathrm{a}}(X_{\tau_\ell}^\nu(1 - \nu_{\tau_\ell}\gamma_{\tau_l})) \,\Big|\, \mathcal{F}_{\tau_\ell \wedge s}\right]$$

$$= \mathbb{E}^{\mathbb{P}}\left[\operatorname*{ess\,sup}_{\pi^0 \in \mathcal{A}_\ell^0(t,\nu)} \mathbb{E}^{\mathbb{P}}\left[\mathbb{1}_{\{\tau_\ell > T\}} p_T(\ell) U(X_T^{\pi^0})\right.\right.$$

$$\left.+ \mathbb{1}_{\{t < \tau_\ell \leq T\}} V_{\tau_\ell}^{\ell,\mathrm{a}}(X_{\tau_\ell}^{\pi^0}(1 - \pi_{\tau_\ell}^0 \gamma_{\tau_\ell})) \,\Big|\, \mathcal{F}_{\tau_\ell \wedge t}\right]$$

$$\left.+ \mathbb{1}_{\{s < \tau_\ell \leq t\}} V_{\tau_\ell}^{\ell,\mathrm{a}}(X_{\tau_\ell}^\nu(1 - \nu_{\tau_\ell}\gamma_{\tau_\ell})) \,\Big|\, \mathcal{F}_{\tau_\ell \wedge s}\right]$$

$$\leq \operatorname*{ess\,sup}_{\pi^0 \in \mathcal{A}_\ell^0(s,\nu)} \mathbb{E}^{\mathbb{P}}\left[\mathbb{1}_{\{\tau_\ell > T\}} p_T(\ell) U(X_T^{\pi^0})\right.$$

$$\left.+ \mathbb{1}_{\{s < \tau_\ell \leq T\}} V_{\tau_\ell}^{\ell,\mathrm{a}}(X_{\tau_\ell}^{\pi^0}(1 - \pi_{\tau_\ell}^0 \gamma_{\tau_\ell})) \,\Big|\, \mathcal{F}_{\tau_\ell \wedge s}\right].$$

Therefore, we obtain

$$\mathbb{E}^{\mathbb{P}}\left[V_t^\ell(X_0, \nu) + \mathbb{1}_{\{\tau_\ell \leq t\}} V_{\tau_\ell}^{\ell,\mathrm{a}}(X_{\tau_\ell}^\nu(1 - \nu_{\tau_\ell}\gamma_{\tau_\ell})) \,\Big|\, \mathcal{F}_{\tau_\ell \wedge s}\right]$$

$$\leq V_t^\ell(X_0, \nu) + \mathbb{1}_{\{\tau_\ell \leq s\}} V_{\tau_\ell}^{\ell,\mathrm{a}}(X_{\tau_\ell}^\nu(1 - \nu_{\tau_\ell}\gamma_{\tau_\ell})).$$

and hence ξ^ν is an $\mathbb{F}^0$-supermartingale on $[0, T]$.

Note that ν^* is an optimal strategy for the problem [3.94] if and only if $\mathbb{E}^{\mathbb{P}}[\xi_T^{\nu^*}] = V_0^\ell(X_0) = \xi_0^{\nu^*}$, namely, ξ^{ν^*} is an $(\mathbb{F}^0, \mathbb{P})$-martingale (since we have proved that it is an $(\mathbb{F}^0, \mathbb{P})$-supermartingale). $\qquad\square$

LEMMA 3.2.– Let $(M_t)_{t \in [0,T]}$ be an $(\mathbb{F}^0, \mathbb{P})$-martingale. Then, there exists an $\mathbb{F}$-predictable process ϕ in $L_{\mathrm{loc}}^2(W)$ such that

$$M_t = M_0 + \int_0^{\tau_\ell \wedge t} \phi_s dW_s, \qquad t \in [0, T].$$

PROOF.– We first prove that $(M_t)_{t \in [0,T]}$ is also an $(\mathbb{F}, \mathbb{P})$-martingale. Indeed, for $s \leq t \leq T$

$$M_s = \mathbb{E}^{\mathbb{P}}[M_t \mid \mathcal{F}_{\tau_\ell \wedge s}] = \mathbb{E}^{\mathbb{P}}[\mathbb{E}^{\mathbb{P}}[M_t \mid \mathcal{F}_{\tau_\ell}] \mid \mathcal{F}_s] = \mathbb{E}^{\mathbb{P}}[M_t \mid \mathcal{F}_s]$$

because M_t is $\mathcal{F}_{\tau_\ell}$-measurable. Thus, by the representation theorem for the $\mathbb{F}$-martingale, and since $(M_t)_{t \in [0,T]}$ is stopped at τ_ℓ, there exists ϕ an $\mathbb{F}$-predictable process in $L_{\mathrm{loc}}^2(W)$ such that $M_t = M_0 + \int_0^{\tau_\ell \wedge t} \phi_s dW_s$. $\qquad\square$

3.5.3. *The logarithmic utility case*

Let $U(x) = \log(x)$ be the logarithmic utility function. By [3.91], for any $\nu \in \mathcal{A}_\ell^0$ we have $V_{\tau_\ell}^{\ell,a}(\cdot) = p_{\tau_\ell}(\ell) \log(\cdot) + J_{\tau_\ell}$. In particular, the process

$$Y_t := V_t^\ell(X_0, \nu) - \mathbb{1}_{\{\tau_\ell > t\}} p_t(\ell) \log(X_t^\nu) + \mathbb{1}_{\{\tau_\ell \le t\}} J_{\tau_\ell}, \quad t \in [0, T] \quad [3.96]$$

does not depend on the choice of the strategy ν since it can be written as

$$\underset{\pi^0 \in \mathcal{A}_\ell^0(t,\nu)}{\text{ess sup}} \; \mathbb{E}^{\mathbb{P}} \left[\mathbb{1}_{\{\tau_\ell > T\}} p_T(\ell) \log\left(\frac{X_T^{\pi^0}}{X_t^\nu} \right) + \mathbb{1}_{\{\tau_\ell \le T\}} J_{\tau_\ell} \right.$$
$$\left. + \mathbb{1}_{\{t < \tau_\ell \le T\}} p_{\tau_\ell}(\ell) \log\left(\frac{X_{\tau_\ell}^{\pi^0}}{X_t^\nu} (1 - \pi_{\tau_\ell}^0 \gamma_{\tau_\ell}) \right) \;\middle|\; \mathcal{F}_{\tau_\ell \wedge t} \right].$$

Note that

$$\xi_t^\nu = Y_t + \mathbb{1}_{\{\tau_\ell > t\}} p_t(\ell) \log(X_t^\nu) + \mathbb{1}_{\{\tau_\ell \le t\}} p_{\tau_\ell}(\ell) \log(X_{\tau_\ell}^\nu (1 - \nu_{\tau_\ell} \gamma_{\tau_\ell}))$$
$$= Y_t + p_{\tau_\ell \wedge t}(\ell) \log(X_{\tau_\ell \wedge t}^\nu) + \mathbb{1}_{\{\tau_\ell \le t\}} p_{\tau_\ell}(\ell) \log(1 - \nu_{\tau_\ell} \gamma_{\tau_\ell}).$$

In particular, the process Y is an $(\mathbb{F}^0, \mathbb{P})$-supermartingale (this can be seen by taking ν to be the zero investment strategy). By the Doob–Meyer decomposition and lemma 3.2, there exists $Z \in L_{\text{loc}}^2(W)$, and a finite variation increasing $\mathbb{F}^0$-predictable process A such that:

$$dY_t = \mathbb{1}_{\{t \le \tau_\ell\}} Z_t dW_t - dA_t, \quad t \in [0, T]. \quad [3.97]$$

By Itô's formula and the stochastic equation, we have

$$d\log(X_t^\nu) = \nu_t \sigma_t^{\mathbb{F}} dW_t + \left(\nu_t \mu_t^{\mathbb{F}} - \frac{1}{2}(\nu_t \sigma_t^{\mathbb{F}})^2 \right) dt.$$

Assuming that the density process $p(\ell)$ is given by the following diffusion equation

$$\frac{dp_t(\ell)}{p_t(\ell)} = c_t(\ell) dW_t.$$

Then, we have

$$d(p_t(\ell) \log(X_t^\nu)) = p_t(\ell) \left[\left(c_t(\ell) \log(X_t^\nu) + \nu_t \sigma_t^{\mathbb{F}} \right) dW_t \right.$$
$$\left. + \left(\nu_t \mu_t^{\mathbb{F}} + \nu_t \sigma_t^{\mathbb{F}} c_t(\ell) - \frac{1}{2}(\nu_t \sigma_t^{\mathbb{F}})^2 \right) dt \right].$$

Therefore, the finite variation part in the Doob–Meyer decomposition of the process ξ^ν is given by $-A^\nu$ with

$$dA_t^\nu = dA_t - \mathbb{1}_{\{\tau_\ell \geq t\}} p_t(\ell) \left(\nu_t \mu_t^{\mathrm{F}} + \nu_t \sigma_t^{\mathrm{F}} c_t(\ell) - \frac{1}{2}(\nu_t \sigma_t^{\mathrm{F}})^2 \right) dt$$
$$- p_{\tau_\ell}(\ell) \log(1 - \nu_{\tau_\ell} \gamma_{\tau_\ell}) d\mathbb{1}_{\{\tau_\ell \leq t\}}.$$

Therefore proposition 3.5 leads to the following result.

PROPOSITION 3.6.– The process Y defined in [3.96] satisfies the following backward stochastic differential equation

$$Y_t = \mathbb{1}_{\{\tau_\ell \leq T\}} \, J_{\tau_\ell} + \mathbb{1}_{\{t < \tau_\ell \leq T\}} p_{\tau_\ell}(\ell) \log(1 - \nu_{\tau_\ell} \gamma_{\tau_\ell})$$
$$+ \int_t^{\tau_\ell \wedge T} f(s) ds - \int_t^{\tau_\ell \wedge T} Z_s dW_s \qquad [3.98]$$

for some $Z \in L_{\mathrm{loc}}^2(W)$, with

$$f(s) = p_s(\ell) \sup_{\pi \in [0,b]} \left(\pi(\mu_s^{\mathrm{F}} + \sigma_s^{\mathrm{F}} c_s(\ell)) - \frac{1}{2}(\pi \sigma_s^{\mathrm{F}})^2 \right). \qquad [3.99]$$

PROOF.– By proposition 3.5 and the above formula for the dynamic of A^ν, we obtain that

$$A_t = \operatorname*{ess\,sup}_{\nu \in \mathcal{A}_\ell^0} \left[\int_0^{\tau_\ell \wedge t} p_s(\ell) \left(\nu_s \mu_s^{\mathrm{F}} + \nu_s \sigma_s^{\mathrm{F}} c_s(\ell) - \frac{1}{2}(\nu_s \sigma_s^{\mathrm{F}})^2 \right) ds \right.$$
$$\left. + \mathbb{1}_{\{\tau_\ell \leq t\}} p_{\tau_\ell}(\ell) \log(1 - \nu_{\tau_\ell} \gamma_{\tau_\ell}) \right].$$

Moreover, by proposition 3.4, in the above formula, it suffices to take the essential supremum with respect to the investment strategies ν such that

$\nu_{\tau_\ell} = b\mathbb{1}_{\{\gamma_{\tau_\ell}<0\}}$. Moreover, the process Y is stopped at time τ_ℓ. Hence, we obtain that

$$
\begin{aligned}
A_t &= \mathbb{1}_{\{\tau \le t\}} p_{\tau_\ell}(\ell) \log(\nu_{\tau_\ell}\gamma_{\tau_\ell}) \\
&\quad + \underset{\nu \in \mathcal{A}_\ell^0}{\text{ess sup}} \int_0^{\tau_\ell \wedge t} p_s(\ell)\left(\nu_s\mu_s^{\mathbb{F}} + \nu_s\sigma_s^{\mathbb{F}}c_s(\ell) - \tfrac{1}{2}(\nu_s\sigma_s^{\mathbb{F}})^2\right)ds \\
&\quad {}_{\nu_{\tau_\ell}=b\mathbb{1}_{\{\gamma_{\tau_\ell}<0\}}} \\
&= \mathbb{1}_{\{\tau \le t\}} p_{\tau_\ell}(\ell) \log(\nu_{\tau_\ell}\gamma_{\tau_\ell}) \\
&\quad + \int_0^{\tau_\ell \wedge t} p_s(\ell) \underset{\substack{\nu \in \mathcal{A}_\ell^0 \\ \nu_{\tau_\ell}=b\mathbb{1}_{\{\gamma_{\tau_\ell}<0\}}}}{\text{ess sup}} \left(\nu_s\mu_s^{\mathbb{F}} + \nu_s\sigma_s^{\mathbb{F}}c_s(\ell) - \tfrac{1}{2}(\nu_s\sigma_s^{\mathbb{F}})^2\right)ds.
\end{aligned}
$$

Finally, by taking an increasing sequence of $\mathbb{F}$-stopping times converging to τ_ℓ, we can show that the essential supremum in the above formula can be taking pointwise. Therefore, the process Y satisfies the backward stochastic differential equation [3.98]. $\qquad\square$

3.5.4. *Power utility case*

We now consider the optimization problem with the power utility function $U(x) = x^p/p$ with $p < 1$, $p \ne 0$. By [3.93], we can write the after-default optimal investment value function $V_{\tau_\ell}^{\ell,\mathrm{a}}(\cdot) = U(\cdot)K_{\tau_\ell}$, where the random variable K_{τ_ℓ} is defined in [3.92]. Therefore, the process

$$
Y_t := \frac{V_t^\ell(X_0, \nu)}{U(X_t^\nu)}, \quad t \in [0, T] \tag{3.100}
$$

does not depend on the choice of $\nu \in \mathcal{A}_\ell^0$ since it can be written as

$$
\begin{aligned}
&\underset{\pi^0 \in \mathcal{A}_\ell^0(t,\nu)}{\text{ess sup}} \mathbb{E}^{\mathbb{P}}\left[\mathbb{1}_{\{\tau_\ell>T\}} p_T(l)\left(\frac{X_T^{\pi^0}}{X_t^\nu}\right)^p \right. \\
&\quad \left. +\mathbb{1}_{\{t<\tau_\ell \le T\}} K_{\tau_l}\left(\frac{X_{\tau_\ell}^{\pi^0}}{X_t^\nu}\right)^p (1-\pi_{\tau_\ell}^0\gamma_{\tau_\ell})\,\middle|\,\mathcal{F}_{\tau_\ell \wedge t}\right]
\end{aligned}
$$

Note that

$$
\xi_t^\nu = Y_t U(X_t^\nu) + \mathbb{1}_{\{\tau_\ell \le t\}} K_{\tau_\ell} U(X_{\tau_\ell}^\nu(1-\nu_{\tau_\ell}\gamma_{\tau_\ell})).
$$

In particular, $(Y_t + \mathbb{1}_{\{\tau_\ell \leq t\}} K_{\tau_\ell},\ t \in [0,T])$ is an $(\mathbb{F}^0, \mathbb{P})$-supermartingale (this can be seen by taking ν to be the zero investment strategy), and hence the process Y is also an $(\mathbb{F}^0, \mathbb{P})$-supermartingale. By the Doob–Meyer decomposition and lemma 3.2, there exists $Z \in L^2_{\text{loc}}(W)$, and a finite variation increasing $\mathbb{F}^0$-predictable process A such that:

$$dY_t = \mathbb{1}_{\{t \leq \tau_\ell\}} Z_t dW_t - dA_t, \quad t \in [0,T].$$

By Itô's formula, we obtain that the finite variation process in the decomposition of the $\mathbb{F}^0$-supermartingale ξ^ν, $\nu \in \mathcal{A}^0_\ell$, is given by $-A^\nu$ with

$$\frac{dA^\nu_t}{U(X^\nu_t)} = dA_t - p\left[\left((\mu^{\mathbb{F}}_t Y_t + \sigma^{\mathbb{F}}_t Z_t \mathbb{1}_{\{\tau_\ell \geq t\}}) \nu_t + \frac{1-p}{2} Y_t |\nu_t \sigma^{\mathbb{F}}_t|^2 \right) dt \right.$$
$$\left. + K_t \frac{(1 - \nu_t \gamma_t)^p}{p} d\mathbb{1}_{\{\tau_\ell \leq t\}} \right].$$

By proposition 3.5, we obtain

$$A_t = p \operatorname*{ess\,sup}_{\nu \in \mathcal{A}^0_\ell} \left[\int_0^t \left((\mu^{\mathbb{F}}_s Y_s + \sigma^{\mathbb{F}}_s Z_s) \nu_s - \frac{1-p}{2} Y_s |\nu_s \sigma^{\mathbb{F}}_s|^2 \right) ds \right.$$
$$\left. + \mathbb{1}_{\{\tau_\ell \leq t\}} K_{\tau_\ell} \frac{(1 - \nu_{\tau_\ell} \gamma_{\tau_\ell})^p}{p} \right].$$

Moreover, by proposition 3.4, in the above formula, it suffices to take the essential supremum with respect to the investment strategies ν such that $\nu_{\tau_\ell} = b\mathbb{1}_{\{\gamma_{\tau_\ell} < 0\}}$. Therefore, we have

$$A_t = p\mathbb{1}_{\{\tau_\ell \leq t\}} K_{\tau_\ell} \frac{(1 - b\gamma_{\tau_\ell} \mathbb{1}_{\{\gamma_{\tau_\ell} < 0\}})^p}{p}$$
$$+ \int_0^t \operatorname*{ess\,sup}_{\substack{\nu \in \mathcal{A}^0_\ell \\ \nu_{\tau_\ell} = b\mathbb{1}_{\{\gamma_{\tau_\ell} < 0\}}}} \left((\mu^{\mathbb{F}}_s Y_s + \sigma^{\mathbb{F}}_s Z_s) \nu_s - \frac{1-p}{2} Y_s |\nu_s \sigma^{\mathbb{F}}_s|^2 \right) ds. \quad [3.101]$$

By taking an increasing sequence of $\mathbb{F}$-stopping times converging to τ_ℓ, we can show that the essential supremum in the above formula can be taking pointwise, namely,

$$A_t = p\mathbb{1}_{\{\tau_\ell \leq t\}} K_{\tau_\ell} \frac{(1 - b\gamma_{\tau_\ell} \mathbb{1}_{\{\gamma_{\tau_\ell} < 0\}})^p}{p}$$
$$+ \int_0^t \sup_{\pi \in [0,b]} \left((\mu^{\mathbb{F}}_s Y_s + \sigma^{\mathbb{F}}_s Z_s) \pi - \frac{1-p}{2} Y_s |\pi \sigma^{\mathbb{F}}_s|^2 \right) ds.$$

Hence, we have the following result.

PROPOSITION 3.7.– The process Y defined in [3.100] satisfies the following backward stochastic differential equation

$$
\begin{aligned}
Y_t = {}& \mathbb{1}_{\{\tau_\ell > T\}} p_T(\ell) + \mathbb{1}_{\{t < \tau_\ell \le T\}} K_{\tau_\ell} \frac{(1 - b\mathbb{1}_{\{\gamma_{\tau_\ell} < 0\}} \gamma_{\tau_\ell})^p}{p} \\
& + \int_t^{\tau_\ell \wedge T} f(s, Y_s, Z_s) ds - \int_t^{\tau_\ell \wedge T} Z_s dW_s,
\end{aligned}
\tag{3.102}
$$

for some $Z \in L^2_{\text{loc}}(W)$, and where

$$
f(s, Y_s, Z_s) = p \sup_{\pi \in [0, b]} \left[\pi (\mu_s^{\mathbb{F}} Y_s + \sigma_s^{\mathbb{F}} Z_s) - \frac{1-p}{2} Y_s (\pi \sigma_s^{\mathbb{F}})^2 \right].
\tag{3.103}
$$

REMARK 3.6.– As in theorem 3.4, the optimal strategy before default is characterized through the optimization of the driver of a BSDE. However, the main difference relies on the fact that, in our case, the driver has a jump at the default time τ_l. Nevertheless, since the jump occurs (if it occurs) only at the terminal date of the BSDE, standard theory on BSDE still applies.

A naive way to determine the optimal investment strategy consists of optimizing ν_s for $s < \tau_\ell$ pointwise. However, the "optimal strategy" thus obtained needs not be predictable. Consider the auxiliary backward stochastic differential equation as follows

$$
\begin{aligned}
Y_t^0 = {}& \mathbb{1}_{\{\tau_\ell \le T\}} J_{\tau_\ell} + \mathbb{1}_{\{t < \tau_\ell \le T\}} p_{\tau_\ell}(\ell) \log(1 - \nu_{\tau_\ell} \gamma_{\tau_\ell}) \\
& + \int_t^{\tau_\ell \wedge T} f^0(s, Y_s^0) ds - \int_t^{\tau_\ell \wedge T} Z_s dW_s
\end{aligned}
\tag{3.104}
$$

with the driver

$$
f^0(s, Y_s^0, Z_s) = \operatorname*{ess\,sup}_{0 \le \nu_s \le b} p[(\mu_s^{\mathbb{F}} Y_s^0 + \sigma_s^{\mathbb{F}} Z_s) \nu_s - \frac{1-p}{2} Y_s^0 |\nu_s \sigma_s^{\mathbb{F}}|^2],
$$

where Y^0 is solution to the BSDE: for $t \in [0, T \wedge \tau_l]$

$$
\begin{aligned}
Y_t^0 = {}& \mathbb{1}_{\{\tau_\ell > T\}} p_T(\ell) + \mathbb{1}_{\{t < \tau_\ell \le T\}} K_{\tau_\ell} \frac{(1 - b\mathbb{1}_{\{\gamma < 0\}} \gamma_{\tau_\ell})^p}{p} \\
& + \int_t^{\tau_\ell \wedge T} f^0(s, Y_s^0, Z_s) ds - \int_t^{\tau_\ell \wedge s} Z_s dW_s,
\end{aligned}
$$

leading to the optimal portfolio $\hat{\pi}_s^0$. Thus, the natural candidate to be the optimal strategy before default is

$$\pi^{\mathrm{np}} := \mathbb{1}_{[0,\tau_l[}\hat{\pi}^0 + b\mathbb{1}_{\{\gamma<0\}}\mathbb{1}_{\tau_l}, \qquad [3.105]$$

but unfortunately π^{np} is not a predictable process. Nevertheless, we will prove the existence of a sequence of predictable strategies in $\mathcal{A}_l^0$ such that the corresponding value function tends to the value function relative to this non-predictable strategy. To do this, for any strategy $\pi^0 \in \mathcal{A}_l^0$, we recall the corresponding value function of the before default global optimization problem

$$\mathcal{X}_0(\pi^0) = \mathbb{E}\left[\mathbb{1}_{T<\tau_l}p_T(l)U(X_T^{\pi^0}(l)) + \mathbb{1}_{T\geq\tau_l}K_{\tau_l}U(X_{\tau_l}^{\pi^0}(l)(1 - \pi_{\tau_l}^0(l)\gamma_{\tau_l}))\right].$$

$$[3.106]$$

Note that [3.106] can also be defined for a strategy π that is predictable only on $[0, \tau_l[$ (and not necessarily on $[0, \tau_l]$). Using proposition 3.4, we have the following result:

PROPOSITION 3.8.– Let $(\tau_n)_{n\in\mathbb{N}^*}$ be an increasing sequence of $\mathbb{F}$-predictable stopping times that converge to τ_l. We consider the strategies $(\pi_n^0 = \mathbb{1}_{[0,\tau_n]}\hat{\pi}^0 + \mathbb{1}_{]\tau_n,\tau_l]}b\mathbb{1}_{\{\gamma<0\}})$ where $\hat{\pi}^0$ is the optimal process for the driver of the following BSDE: for $t \in [0, T \wedge \tau_l[$

$$Y_t^0 = \mathbb{1}_{T<\tau_l}p_T(l) + \mathbb{1}_{t<\tau_l\leq T}K_{\tau_l}\frac{(1 - b\mathbb{1}_{\{\gamma<0\}}\gamma_{\tau_l})^p}{p}$$

$$+ \int_t^{T\wedge\tau_l} f^0(\theta, Y_\theta^0, \phi_\theta^0)d\theta - \int_t^{T\wedge\tau_l} \phi_\theta^0 dW_\theta,$$

$$f^0(s, y, \phi) = p \sup_{0\leq\nu\leq b}\left[(\mu_s^0 y + \sigma_s^0\phi)\nu - \frac{1-p}{2}y|\nu\sigma_s^0|^2\right].$$

Those strategies are in $\mathcal{A}_l^0$ and satisfy

$$\lim_{n\to+\infty} \mathcal{X}_0(\pi_n^0) = V_0(l)$$

$$= \mathbb{E}\left[\mathbb{1}_{T<\tau_l}p_T(l)U(X_T^{\hat{\pi}^0}(l)) + \mathbb{1}_{T\geq\tau_l}K_{\tau_l}U(X_{\tau_l}^{\hat{\pi}^0}(l)(1 - b\mathbb{1}_{\{\gamma<0\}}\gamma_{\tau_l}))\right].$$

PROOF.– For any $n \in \mathbb{N}^*$, the strategy $\pi_n^0 := \mathbb{1}_{[0,\tau_n]}\hat{\pi}^0 + \mathbb{1}_{]\tau_n,\tau_l]}b\mathbb{1}_{\{\gamma<0\}}$ is in $\mathcal{A}_l^0$, and π_n^0 converges to the non-predictable optimal strategy π^{np} defined in [3.105] when $n \to \infty$. Moreover, for any $n \in \mathbb{N}^*$, $\mathcal{X}_0(\pi_n^0) \le \mathcal{X}_0(\pi^{\mathrm{np}})$ and by proposition 3.4

$$\mathcal{X}_0(\pi^{\mathrm{np}}) \ge \lim_{n \to +\infty} \mathcal{X}_0(\pi_n^0) \ge \mathcal{X}_0(\hat{\pi}^0).$$

But the proof of proposition 3.4 still holds if we change the value at time τ_l of the portfolio π^0, thus the converse inequality $\mathcal{X}_0(\pi^{\mathrm{np}}) \le \lim_{n \to +\infty} \mathcal{X}_0(\pi_n^0)$ holds and

$$\mathbb{E}\left[\mathbb{1}_{T<\tau_l}p_T(l)U(X_T^{\hat{\pi}^0}(l)) + \mathbb{1}_{T\ge\tau_l}K_{\tau_l}U(X_{\tau_l}^{\hat{\pi}^0}(l)(1 - b\mathbb{1}_{\{\gamma<0\}}\gamma_{\tau_l}))\right]$$

$$= \mathcal{X}_0(\pi^{\mathrm{np}}) = \mathcal{X}_0(\mathbb{1}_{[0,\tau_l]}\hat{\pi}^0 + b\mathbb{1}_{\{\gamma<0\}}\mathbb{1}_{\tau_l})$$

$$= \lim_{n \to +\infty} \mathcal{X}_0(\mathbb{1}_{[0,\tau_n]}\hat{\pi}^0 + \mathbb{1}_{]\tau_n,\tau_l]}b\mathbb{1}_{\{\gamma<0\}})$$

$$= \lim_{n \to +\infty} \mathcal{X}_0(\pi_n^0)$$

$$\square$$

3.6. Numerical illustrations

We will now illustrate our previous results using explicit models and we aim to compare the optimization results for an insider, a standard investor and a Merton investor. We recall that all investors start with an initial wealth X_0. For the purpose of comparison, we choose a similar model as the one studied in section 3.3.4. More precisely, we let the parameters $\mu^{\mathbb{F}}$, $\sigma^{\mathbb{F}}$ and γ be constant, and let $\mu(\theta)$, $\sigma(\theta)$ be deterministic functions of θ given by

$$\mu(\theta) = \mu^{\mathbb{F}}\frac{\theta}{T}, \quad \sigma(\theta) = \sigma^{\mathbb{F}}\left(2 - \frac{\theta}{T}\right), \quad \theta \in [0,T], \qquad [3.107]$$

which means that the ratio of the after-default and before-default for the return rate of the asset is smaller than 1 and for the volatility is larger than 1. Moreover, these ratios increase or decrease linearly with the default time, respectively: the after-default rate of return drops to zero, when the default time occurs near the initial date, and converges to the before-default rate of return, when the default time occurs near the finite investment horizon. For the volatility, this ratio converges to the double (respectively, initial) value of the before-default volatility, when the default time goes to the initial (respectively, terminal horizon) time. Moreover, in order to satisfy the hypothesis in the simulation of section 3.3.4, we assume that the default barrier L has no atoms (to ensure the density hypothesis) and that L is independent of the filtration $\mathbb{F}$ (so that the default density is a deterministic function). In this case, $p_T(L) = 1$. For the default event, we consider a simple case where the process $(\lambda_t, t \geq 0)$ is a constant $\lambda > 0$ and the default threshold L follows the uni-exponential law. Hence, $\mathbb{P}(\tau > t) = e^{-\lambda t}$ and the default density is a deterministic function $\alpha(\theta) = \lambda e^{-\lambda \theta}$ for all $\theta \geq 0$.

Consider the power utility function $U(x) = x^p/p$, $0 < p < 1$, the after-default value function is given from [3.93] by

$$V_{\tau_\ell}^{\ell,\mathrm{a}}(\cdot) = K_{\tau_\ell} U(\cdot)$$

where

$$K_{\tau_\ell} = \mathbb{E}^{\mathbb{P}}\left[Z_T(\tau_\ell)^{p/p-1}\right]^{1-p} = \exp\left(\frac{p}{2(1-p)}\left(\frac{\mu(\tau_\ell)}{\sigma(\tau_\ell)}\right)^2(\tau_\ell \vee T - \tau_\ell)\right)$$

Furthermore, the solution of the before-default optimization problem [3.85] is given by

$$V_0^\ell(X_0) = Y_0 U(X_0)$$

where Y is the solution of the backward stochastic differential equation [3.102] while letting $Z = 0$, namely,

$$Y_t = \mathbb{1}_{\{\tau_\ell > T\}} + \mathbb{1}_{\{t < \tau_\ell \leq T\}} K_{\tau_\ell} \frac{(1 - b\gamma \mathbb{1}_{\{\gamma<0\}})^p}{p} + \int_t^{\tau_\ell \wedge T} f(\theta, Y_\theta)d\theta \quad [3.108]$$

where

$$f(t, y) = py \operatorname*{ess\,sup}_{\nu \in \mathcal{A}_\ell^0, \, \nu_{\tau_\ell} = b\mathbb{1}_{\{\gamma<0\}}} \left(\mu^{\mathbb{F}}\nu_t - \frac{1-p}{2}(\nu_t \sigma^{\mathbb{F}})^2\right).$$

We notice that in the case where the default time τ_ℓ occurs after the maturity T, the optimal strategy coincides with the classical Merton strategy with constraint $\pi \in [0, \frac{1}{\gamma}\mathbb{1}_{\{\gamma>0\}} + b\mathbb{1}_{\{\gamma<0\}}[$ (Merton strategy does not take into account the eventuality of the default). In the case where τ_ℓ occurs before T, the process Y is stopped at τ_ℓ, with the terminal value depending on the quantity K_{τ_ℓ}, and the strategy at τ_ℓ is equal to the trading constraint. We use an iterative Howard algorithm [HOW 60] to solve equation [3.108]. The following results are based on the model parameters described below: $\mu^{\mathbb{F}} = 0.03$, $\sigma^{\mathbb{F}} = 0.2$, $T = 1$, the risk aversion parameter $p = 0.7$ and the buying constraint $b = 1$. In addition, we fix the default intensity $\lambda = 0.3$. This corresponds to a relatively high default risk.

Figure 3.5 compares, for the insider, standard and Merton investors, the optimal value function and the wealth process for one given trajectory in the case of positive values for γ (that is a loss of the risky asset at the default time). The loss given default is $\gamma = 0.3$. At the default time which occurs before the maturity, the value function and the wealth process suffer a brutal loss for all the three strategies. For the value function, the insider outperforms the other two investors before and after the default occurs. Before the default, the value function for the standard investor is smaller than the Merton one because the latter does not consider the potential default risk at all. However, when the default occurs, the investor outperforms the Merton strategy since the default risk is taken into account from the beginning. For the wealth process, we observe that the insider's wealth coincides with that of the Merton investor for a long time before the default occurs. However, due to her information on the default event, she can adjust the strategy just before the default in order not to be impacted by the loss of the risky asset. On the contrary, both the standard and Merton investors' wealth suffer a loss at the default time, the loss of the standard investor being less than for the Merton investor. Therefore, the insider obtains the largest wealth after default.

Figures 3.6 and 3.7 consider the case of negative γ (that is a gain of the risk asset at the default time) with the other parameters being unchanged. We observe a similar phenomenon for the optimal value function with a loss at the default time for all investors. However, for all the three types of investors, the wealth process has a gain since the jump of the risky asset is positive. Besides, the profit of the insider is more important as the jump size $|\gamma|$ is larger.

Finally, we discuss by numerical tests the possibility to relax the short-selling constraint, that is instead of prohibiting completely the short-selling strategy, we suppose that the investors can effectuate short-selling trading under a given constraint δ_s. The results for different values of δ_s are illustrated in Figure 3.8: not surprisingly, for the case of a loss at default, the optimal value function of both the insider and the standard investor is an increasing function of δ_s. Moreover, the gain is more significant for the insider.

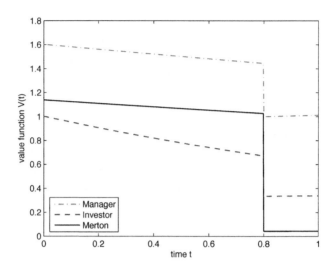

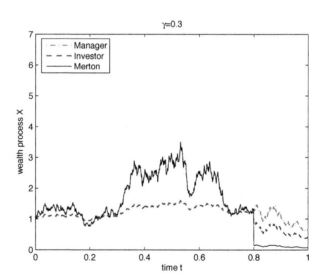

Figure 3.5. *Value function and wealth process for insider, investor and Merton:* $\gamma = 0.3$.

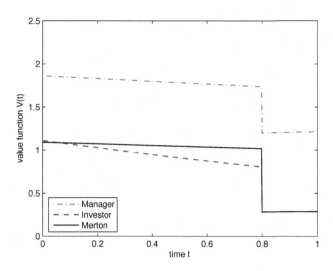

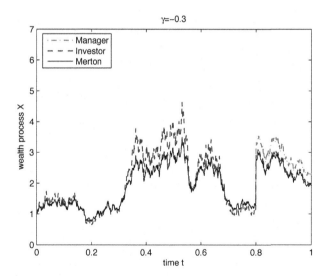

Figure 3.6. *Value function and wealth process for insider, investor and Merton:* $\gamma = -0.3$

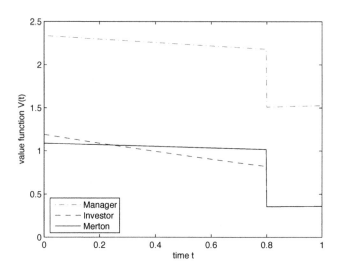

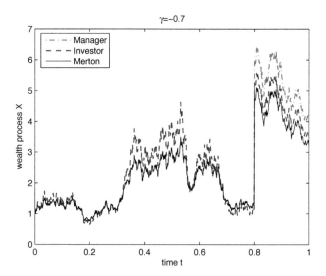

Figure 3.7. *Value function and wealth process for insider, investor and Merton:* $\gamma = -0.7$

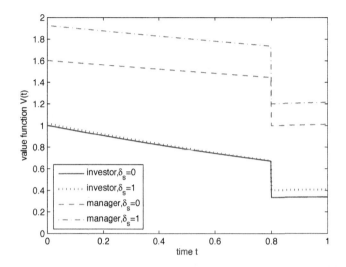

Figure 3.8. *The impact of the short-selling*
constraint $\lambda = 0.3$ *and* $\gamma = 0.3$

4

Portfolio Optimization with Information Asymmetry

This chapter focuses on the characterization and simulation of the optimal strategy of investors that possess some side-information about the market structure, with the purpose of comparing it with non-insider's optimal strategy. The investors strive to maximize their expected discounted utility of terminal wealth on $[0, T]$, where $T > 0$ is a fixed finite time horizon. The investors observe the same stock prices, but their total information may differ due to some extra information that has been obtained in some other way. This is naturally related to the enlargement of filtration problem. As seen in Chapter 2, mathematically, the problem is determining the semimartingale decomposition of the Wiener and the Poisson processes in the filtration enlarged with the additional information of the insider, leading to the computation of the so-called information drift. Thus, we can express the dynamics of the prices for this insider and compute her optimal investment strategy.

Private information that is too informative may lead to arbitrage opportunity for the insider: for example, if she knows the exact asset price at the end of a time interval, then she will make an infinite amount of money at the end of this time interval. More generally, the optimal utility of the insider will be infinite if the information drift degenerates at the terminal time T. This is the case in the pioneering paper of Karatzas-Pikovsky [PIK 96], who studied optimal strategies in some examples of real or vectorial random variables (such as the value at time T of the Wiener process). [PIK 96] showed that those optimal insider strategies blow up at time T and the optimal utility of the insider becomes infinite. Grorud and Pontier [GRO 98] also provide arbitrage strategies in other examples of private-information, such as the knowledge of the ratio at time T of two asset prices. The idea of Corcuera *et al.* [COR 04] of adding a vanishing independent noise to the private information (see section 2.2.3) is useful in any situation where the information drift degenerates at some points: more precisely, Corcuera *et al.* [COR 04] proved that if the rate at which the insider improves her views on future events is slow enough, then the optimal utility is finite.

In this chapter, we consider private information that does not imply arbitrage strategies for the insider. Thus, we assume a density hypothesis (also called Jacod equivalence condition) for the additional information, because as shown by Grorud-Pontier [GRO 98] or Amendinger [AME 98], it implies the existence of equivalent martingale measure and thus No Free Lunch with Vanishing Risk.

The mathematical framework is the following: let $(\Omega, \mathbb{F}, \mathbb{P})$ be a filtered probability space with a multidimensional Brownian motion W and a multidimensional Poisson process N. We consider a market model with one bond and discontinuous risky assets. All investors are price takers, that is none of them can change the value of the assets by using her trading strategies. For the case of large insiders who influence the dynamics of the stock, we refer for instance to the works of Grorud and Pontier [GRO 06], Kohatsu-Higa *et al.* [KOH 06, KOH 08].

We consider two types of side information: a "full strong" information and a "noisy strong" information.

The first type of side-information, called "full strong" information, consists of the knowledge, from the beginning, of extra information about the outcome of some variable L of the prices. The cornerstone of this modelization is the theory of initial enlargement of filtration covered in section 2.2. This problem has been considered first by Karatzas-Pikovsky [PIK 96], with many generalizations in the case of a purely diffusive market model, such as -among others- Grorud and Pontier [GRO 98], Amendinger *et al.* [AME 98, AME 03] and Imkeller [IMK 02, IMK 03]. Some papers are devoted to insider trading in the case where the prices are discontinuous semimartingales. For instance, in a mixed diffusive-jump market model, Elliott and Jeanblanc [ELL 99] and Grorud [GRO 00] studied the case where L is the number of jumps over the interval. Gasbarra *et al.* [GAS 06] apply a dynamical Bayesian approach to some problems concerning initial enlargement of filtrations theory, in a context of a Lévy market. They propose a Bayesian interpretation of utility gain related to asymmetric information.

Kohatsu and Yamazoto [KOH 08] propose a reformulation of Jacod's theorem to deal with perturbed random times in the framework of jump processes. In those papers, it appears that the presence of jumps in the dynamics of price processes tends to mitigate the value of the private information.

The second type of side-information is the "noisy strong" information: the insider's information is perturbed by an independent noise changing throughout time. This case deals with the theory of a noisy enlargement of filtration, recalled in section 2.2.3, and in the sense of Corcuera et al. [COR 04]. Using Malliavin's calculus, they obtained in [COR 04] the formula of the compensator in some examples of information, such as a function of the terminal value of the Brownian motion, disturbed by an independent noise.

We study the agent's problem of maximizing the expectation of the logarithm of her terminal wealth. In some examples of side-information, we compute the explicit formula of the insiders' strategy (optimal wealth and portfolio) in our mixed diffusive-jump market model. We simulate them and compare them to each other and to the non-insider's optimal strategy.

We more especially consider two examples of full strong information that can occur in a case of a merger between two companies: the insider knows that an asset price will be or not at future fixed date T in a given margin, or she knows the ratio at time T of two asset prices. We compute the difference of strategies between a non-insider and an insider in both cases : a purely diffusive market model or a mixed diffusive-jump market model. We simulate the above strategies in a diffusive-jump market model with four risky assets and we specify qualitatively the optimal investments.

4.1. The market

We consider a mixed jump-diffusive model, with $\mathbb{F}$ the filtration generated by an m-dimensional Brownian motion W and an m'-dimensional Poisson process N, as described in section 1.5. Let $d = m + m'$. The agents on the financial market can invest in d risky assets, the prices of which are driven by the following stochastic differential equations :

$$dS_t^i = S_{t-}^i [\mu_t^i dt + \sigma_t^i . d(W_t, N_t)] \qquad i = 1, \cdots, d. \qquad [4.1]$$

(for simplicity, we assume that the prices are discounted and the non-risky asset S^0 is the constant and equal to 1). The volatility σ is a given strongly non-degenerate deterministic $d \times d$-matrix-valued process, σ^i denotes its ith line. The drift process μ is assumed to be deterministic and bounded on $[0, T]$. We assume that $\sigma^{ij} > -1$ for all $m + 1 \leq j \leq d$ and $1 \leq i \leq d$. Thus, $\mathbb{F}$ and the filtration generated by the prices are identical.

If the agent has private information, she receives an individual flow of side-information, represented by the filtration $\mathbb{H} := (\mathcal{H}_t)_{t \in [0,T]}$. Thus, we introduce the individual agent's filtration $\mathbb{G} := (\mathcal{G}_t)_{t \in [0,T]}$ of available information, with

$$\mathcal{G}_t := \mathcal{F}_t \vee \mathcal{H}_t, \qquad 0 \leq t \leq T.$$

In other words, this agent possesses all information about the market up to the present time t, plus her own side-information that she does not reveal to the other agents (except indirectly, by her market strategies).

DEFINITION 4.1.– *A $\mathbb{G}$-admissible strategy is a portfolio ϕ such that for all $i = 1, \cdots, d$, ϕ^i is $\mathbb{G}$-predictable and satisfies the integrability requirement $\int_0^T |\mu_t.(\phi_t * S_t)| + \|\sigma_t(\phi_t * S_t)\|^2 dt < \infty$ $\mathbb{P}$-almost surely and so that the corresponding wealth process X is bounded from below and satisfies $X_T \geq 0$ $\mathbb{P}$-almost surely.*

The amount ϕ_t^i represents the quantity at time t of the ith stock $(i = 1, \cdots, d)$ invested by the agent. The agent has an initial wealth $X_0 \in L^1(\mathcal{G}_0)$. She chooses her strategy so as to optimize her terminal wealth. As usually, we assume that the strategy is self-financing, so the agent's discounted wealth is given by

$$X_t^\phi = X_0 + \int_0^t \phi_s * S_s \mu_s ds + \int_0^t \phi_{s^-} * S_{s^-}.\sigma_s d(W, N)_s. \qquad [4.2]$$

But on the enlarged filtered probability space $(\mathbb{G}, \mathbb{P})$, the process (W, N) could no more be a semimartingale. Chapter 2 gives sufficient conditions to obtain a meaningful wealth equation for an insider: the wealth equation (4.2) is meaningful under hypotheses 2.1 or hypotheses 2.2.

Let us recall some notations:

– $I_n = (1, \cdots, 1)' \in \mathbb{R}^n$;

– if v_1 and v_2 are two vectors of same dimension d, we note $v_1 * v_2$ the vector with components $(v_1 * v_2)_i = v_{1,i}.v_{2,i}$, $i = 1, \cdots, d$.

– $\mathcal{E}$ denotes the Doléans-Dade exponential.

We define the m-dimensional process Θ and the m'-dimensional process q such that

$$(\Theta_t, -q_t) = \sigma_t^{-1}\mu_t. \tag{4.3}$$

We assume that

HYPOTHESES 4.1.– q is a process with positive components

Otherwise, arbitrage opportunities can occur (see [JEA 90]).

$$\widehat{W}_t := W_t + \int_0^t \Theta_s ds, \quad \widehat{M}_t := N_t - \int_0^t q_s ds, \quad t \in [0, T]. \tag{4.4}$$

$$X_t^\phi = X_0 + \int_0^t \phi_{s-} * S_{s-}\sigma_s d(\widehat{W}, \widehat{M})_s. \tag{4.5}$$

$$\widehat{\mathbb{P}^0} := Y^0 \mathbb{P} \quad \text{where} \quad Y^0 = \mathcal{E}\left(\int_0^\cdot \left(-\Theta_s.dW_s + \left(\frac{q_s}{\lambda_s} - I_n \right).dM_s \right) \right) \tag{4.6}$$

is the "risk neutral probability measure" for a non-insider, as soon as this local martingale Y^0 is a martingale.

4.1.1. *Risk neutral probabilities measures for insider*

We recall that under hypotheses 2.1 or hypotheses 2.2, $\widetilde{W}. = W - \int_0^\cdot \rho_s^1 ds$ is a $(\mathbb{G}, \mathbb{P})$-Brownian motion and $\widetilde{M}. = N - \int_0^\cdot \rho_s^2 ds$ is the compensated process of a $(\mathbb{G}, \mathbb{P})$-Poisson process with intensity ρ^2 (see definition 2.3 and theorem 2.1, respectively).

DEFINITION 4.2.–

$$Y_. := \mathcal{E}\left(\int_0^\cdot \left(-(\Theta + \rho_s^1).d\widetilde{W}_s + \left(\frac{q}{\rho_s^2} - I_n \right).d\widetilde{M}_s \right) \right).$$

Y is a positive $(\mathbb{G}, \mathbb{P})$-local martingale. A straightforward calculus yields:

$$d(Y_t^{-1}) = Y_{t-}^{-1} l_t d(\widehat{W}, \widehat{M})_t \quad \text{with} \quad l := \left((\Theta + \rho^1), (\tfrac{\rho^2}{q} - I_n) \right).$$

$C_t := \int_0^t \left(-(\Theta_s + \rho_s^1).d\widetilde{W}_s + \left(\tfrac{q_s}{\rho_s^2} - I_n \right).d\widetilde{M}_s \right).$ $\Delta C > -1$ so Y is a positive $(\mathbb{G}, \mathbb{P})$-local martingale. For instance, according to Lépingle and Mémin, theorem 3.1 p. 185 [LÉP 78], Y is a $(\mathbb{G}, \mathbb{P})$-martingale if

$$E_{\mathbb{P}} \left[\exp \left(\frac{1}{2} \langle C^c, C^c \rangle_T + \sum_{s \leq T} (1 + \Delta C_s) \log(1 + \Delta C_s) - \Delta C_s \right) \right] < +\infty.$$

THEOREM 4.1.– We assume 2.1 or 2.2 and that Y defined in definition 4.2 is a $(\mathbb{G}, \mathbb{P})$-martingale. Then, $\widehat{\mathbb{P}} := Y\mathbb{P}$ is a "risk neutral probability measure" for the insider.

$\widehat{W}$ and $\widehat{M}$ (definition 4.4) are, respectively, a $(\mathbb{G}, \widehat{\mathbb{P}})$-Brownian motion and the compensated process of a $(\mathbb{G}, \widehat{\mathbb{P}})$-Poisson process with intensity q.

Furthermore, under hypotheses 2.1, the market is complete for the insider possessing full information: if $\widehat{A}$ is a $(\mathcal{G}_T, \widehat{\mathbb{P}})$-local martingale, there exists $\psi \in L^1_{loc}((\widehat{W}, \widehat{M}), \mathbb{G}, \widehat{\mathbb{P}})$ such that $\widehat{A}_t = \widehat{A}_0 + \int_0^t \psi_s.d(\widehat{W}, \widehat{M})_s$ for all $(t, \omega) \in [0, T] \times \Omega$.

PROOF.– By Girsanov's theorem, $\widehat{W}. := W. + \int_0^\cdot \Theta_s ds = \widetilde{W}. + \int_0^\cdot (\Theta_s + \rho_s^1) ds$ is a $(\mathbb{G}, \widehat{\mathbb{P}})$-Brownian motion and $\widehat{M}. := N. - \int_0^\cdot q_s ds = \widetilde{M}. + \int_0^\cdot (\rho_s^2 - q_s) ds$ is the compensated process of a $(\mathbb{G}, \widehat{\mathbb{P}})$-Poisson process with intensity q. It follows that under the probability $\widehat{\mathbb{P}}$, the (discounted) price processes S^i, $i = 1, \cdots, d$, are $\mathbb{G}$-local martingales, i.e. $\widehat{\mathbb{P}}$ is the so-called "risk neutral probability measure" for the agent.

$$dS_t^i = S_{t-}^i \sigma_t^i d(\widehat{W}, \widehat{M})_t$$

The martingale representation theorem under hypotheses 2.1 follows from theorem 8 of Grorud [GRO 00]. □

4.1.2. *Solution of the optimization problem*

Let $T < T'$. An insider wants to maximize the logarithmic utility of her terminal wealth, given its initial value. That is, she maximizes the mapping

$$(\phi, X) \to V(\phi, X) := \mathbb{E}^{\mathbb{P}}\left[\log(X_A^\phi)) \mid \mathcal{G}_0\right]$$

over all $\mathbb{G}$-admissible strategies. We assume that the initial wealth is positive ($X_0 > 0$ $\mathbb{P}$-almost surely). Then, for the two types of insiders, the optimal wealth and portfolio are given by

$$\forall t \in [0, T], \quad \begin{cases} X_t^* = X_0 \frac{1}{Y_t} \\ \phi_t^* = (\sigma_t)^{-1} \frac{Y_t}{Y_{t-}} \frac{X_t^*}{S_t} l_t \end{cases} \tag{4.7}$$

with the corresponding processes $\frac{1}{Y}$ and l. The optimal proportional investment strategy is then given by

$$\forall t \in [0, T], \quad \pi_t^* = (\sigma_t)^{-1} \frac{Y_t}{Y_{t-}} l_t.$$

We remark here that the optimal wealth is proportional to the process $\frac{1}{Y}$. Moreover, this process "summarizes" the information available for the agent. Therefore, the key of the following computations will be the computation of the process Y.

4.2. Optimal strategies in some examples of side-information

For two examples of full strong side information that can occur in a case of a merger between two companies, we compute the optimal strategy (wealth and part of the wealth invested in each asset) and we compare it to the optimal strategy of a non-insider.

4.2.1. *Initial strong insider*

We recall that Y^0 (see equation [4.6]) denotes the state process of a non-insider. Thus, the state process of an insider can be written as

$$Y = \frac{Y^0}{p.(L)}. \tag{4.8}$$

Indeed,

$$dp_t(L) = p_{t-}(L))[\rho_t^1 dW_t + (\frac{\rho_t^2}{\lambda_t} - I_{m'})dM_t]$$

therefore,

$$\frac{1}{p.(L)} = \mathcal{E}\left(\int_0^. \left(-\rho_s^1 d\widetilde{W}_s + (\frac{\lambda_s}{\rho_s^2} - I_{m'})d\widetilde{M}_s \right) \right).$$

Furthermore,

$$Y^0 = \mathcal{E}\left(\int_0^. \left(-\Theta_s dW_s + (\frac{q_s}{\lambda_s} - I_{m'})dM_s \right) \right).$$

Since $\mathcal{E}(X)\mathcal{E}(Y) = \mathcal{E}(X + Y - [X, Y])$ and with the definition 4.2 of Y, we obtain

$$\frac{Y^0}{p.(L)} = \mathcal{E}\left(\int_0^. \left(-(\Theta_s + \rho_s^1)d\widetilde{W}_s + (\frac{q}{\rho_s^2} - I_{m'})d\widetilde{M}_s \right) \right) = Y.$$

The following two examples 4.2.2 and 4.2.3 are initial full information. We imagine a case of a merger between two companies. The acquirer can buy the target in cash or shares at the time T' (with $T' > T$ to exclude arbitrage opportunities). If she does it in cash, the acquirer bids for a given price P_{bid} for each share of the target, at the maturity T'. Therefore, an insider will know that the spot of the target at time T' will be in a range around P_{bid}: this situation corresponds to the information in 4.2.2. If the acquisition is done with shares, the acquirer will exchange N_t shares of the target for N_a shares of the acquirer. Therefore, an insider will know that at the acquisition time T', the ratio of the asset prices of the target and the acquirer will be equal to $\frac{N_t}{N_a}$: this situation corresponds to the information in 4.2.3.

We denote σ^{iW} (respectively, σ^{iN}) the m first (respectively, the m' last) components of σ^i the ith line of σ : $\sigma^i = (\sigma^{iW}, \sigma^{iN})$. For the sake of simplicity, we assume λ is constant.

4.2.2. There exist i, $1 \leq i \leq d$, **such that** $L = \mathbf{1}_{[a,b]}(S^i_{T'})$, $0 < a < b$

The insider knows whether or not the terminal price of the ith asset will be between a and b. We introduce $\Sigma_t := \int_t^{T'} ||\sigma_s^{iW}||^2 ds$,

$$
k_x(t) := \log x - \log(S^i_0) - \int_0^{T'} (\mu_s^i - \frac{1}{2}||\sigma_s^{iW}||^2)ds
$$
$$
- \left(\int_0^t \sigma_s^{iW} dW_s + \log(1 + \sigma_s^{iN})dN_s \right), \qquad [4.9]
$$

$$
(F_{t,T',k_j})^{m'} := \left\{ (t_{jl_j})_{\substack{1 \leq j \leq m' \\ 1 \leq l_j \leq k_j}} \in \mathbb{R}^{k_1 + \cdots + k_{m'}} | \forall\ 1 \leq j \leq m', \right.
$$
$$
\left. t \leq t_{jl_1} \leq \cdots \leq t_{jl_{k_j}} \leq T' \right\} \qquad [4.10]
$$

and for $(t_{jl_j})_{\substack{1 \leq j \leq m' \\ 1 \leq l_j \leq k_j}} \in (F_{t,T',k_j})^n$,

$$
f_{(t_{jl_j})}(x) := \exp\left(\frac{-(x - \sum_{j=1}^{m'} \sum_{l_j=1}^{k_j} \log(1 + \sigma_{(t_{jl_j})}^{ij}))^2}{2\Sigma_t} \right). \qquad [4.11]
$$

$$
\xi_{m',k_j,l_j}(x) := x + \sum_{j=1}^{m'} \sum_{l_j=1}^{k_j} \log(1 + \sigma_{(t_{jl_j})}^{ij}).
$$

Let us introduce the scalar a_t for $t \in [0, T]$

$$
a_t :=
$$
$$
\frac{\prod_{j=1}^{m'} \sum_{k_j \geq 0} \frac{e^{-\lambda_j(T'-t)}}{\sqrt{2\pi\Sigma_t}} \lambda_j^{k_j} \int_{(F_{t,T',k_j})^{m'}} \left(f_{(t_{jl_j})}(k_a(t)) - f_{(t_{jl_j})}(k_b(t)) \right) \prod_{l_j=1}^{k_j} dt_{jl_j}\ \mathbf{1}_{(L=1)}}{\int_{\mathbb{R}} \prod_{j=1}^{m'} \sum_{k_j \geq 0} \frac{e^{-\lambda_j(T'-t)-\frac{x^2}{2\Sigma_t}}}{\sqrt{2\pi\Sigma_t}} \lambda_j^{k_j} \int_{(F_{t,T',k_j})^{m'}} \mathbf{1}_{[k_a(t),k_b(t)]} \xi_{m',k_j,l_j}(x) dx \prod_{l_j=1}^{k_j} dt_{jl_j}}
$$
$$
+ \frac{\prod_{j=1}^{m'} \sum_{k_j \geq 0} \frac{e^{-\lambda_j(T'-t)}}{\sqrt{2\pi\Sigma_t}} \lambda_j^{k_j} \int_{(F_{t,T',k_j})^{m'}} \left(f_{(t_{jl_j})}(k_b(t)) - f_{(t_{jl_j})}(k_a(t)) \right) \prod_{l_j=1}^{k_j} dt_{jl_j}\ \mathbf{1}_{(L=0)}}{\int_{\mathbb{R}} \prod_{j=1}^{m'} \sum_{k_j \geq 0} \frac{e^{-\lambda_j(T'-t)-\frac{x^2}{2\Sigma_t}}}{\sqrt{2\pi\Sigma_t}} \lambda_j^{k_j} \int_{(F_{t,T',k_j})^{m'}} \mathbf{1}_{[k_a(t),k_b(t)]^C} \xi_{m',k_j,l_j}(x) dx \prod_{l_j=1}^{k_j} dt_{jl_j}}
$$

PROPOSITION 4.1.– If the insider knows $L = \mathbf{1}_{[a,b]}(S^i_{T'})$ for some i ($0 < a < b$ and $1 \leq i \leq d$), then $p_t(L) = p_t(1)\mathbf{1}_{(L=1)} + p_t(0)\mathbf{1}_{(L=0)}$ with

$p_t(1)$

$$= \frac{\int_\mathbb{R} \prod_{j=1}^{m'} \sum_{k_j \geq 0} \frac{e^{-\lambda_j(T'-t)-\frac{x^2}{2\Sigma_t}}}{\sqrt{2\pi\Sigma_t}} \lambda_j^{k_j} \int_{(F_{t,T',k_j})^{m'}} \mathbf{1}_{[k_a(t),k_b(t)]}\xi_{m',k_j,l_j}(x)dx \prod_{l_j=1}^{k_j} dt_{jl_j}}{\int_\mathbb{R} \prod_{j=1}^{m'} \sum_{k_j \geq 0} \frac{e^{-\lambda_j T'-\frac{x^2}{2\Sigma_0}}}{\sqrt{2\pi\Sigma_0}} \lambda_j^{k_j} \int_{(F_{0,T',k_j})^{m'}} \mathbf{1}_{[k_a(0),k_b(0)]}\xi_{m',k_j,l_j}(x)dx \prod_{l_j=1}^{k_j} dt_{jl_j}}$$

$p_t(0)$

$$= \frac{\int_\mathbb{R} \prod_{j=1}^{m'} \sum_{k_j \geq 0} \frac{e^{-\lambda_j(T'-t)-\frac{x^2}{2\Sigma_t}}}{\sqrt{2\pi\Sigma_t}} \lambda_j^{k_j} \int_{(F_{t,T',k_j})^{m'}} \mathbf{1}_{[k_a(t),k_b(t)]^C}\xi_{m',k_j,l_j}(x)dx \prod_{l_j=1}^{k_j} dt_{jl_j}}{\int_\mathbb{R} \prod_{j=1}^{m'} \sum_{k_j \geq 0} \frac{e^{-\lambda_j T'-\frac{x^2}{2\Sigma_0}}}{\sqrt{2\pi\Sigma_0}} \lambda_j^{k_j} \int_{(F_{0,T,k_j})^{m'}} \mathbf{1}_{[k_a(0),k_b(0)]^C}\xi_{m',k_j,l_j}(x)dx \prod_{l_j=1}^{k_j} dt_{jl_j}}$$

Besides, the drift information is

$$\rho^1_t = a_t\sigma^{iW}_t \quad \text{and} \quad \rho^2_t = \lambda_t + a_t\lambda_t * \log(1 + \sigma^{iN}_t).$$

REMARK 4.1.– For a purely diffusive market model, the formulas are more simple:

$$p_t(1) = \frac{F(t,k_b(t)) - F(t,k_a(t))}{F(0,k_b(0)) - F(0,k_a(0))},$$

$$p_t(0) = \frac{1 - F(t,k_b(t)) + F(t,k_a(t))}{1 - F(0,k_b(0)) + F(0,k_a(0))},$$

$$a_t = \frac{\frac{\partial F}{\partial x}(t,k_b(t)) - \frac{\partial F}{\partial x}(t,k_a(t))}{1 - F(t,k_b(t)) + F(t,k_a(t))}\mathbf{1}_{(L=0)}$$

$$- \frac{\frac{\partial F}{\partial x}(t,k_b(t)) - \frac{\partial F}{\partial x}(t,k_a(t))}{F(t,k_b(t)) - F(t,k_a(t))}\mathbf{1}_{(L=1)}$$

where $F(t,\cdot)$ is the cumulative distribution function of a Gaussian $\mathcal{N}(0,\Sigma_t)$ with mean 0 and variance $\Sigma_t = \int_t^{T'}||\sigma^i_s||^2 ds$.   □

PROOF.– The insider knows whether or not the terminal price of the ith asset will be between a and b : $L = \mathbf{1}_{[a,b]}(S^i_{T'})$.

$$\log(S^i_{T'}) = \log(S^i_0) + \int_0^{T'} (\mu^i_s - \frac{1}{2}||\sigma^{iW}_s||^2)ds + \int_0^{T'} \sigma^{iW}_s dW_s$$

$$+ \int_0^{T'} \log(1 + \sigma^{iN}_s)dN_s.$$

$$\mathbb{P}\left[L = 1 | \mathcal{F}_t\right] = \mathbb{P}\left[\log a \leq \log(S^i_{T'}) \leq \log b | \mathcal{F}_t\right]$$

$$= \mathbb{P}\left[k_a(t) \leq \int_t^{T'} \sigma^{iW}_s dW_s + \log(1 + \sigma^{iN}_s)dN_s \leq k_b(t)\right]$$

because $\int_t^{T'} \sigma^{iW}_s dW_s + \log(1 + \sigma^{iN}_s)dN_s$ is independent of $\mathcal{F}_t$ and $\forall x \in \mathbb{R}$, k_x (defined in [5.9]) is $\mathcal{F}_t$-measurable. We first investigate the law of $\int_t^{T'} \sigma^{iW}_s dW_s + \log(1 + \sigma^{iN}_s)dN_s$. Since N^j is a Poisson process with intensity λ_j, if τ^j_i is the ith time of jump of N^j, the random variables $(\tau^j_{i+1} - \tau^j_i)_{i \geq 1}$ are independent; their law is exponential with parameter λ_j. Thus, the law of $(\tau^j_1, \cdots, \tau^j_k)$ has for density $\mathbf{1}_{0 \leq t_1 \leq \cdots \leq t_k} \lambda^k_j e^{-\lambda_j t_k} dt_1 \cdots dt_k$ with respect to the Lebesgue measure on $\mathbb{R}^k$. Therefore, let f be a bounded real measurable function and we introduce the sets

$$D_{t,T',k} = \left\{(t_1, \cdots, t_{p+k}) \in \mathbb{R}^{p+k} | 0 \leq t_1 \leq \cdots \leq t_{p-1} \leq t \leq t_p\right.$$

$$\left. \leq \cdots \leq t_{p+k-1} \leq T' \leq t_{p+k}\right\},$$

$$F_{t,T',k} = \left\{(t_1, \cdots, t_k) \in \mathbb{R}^k | 0 \leq t \leq t_1 \leq \cdots \leq t_k \leq T'\right\}.$$

$$\mathbb{E}^{\mathbb{P}}\left(f(\int_t^{T'} \log(1 + \sigma^{ij}_s)dN_j(s))\right)$$

$$= \sum_{k \geq 0}\sum_{p \geq 1} \lambda^{p+k}_j \int_{D_{t,T',k}} f(\sum_{l=0}^{k-1} \log(1 + \sigma^{ij}_{(t_{p+l})}))e^{-\lambda_j t_{p+k}} dt_1 \cdots dt_{p+k}$$

$$= \sum_{k \geq 0} \lambda^k_j \sum_{p \geq 1} \lambda^p_j \left(\int_{0 \leq t_1 \leq \cdots \leq t_{p-1} \leq t} dt_1 \cdots dt_{p-1}\right)$$

$$\cdot \left(\int_{T' \leq t_{p+k}} e^{-\lambda_j t_{p+k}} dt_{p+k} \right)$$

$$\cdot \left(\int_{t \leq t_p \leq \cdots \leq t_{p+k-1} \leq T'} f(\sum_{l=0}^{k-1} \log(1 + \sigma^{ij}_{(t_{p+l})})) dt_p \cdots dt_{p+k-1} \right)$$

$$= \sum_{k \geq 0} e^{-\lambda_j(T'-t)} \lambda_j^k \int_{F_{t,T',k}} f(\sum_{l=1}^{k} \log(1 + \sigma^{ij}_{(t_l)})) \, dt_1 \cdots dt_k$$

We use the convention that $\int_{F_{t,T',k}} f(x + \sum_{l=1}^{k} \log(1 + \sigma^{ij}_{(t_l)})) \, dt_1 \cdots dt_k = f(x)$ if $k = 0$. The last equality follows from a change of index in the last bracket and from the fact that

$$\sum_{p \geq 1} \lambda_j^p \left(\int_{0 \leq t_1 \leq \cdots \leq t_{p-1} \leq t} dt_1 \cdots dt_{p-1} \right) \left(\int_{T' \leq t_{p+k}} e^{-\lambda_j t_{p+k}} dt_{p+k} \right)$$

$$= \sum_{p \geq 1} \frac{(\lambda_j t)^{p-1}}{(p-1)!} e^{-\lambda_j T'} = e^{-\lambda_j(T'-t)}.$$

Since the Poisson processes $N^1, \cdots, N^{m'}$ are mutually independent,

$$\mathbb{E}^{\mathbb{P}} \left(f(\int_t^{T'} \log(1 + \sigma_s^{iN}) dN_s) \right)$$

$$= \prod_{j=1}^{m'} \sum_{k_j \geq 0} e^{-\lambda_j(T'-t)} \lambda_j^{k_j} \int_{(F_{t,T',k_j})^{m'}} f\left(\sum_{j=1}^{m'} \sum_{l_j=1}^{k_j} \log(1 + \sigma^{ij}_{(t_{jl_j})}) \right) \prod_{l_j=1}^{k_j} dt_{jl_j}$$

with $(F_{t,T',k_j})^{m'}$ defined in (4.10). $\int_t^{T'} \sigma_s^{iW} dW_s$ is independent of $(N^1, \cdots, N^{m'})$, its law is a Gaussian law with mean 0 and variance $\Sigma_t = \int_t^{T'} ||\sigma_s^{iW}||^2 ds$, thus

$$\mathbb{E}^{\mathbb{P}} \left(f(\int_t^{T'} \sigma_s^{iW} dW_s + \log(1 + \sigma_s^{iN}) dN_s) \right)$$

$$= \int_{\mathbb{R}} \prod_{j=1}^{m'} \sum_{k_j \geq 0} e^{-\lambda_j(T'-t)} \lambda_j^{k_j}$$

$$\int_{(F_{t,T',k_j})^{m'}} f(\xi_{m',k_j,l_j}(x)) \frac{\exp(\frac{-x^2}{2\Sigma_t})}{\sqrt{2\pi\Sigma_t}} dx \prod_{l_j=1}^{k_j} .dt_{jl_j}$$

Therefore

$$\mathbb{P}\left[\mathbf{1}_{[a,b]}(S_{T'}^i) = 1 | \mathcal{F}_t\right]$$

$$= \int_{\mathbb{R}} \prod_{j=1}^{m'} \sum_{k_j \geq 0} e^{-\lambda_j(T'-t)} \lambda_j^{k_j}$$

$$\int_{(F_{t,T',k_j})^{m'}} \mathbf{1}_{[k_a(t),k_b(t)]} \xi_{m',k_j,l_j}(x) \frac{\exp(\frac{-x^2}{2\Sigma_t})}{\sqrt{2\pi\Sigma_t}} dx \prod_{l_j=1}^{k_j} dt_{jl_j}$$

This yields the formulas of $p_t^*(1)$ and $p_t(0)$ given in Proposition 4.1.

The coefficient of $dp_t(1)$ on dW_t is

$$\frac{\prod_{j=1}^{m'} \sum_{k_j \geq 0} \frac{e^{-\lambda_j(T'-t)}}{\sqrt{2\pi\Sigma_t}} \lambda_j^{k_j} \int_{(F_{t,T',k_j})^{m'}} \left(f_{(t_{jl_j})}(k_a(t)) - f_{(t_{jl_j})}(k_b(t))\right) \prod_{l_j=1}^{k_j} dt_{jl_j} \quad \sigma_t^{iW}}{\int_{\mathbb{R}} \prod_{j=1}^{m'} \sum_{k_j \geq 0} \frac{e^{-\lambda_j T' - \frac{x^2}{2\Sigma_0}}}{\sqrt{2\pi\Sigma_0}} \lambda_j^{k_j} \int_{(F_{0,T',k_j})^{m'}} \mathbf{1}_{[k_a(0),k_b(0)]} \xi_{m',k_j,l_j}(x) dx \prod_{l_j=1}^{k_j} dt_{jl_j}}$$

with $f_{(t_{jl_j})}$ defined in (4.11). The coefficient of $dp_t(0)$ on dW_t is

$$\frac{\prod_{j=1}^{m'} \sum_{k_j \geq 0} \frac{e^{-\lambda_j(T'-t)}}{\sqrt{2\pi\Sigma_t}} \lambda_j^{k_j} \int_{(F_{t,T',k_j})^{m'}} \left(f_{(t_{jl_j})}(k_b(t)) - f_{(t_{jl_j})}(k_a(t))\right) \prod_{l_j=1}^{k_j} dt_{jl_j} \quad \sigma_t^{iW}}{\int_{\mathbb{R}} \prod_{j=1}^{m'} \sum_{k_j \geq 0} \frac{e^{-\lambda_j T' - \frac{x^2}{2\Sigma_0}}}{\sqrt{2\pi\Sigma_0}} \lambda_j^{k_j} \int_{(F_{0,T',k_j})^{m'}} \mathbf{1}_{[k_a(0),k_b(0)]^C} \xi_{m',k_j,l_j}(x) dx \prod_{l_j=1}^{k_j} dt_{jl_j}}$$

Thus we obtain the expression of ρ^1 and ρ^2 given in Proposition 4.1, with a_t defined page 149. $\qquad \square$

We will now compare the insider's strategy to the optimal strategy of a non-insider (the index 0 refers to the non- insider).

PROPOSITION 4.2.– If the insider knows $L = 1_{[a,b]}(S_{T'}^i)$ for some i ($0 < a < b$ and $1 \leq i \leq d$), then if t is not a time of jump

$$\pi_t^* - \pi_t^{0,*} = (\sigma')^{-1} \left(\sigma_t^{iW}, \frac{\log(1 + \sigma_t^{iN})}{q} \right)' a_t.$$

In a purely diffusive market model, the part of the wealth invested in the assets j ($1 \leq j \leq d$ and $j \neq i$) is the same for this insider and a non-insider.

PROOF.– Let t be not a time of jump. Thus, equation 4.7 yields $\pi_t^* = (\sigma_t')^{-1} l_t$. Therefore, the difference between the part of the wealth invested in the four assets by an insider and a non-insider is

$$\pi_t^* - \pi_t^{0,*} = (\sigma_t')^{-1}(l_t - l_t^0) = (\sigma_t')^{-1} \left((\rho_t^1)', (\frac{\rho_t^2 - 1_2}{q_t})' \right)'$$

$$= (\sigma_t')^{-1} \left(\sigma_t^{iW}, \frac{\log(1 + \sigma_t^{iN})}{q_t} \right)' a_t$$

where a_t is a scalar. In a purely diffusive market model,

$$\overset{\text{component } i}{\pi_t^* - \pi_t^{0,*} = (\sigma_t')^{-1}(\sigma_t^i)' a_t = (0, \cdots, 0, \overbrace{a_t}, 0, \cdots, 0)^*}$$

because $(\sigma'(t))^{-1}\sigma_1'(t)$ is the ith row of $(\sigma_t')^{-1}\sigma_t' = (\sigma_t\sigma_t)^{-1})'$ which is the identity $d \times d$-matrix. Therefore, in a purely diffusive market model, the part of the wealth invested in the assets j ($1 \leq j \leq d$ and $j \neq i$) is the same for an insider and a non-insider.

But this is not true in a mixed diffusive-jump market model (see Figures 4.3 and 4.4 page 161 for a simulation in a diffusive-jump market model with four risky assets) because

$$\overset{\text{component } i}{(\sigma_t')^{-1} \left(\sigma_t^{iW}, \frac{\log(1 + \sigma_t^{iN})}{q_t} \right)' \neq (0, \cdots, 0, \overbrace{1}, 0, \cdots, 0)'.}$$

From a mathematical point of view, this difference comes from the expression of the logarithm of the prices, because the log function appears in the jump part. From a heuristic point of view, it seems that the insider uses her side information to learn about the jump process and reflect it in all the assets. □

4.2.3. $L = \log(S_{T'}^{i_1}) - \log(S_{T'}^{i_2})$

The insider knows the ratio of assets i_1 and i_2 prices at time T'. We introduce

$$
m_t := \int_0^{T'} \left((\mu_s^{i_1} - \mu_s^{i_2}) - \frac{1}{2}(||\sigma_s^{i_1 W}||^2 - ||\sigma_s^{i_2 W}||^2) \right) ds
$$
$$
+ \int_0^t (\sigma_s^{i_1 W} - \sigma_s^{i_2 W}) dW_s + \int_0^t \log\left(\frac{1 + \sigma_s^{i_1 N}}{1 + \sigma_s^{i_2 N}} \right) dN_s.
$$

Thus, we have

$$
L = m_t + \int_t^{T'} (\sigma_s^{i_1 W} - \sigma_s^{i_2 W}) dW_s + \int_t^{T'} \log\left(\frac{1 + \sigma_s^{i_1 N}}{1 + \sigma_s^{i_2 N}} \right) dN_s).
$$

$(F_{t,T',k_j})^{m'}$ and $f_{(t_{jl_j})}$ are defined in [4.10] and [4.11].

In this section, $\Sigma_t := \int_t^{T'} ||\sigma_s^{i_1 W} - \sigma_s^{i_2 W}||^2 ds$ and

$$
\xi_{m',k_j,l_j} := \sum_{j=1}^{m'} \sum_{l_j=1}^{k_j} \log\left(\frac{1 + \sigma_{(t_{jl_j})}^{i_1 j}}{1 + \sigma_{(t_{jl_j})}^{i_2 j}} \right).
$$

$$
a_t := \frac{\displaystyle\prod_{j=1}^{m'} \sum_{k_j \geq 0} \frac{1}{\Sigma_t} \lambda_j^{k_j} \int_{(F_{t,T',k_j})^{m'}} f_{(t_{jl_j})}(L - m_t)(L - m_t - \xi_{m',k_j,l_j}) \prod_{l_j=1}^{k_j} dt_{jl_j}}{\displaystyle\prod_{j=1}^{m'} \sum_{k_j \geq 0} \lambda_j^{k_j} \int_{(F_{t,T',k_j})^{m'}} f_{(t_{jl_j})}(L - m_t) \prod_{l_j=1}^{k_j} dt_{jl_j}}.
$$

Using similar methods as for 4.2.2, we obtain

PROPOSITION 4.3.– If the insider knows $L = \log(S_{T'}^{i_1}) - \log(S_{T'}^{i_2})$, then

$$
p_t(x) = \frac{\displaystyle\prod_{j=1}^{m'} \sum_{k_j \geq 0} \frac{e^{-\lambda_j(T'-t)}}{\sqrt{2\pi\Sigma_t}} \lambda_j^{k_j} \int_{(F_{t,T',k_j})^{m'}} \exp\left(\frac{-(x - m_t - \xi_{m',k_j,l_j})^2}{2\Sigma_t} \right) \prod_{l_j=1}^{k_j} dt_{jl_j}}{\displaystyle\prod_{j=1}^{m'} \sum_{k_j \geq 0} \frac{e^{-\lambda_j T'}}{\sqrt{2\pi\Sigma_0}} \lambda_j^{k_j} \int_{(F_{0,T',k_j})^{m'}} \exp\left(\frac{-(x - m_0 - \xi_{m',k_j,l_j})^2}{2\Sigma_0} \right) \prod_{l_j=1}^{k_j} dt_{jl_j}}.
$$

Furthermore, the information drift is

$$\rho_t^1 = a_t(\sigma_t^{i_1 W} - \sigma_t^{i_2 W}) \quad \text{and} \quad \rho_t^2 = \lambda_t + a_t \lambda_t * \log\left(\frac{1 + \sigma_t^{i_1 N}}{1 + \sigma_t^{i_2 N}}\right).$$

REMARK 4.2.– For a purely diffusive market model, the formulas are more simple:

$$p_t(L) = \frac{\sqrt{2\pi \Sigma_0}}{\sqrt{2\pi \Sigma_t}} \exp\left(\frac{-(\int_t^{T'} (\sigma_s^{i_1} - \sigma_s^{i_2})dW_s)^2}{2\Sigma_t} + \frac{(\int_0^{T'} (\sigma_s^{i_1} - \sigma_s^{i_2})dW_s)^2}{2\Sigma_0}\right),$$

$$a_t = \frac{\int_t^{T'} (\sigma_s^{i_1} - \sigma_s^{i_2})dW_s}{\Sigma_t} \quad \text{where} \quad \Sigma_t := \int_t^{T'} ||\sigma_s^{i_1} - \sigma_s^{i_2}||^2 ds. \quad \square$$

The following proposition compare this insider's strategy with the optimal strategy of a non-insider.

PROPOSITION 4.4.– If the insider knows $L = \log(S_{T'}^{i_1}) - \log(S_{T'}^{i_2})$, then if t is not a time of jump

$$\pi_t^* - \pi_t^{0,*} = (\sigma_t')^{-1}\left((\sigma_t^{i_1 W} - \sigma_t^{i_2 W}), \frac{1}{q_t}\log\left(\frac{1 + \sigma_t^{i_1 N}}{1 + \sigma_t^{i_2 N}}\right)\right)' a_t.$$

n a purely diffusive market model, the part of the wealth invested in the bond and the assets j ($1 \leq j \leq d$, $j \neq i_1$ and $j \neq i_2$) is the same for this insider and a non-insider.

PROOF.– Let t be not a time of jump. Thus, the difference between the part of the wealth invested in the four assets by an insider and a non-insider is

$$\pi_t^* - \pi_t^{0,*} = (\sigma_t')^{-1}\left((\sigma_t^{i_1 W} - \sigma_t^{i_2 W}), \frac{1}{q_t}\log\left(\frac{1 + \sigma_t^{i_1 N}}{1 + \sigma_t^{i_2 N}}\right)\right)' a_t.$$

where a_t is a scalar. In a purely diffusive market model,

$$(\sigma_t')^{-1}\left(\sigma^{i_1 W} - \sigma^{i_2 W}\right)'(t) = (0, \cdots, 0, \overbrace{1}^{\text{component } i_1},$$

$$0, \cdots, 0, \overbrace{-1}^{\text{component } i_2}, 0, \cdots, 0)'.$$

Since the fraction of the wealth invested in the bond is equal to $1 - \sum_{i=1}^{d} \pi^i$, the part of the wealth invested in the bond and the assets j ($1 \leq j \leq d, j \neq i_1$ and $j \neq i_2$) is the same for an insider and a non-insider. But this is not true in a mixed diffusive-jump market model (see Figures 4.6 and 4.9 for a simulation in a diffusive-jump market model with four risky assets). □

4.3. Numerical illustrations

We simulate the strategy of an insider optimizing her terminal wealth on $[0, T]$ ($T < T'$). Here are the data that we have used for our simulations. $T = 0.95$ and $T' = 1$ and the initial wealth is equal to 1: $X_0 = 1$. Both Brownian motion and Poisson process are two-dimensional: $m = m' = 2$. The intensity of the Poisson process is $\lambda = (3, 2)$. We choose constant market coefficients, but the simulations could be easily extended with time-varying market coefficients. The annual interest rate is 0.02 for all t and the drift $(0.15, 0.1, 0.084, 0.1)$. Thus, the drift vector of the discounted assets is

$$\mu_t = \begin{pmatrix} 0.13 \\ 0.08 \\ 0.064 \\ 0.08 \end{pmatrix} \quad \forall t \in [0, T'].$$

$$\text{The volatility } \sigma_t = \begin{pmatrix} -0.4 & -0.1 & -0.15 & 0.17 \\ -0.09 & -0.4 & -0.03 & 0.035 \\ 0.048 & -0.12 & 0.1 & -0.12 \\ 0.075 & 0.26 & 0.31 & -0.28 \end{pmatrix} \quad \forall t \in [0, T'],$$

Therefore, $q = \lambda * (1.3496, 1.9731) = (4.05, 3.95)$ has positive components. The first two rows of σ are the components of the volatility on the diffusion part (in practice, the standard variation of a purely diffusive asset is in the range [0.1,0.4]). The last two rows of σ are the components of the volatility on the jump part. We choose σ_{3i} and σ_{4i} ($i = 1, \cdots, 4$) in the same range and of opposite sign so that the price of asset i does not increase (or decrease) at each jump time. The prices of the assets at time $t = 0$ are 1.

We simulate the optimal strategy (wealth and part of the wealth invested in each asset) of a non-insider and an insider. In 4.3.1 (respectively, in 4.3.2), the insider has the side-information of example 4.2.2 (respectively of example 4.2.3). Our aim is to qualitatively determine the optimal strategy and to show that the simulated optimal investments are in agreement with what we could have expected.

4.3.1. $L = 1_{[a,b]}(S^1_{T'})$, $0 < a < b$

See section 4.3.3 page 160 for the figures. In our simulation,

$$\mathbb{E}^{\mathbb{P}}(S^1_{T'})$$

$$= S^1_0 \exp\left(T'(\mu_1 - \frac{1}{2}||\sigma^{1W}||^2)\right)(1 + \sigma_{13})^{\lambda_1 T'}(1 + \sigma_{14})^{\lambda_2 T'}$$

$$= 0.8971.$$

We notice in Figure 4.1 that $\frac{1}{Y}$ is bigger than $\frac{1}{Y^0}$, therefore the wealth of the insider is larger than that of a non-insider. If $S^1_{T'}$ is in $[a, b]$, the further away $[a, b]$ is from its expectation $\mathbb{E}^{\mathbb{P}}(S^1_{T'})$, the better the gain is. We can explain this by the fact that in this case, the insider knows an event that occurs with a low probability, therefore her side information is important. Thus, the more relevant the side-information is, the bigger the process $\frac{1}{Y}$ (and therefore the optimal wealth) is. We also notice that the bigger $S^1_{T'}$ is, the bigger $\frac{1}{Y}$ and $\frac{1}{Y^0}$ are.

Furthermore, as noticed in proposition 4.2, the parts of the wealth invested in each asset by an insider and a non-insider are different (see Figures 4.2, 4.3 and 4.4). If t is not a time of jump, the fact that the market coefficients r, b and σ are constant implies that $\pi^{0,*}$ of a non-insider is constant, and that the parts of wealth invested by the insider in the bond and each of the four risky assets are proportional to each other.

We notice that the insider's strategy in our simulations is very rational and is as we can expect: the strategy depends on the value of L and if $\mathbb{E}^{\mathbb{P}}(S^i_{T'})$ is in $[a, b]$ or not.

– *Case 1*: $S^1_{T'} \notin [a, b]$ and $\mathbb{E}^{\mathbb{P}}(S^1_{T'}) \notin [a, b]$.

The side-information is not very relevant. The insider's strategy is the following.

If $a < b < \mathbb{E}^{\mathbb{P}}(S^1_{T'})$, then $\mathbb{P}\left[S^1_{T'} > \mathbb{E}^{\mathbb{P}}(S^1_{T'})\right] > \mathbb{P}\left[S^1_{T'} < \mathbb{E}^{\mathbb{P}}(S^1_{T'})\right]$. Thus, the insider (compared to a non-insider) invests more in the first asset and less in the bond, regardless of the first asset price. Conversely if $\mathbb{E}^{\mathbb{P}}(S^1_{T'}) < a < b$, the insider invests less in the first asset and more in the bond.

– *Case 2*: $S^1_{T'} \notin [a,b]$ and $\mathbb{E}^{\mathbb{P}}(S^1_{T'}) \in [a,b]$.

The insider follows the first asset price. At time t, if $S^1_t < \mathbb{E}^{\mathbb{P}}(S^1_{T'})$ the insider thinks that $S^1_{T'} < a$ and invests less in the first asset and more in the bond. Conversely, if $S^1_t > \mathbb{E}^{\mathbb{P}}(S^1_{T'})$, the insider invests more in the first asset and less in the bond.

– *Case 3*: $S^1_{T'} \in [a,b]$ and $\mathbb{E}^{\mathbb{P}}(S^1_{T'}) \notin [a,b]$.

The side-information is very relevant, the insider knows exactly if S^1_T is bigger or not than its expectation. Her gain is important. If $S^1_{T'} > \mathbb{E}^{\mathbb{P}}(S^1_{T'})$, she invests more in the first asset. Conversely, if $S^1_{T'} < \mathbb{E}^{\mathbb{P}}(S^1_{T'})$, she invests less in the first asset.

– *Case 4*: $S^1_{T'} \in [a,b]$ and $\mathbb{E}^{\mathbb{P}}(S^1_{T'}) \in [a,b]$.

The insider follows the first asset price. At time t, she invests more in the first asset if S^1_t is near the bottom range a (because she knows that $S^1_{T'} > a$ and thus S^1 will increase) and if S^1_t is near the top range b, she invests less in the first asset.

4.3.2. $L = \log(S^1_{T'}) - \log(S^2_{T'})$

See section 4.3.4 page 160 for the figures. In our simulation,

$$\mathbb{E}^{\mathbb{P}}(\log(S^1_{T'}) - \log(S^2_{T'})) = \left(T'(\mu_1 - \mu_2) - \frac{1}{2}(||\sigma^{1W}||^2) - (||\sigma^{2W}||^2) \right)$$

$$+ \lambda^1 T' \log\left(\frac{1+\sigma^{13}}{1+\sigma^{23}}\right) + \lambda_2 T' \log\left(\frac{1+\sigma^{14}}{1+\sigma^{24}}\right)$$

$$= -0.1019.$$

We notice in Figure 4.5 that $\frac{1}{Y}$ is bigger than $\frac{1}{Y^0}$. The insider strategy on assets 1 and 2 depends on the position of $\log(\frac{S^1_t}{S^2_t})$ (the ratio of assets 1 and 2 at time t) compared to the value of L (which is the same ratio at time T'). If $\log\frac{S^1_t}{S^2_t} > L$ (see Figure 4.7 for the graph of $\log(\frac{S^1}{S^2})$), the fraction of the wealth at time t invested in asset 1 (respectively, in asset 2) is smaller (respectively, bigger) than those of a non-insider. Indeed, the insider knows that at maturity time T', the ratio $\log(\frac{S^1}{S^2})$ will be smaller than it is now, meaning that the price of asset 1 will decrease compared to the price of asset 2. Inversely, if $\log(\frac{S^1_t}{S^2_t}) < L$, the insider invests more in asset 1 and less in asset 2 (see Figure 4.8).

Furthermore, as noticed in proposition 4.4, the parts of the wealth invested in each asset by an insider and a non-insider are different (see Figures 4.6, 4.8 and 4.9).

4.3.3. $L = 1_{[a,b]}(S^1_{T'})$

In this simulation, $a = 0.7$, $b = 1.1$, $S^1_{T'} = 2.42$. See Figures 4.1, 4.2, 4.3 and 4.4.

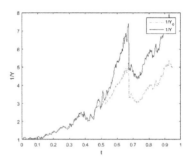

Figure 4.1. *Processes $\frac{1}{Y^0}$ and $\frac{1}{Y}$*

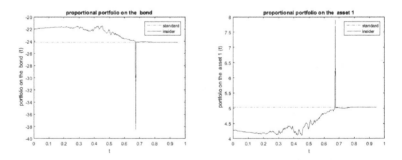

Figure 4.2. *Portfolio on the bond (left), portfolio on asset 1 (right)*

4.3.4. $L = \log(S^1_{T'}) - \log(S^2_{T'})$

In this simulation, $L = -0.0894$. See Figures 4.5, 4.6, 4.7, 4.8 and 4.9.

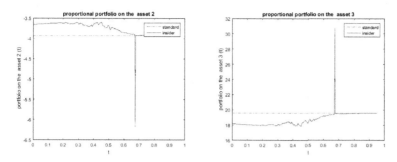

Figure 4.3. *Portfolio on asset 2 (left), portfolio on asset 3 (right)*

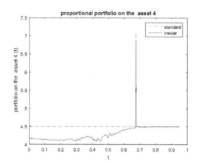

Figure 4.4. *Portfolio on asset 4*

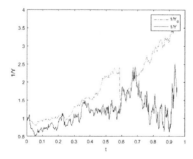

Figure 4.5. *Processes $\frac{1}{Y^0}$ and $\frac{1}{Y}$*

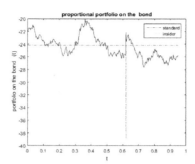

Figure 4.6. *Portfolio on the bond*

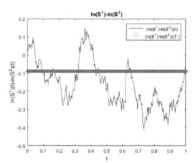

Figure 4.7. $\log(S_t^1) - \log(S_t^2)$

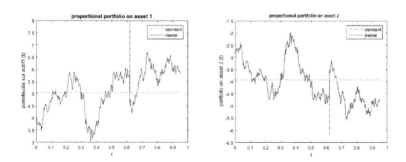

Figure 4.8. *Portfolio on asset 1 (left), portfolio on asset 2 (right)*

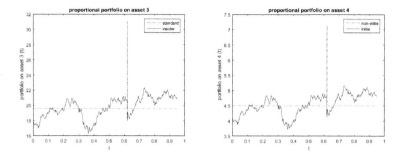

Figure 4.9. *Portfolio on asset 3 (left), portfolio on asset 4 (right)*

Bibliography

[AKS 14a] AKSAMIT A., Random times, enlargement of filtration and arbitrages, PhD Thesis, University of Evry, available at: https://tel.archives-ouvertes.fr/tel-01016672/, 2014.

[AKS 14b] AKSAMIT A., CHOULLI T., DENG J. *et al.*, "Arbitrages in a progressive enlargement setting", in *Arbitrage, Credit and Informational Risks*, World Science Publication, Hackensack, 2014.

[AKS 16] AKSAMIT A., JEANBLANC M., *Enlargements of Filtrations with Finance in View*, Springer, 2016.

[AME 98] AMENDINGER J., IMKELLER P., SCHWEIZER M., "Additional logarithmic utility of an insider", *Stochastic Processes and their Applications*, vol. 75, no. 2, pp. 263–286, 1998.

[AME 99] AMENDINGER J., Initial enlargement of filtrations and additional information in financial markets, PhD Thesis, Technischen Universität Berlin, 1999.

[AME 00] AMENDINGER J., "Martingale representation theorems for initially enlarged filtrations", *Stochastic Processes and their Applications*, vol. 89, no. 1, pp. 101–116, 2000.

[AME 03] AMENDINGER J., BECHERER D., SCHWEIZER M., "A monetary value for initial information in portfolio optimization", *Finance and Stochastics*, vol. 7, no. 1, pp. 29–46, 2003.

[ANK 05] ANKIRCHNER S., Information and semimartingales, PhD Thesis, Humboldt Universität, Berlin, 2005.

[ANK 06] ANKIRCHNER S., DEREICH S., IMKELLER P., "The Shannon information of filtrations and the additional logarithmic utility of insiders", *The Annals of Probability*, vol. 34, no. 2, pp. 743–778, 2006.

[ANK 08] ANKIRCHNER S., "On filtration enlargements and purely discontinuous martingales", *Stochastic Processes and their Applications*, vol. 118, no. 9, pp. 1662–1678, 2008.

[ANK 10] ANKIRCHNER S., BLANCHET-SCALLIET C., EYRAUD-LOISEL A., "Credit risk premia and quadratic BSDEs with a single jump", *International Journal of Theoretical and Applied Finance*, vol. 13, no. 7, pp. 1103–1129, 2010.

[BAR 78] BARLOW M.T., "Study of a filtration expanded to include an honest time", *Zeitschrift für Wahrscheinlichkeitstheorie und Verwandte Gebiete*, vol. 44, no. 4, pp. 307–323, 1978.

[BAU 01] BAUDOIN F., Portfolio optimization associated with a weak information, Technical report, Pierre and Marie Curie University, 2001.

[BAU 02] BAUDOIN F., "Conditioned stochastic differential equations: theory, examples and application to finance", *Stochastic Processes and their Applications*, vol. 100, pp. 109–145, 2002.

[BEL 01] BELLAMY N., "Wealth optimization in an incomplete market driven by a jumpdiffusion process", *Journal of Mathematical Economics*, vol. 35, no. 2, pp. 259–287, 2001.

[BEN 70] BENE V.E., "Existence of optimal strategies based on specified information, for a class of stochastic decision problems", *SIAM Journal on Control and Optimization*, vol. 8, pp. 179–188, 1970.

[BIA 05] BIAGINI F., ØKSENDAL B., "A general stochastic calculus approach to insider trading", *Applied Mathematics and Optimization. An International Journal with Applications to Stochastics*, vol. 52, no. 2, pp. 167–181, 2005.

[BIE 02] BIELECKI T.R., RUTKOWSKI M., *Credit Risk: Modelling, Valuation and Hedging*, Springer, Berlin, 2002.

[BIE 04] BIELECKI T.R., JEANBLANC M., RUTKOWSKI M., "Modeling and valuation of credit risk", in *Stochastic Methods in Finance*, of *Lecture Notes in Mathematics*, Springer, Berlin, vol. 1856 pp. 27–126, 2004.

[BLA 08] BLANCHET-SCALLIET C., EL KAROUI N., JEANBLANC M. *et al.*, "Optimal investment decisions when time-horizon is uncertain", *Journal of Mathematical Economics*, vol. 44, no. 11, pp. 1100–1113, 2008.

[BLA 16] BLANCHET-SCALLIET C., HILLAIRET C., JIAO Y., "Successive enlargement of filtrations and application to insider information", *Advances in Applied Probability*, 2016.

[BLÜ 16] BLÜMMEL T., RHEINLÄNDER T., Financial markets with a large trader, preprint, Vienna University of Technology, 2016.

[BOU 04] BOUCHARD B., PHAM H., "Wealth-path dependent utility maximization in incomplete markets", *Finance and Stochastics*, vol. 8, no. 4, pp. 579–603, 2004.

[BRÉ 78] Brémaud P., Yor M., "Changes of filtrations and of probability measures", *Zeitschrift für Wahrscheinlichkeitstheorie und Verwandte Gebiete*, vol. 45, no. 4, pp. 269–295, 1978.

[BRÉ 81] Brémaud P., *Point Processes and Queues, Martingale Dynamics*, Springer-Verlag, New York-Berlin, 1981.

[BRI 13] Brigo D., Morini M., Pallavicini A., *Counterparty Credit Risk, Collateral and Funding*, Wiley, 2013.

[CAL 06] Callegaro G., Di Masi G., Runggaldier W.J., "Portfolio optimization in discontinuous markets under incomplete information", *Asia Pacific Financial Markets*, vol. 13, no. 4, pp. 373–394, 2006.

[CAL 15] Callegaro G., Gaigi M., Scotti S. *et al.*, "Optimal investment in markets with over and under-reaction to information", *Mathematics and Financial Economics*, DOI 10.1007/s11579-016-0182-8, 2016.

[CHA 15] Chau H.N., Tankov P., "Market models with optimal arbitrage", *SIAM Journal on Financial Mathematics*, vol. 6, no. 1, pp. 66–85, 2015.

[CHO 14] Choulli T., Deng J., "Non-arbitrage for informational discrete time market", *Stochastics*, arXiv :1407.1453, 2014.

[COL 07] Collin Dufresne P., Hugonnier J., "Pricing and hedging in the presence of extraneous risks", *Stochastic Processes and their Applications*, vol. 117, no. 6, pp. 742–765, 2007.

[COR 04] Corcuera J.M., Imkeller P., Kohatsu-Higa A. *et al.*, "Additional utility of insiders with imperfect dynamical information", *Finance and Stochastics*, vol. 8, no. 3, pp. 437–450, 2004.

[CRE 14] Crepey S., Bielecki T.R., Brigo D., *Counterparty Risk and Funding: A Tale of Two Puzzles*, Chapman and Hall/CRC, 2014.

[DAN 03] Dana R.-A., Jeanblanc M., *Financial Markets in Continuous Time*, Springer-Verlag, Berlin, 2003.

[DEL 75] Dellacherie C., Meyer P.-A., *Probabilités et potentiel*, Hermann, Paris, 1975.

[DEL 80] Dellacherie C., Meyer P.-A., *Probabilités et potentiel*, Hermann, Paris, 1980.

[DEL 94] Delbaen F., Schachermayer W., "A general version of the fundamental theorem of asset pricing", *Mathematische Annalen*, vol. 300, no. 3, pp. 463–520, 1994.

[DIN 06] Di Nunno G., Meyer-Brandis T., Øksendal B. *et al.*, "Optimal portfolio for an insider in a market driven by Lévy processes", *Quantitative Finance*, vol. 6, no. 1, pp. 83–94, 2006.

[ELK 81] EL KAROUI N., "Les aspects probabilistes du contrôle stochastique", in *Ninth Saint Flour Probability Summer School – 1979*, Springer, Berlin, vol. 876, 1981.

[ELK 95] EL KAROUI N., QUENEZ M.-C., "Dynamic programming and pricing of contingent claims in an incomplete market", *SIAM Journal on Control and Optimization*, vol. 33, no. 1, pp. 29–66, 1995.

[ELK 97] EL KAROUI N., PENG S., QUENEZ M.-C., "Backward stochastic differential equations in finance", *Mathematical Finance. An International Journal of Mathematics, Statistics and Financial Economics*, vol. 7, no. 1, pp. 1–71, 1997.

[ELK 10] EL KAROUI N., JEANBLANC M., JIAO Y., "What happens after a default: the conditional density approach", *Stochastic Processes and their Applications*, vol. 120, no. 7, pp. 1011–1032, 2010.

[ELK 13] EL KAROUI N., MRAD M., "An exact connection between two solvable SDEs and a nonlinear utility stochastic PDE", *SIAM Journal on Financial Mathematics*, vol. 4, no. 1, pp. 697–736, 2013.

[ELK 15] EL KAROUI N., JEANBLANC M., JIAO Y., "Dynamics of multivariate default system in random environment", preprint arXiv :1509.09133, 2015.

[ELL 99] ELLIOTT R.J., JEANBLANC M., "Incomplete markets with jumps and informed agents", *Mathematical Methods of Operations Research*, vol. 50, no. 3, pp. 475–492, 1999.

[ELL 00] ELLIOTT R.J., JEANBLANC M., YOR M., "On models of default risk", *Mathematical Finance. An International Journal of Mathematics, Statistics and Financial Economics*, vol. 10, no. 2, pp. 179–195, 2000.

[FOL 93] FÖLLMER H., IMKELLER P., "Anticipation cancelled by a Girsanov transformation: a paradox on Wiener space", *Annales de l'Institut Henri Poincaré. Probabilités et Statistiques*, vol. 29, no. 4, pp. 569–586, 1993.

[FON 14] FONTANA C., JEANBLANC M., SONG S., "On arbitrages arising with honest times", *Finance and Stochastics*, vol. 18, no. 3, pp. 515–543, 2014.

[FON 15a] FONTANA C., "The strong predictable representation property in initially enlarged filtrations under the density hypothesis", *Stochastic Processes and Applications*, arXiv :1508.03282, 2015.

[FON 15b] FONTANA C., "Weak and strong no-arbitrage conditions for continuous financial markets", *International Journal of Theoretical and Applied Finance*, vol. 18, no. 1, pp. 1550005, 2015.

[FRE 11] FREY R., SCHMIDT T., "Filtering and incomplete information", in BIELECKI T., BRIGO D., PATRAS F. (eds), *Credit Risk Frontiers: Subprime Crisis, Pricing and Hedging, CVA, MBS, Ratings, and Liquidity*, John Wiley & Sons, 2011.

[FUJ 13] FUJIMOTO K., NAGAI H., RUNGGALDIER W.J., "Expected power-utility maximization under incomplete information and with Cox-process observations", *Applied Mathematics and Optimization. An International Journal with Applications to Stochastics*, vol. 67, no. 1, pp. 33–72, 2013.

[GAS 06] GASBARRA D., VALKEIKA E., VOSTRIKOVA L., "Enlargement of filtration and additional information in pricing models: a Bayesian approach", in KABANOV Y., LIPSTER R., STOYANOV J. (eds.), *From Stochastic Calculus to Mathematical Finance: The Shiryaev Festschrift*, Springer, Berlin Heidelberg, 2006.

[GEN 86] GENNOTTE G., "Optimal portfolio choice under incomplete information", *The Journal of Finance*, vol. 41, no. 3, pp. 733–746, 1986.

[GRO 98] GRORUD A., PONTIER M., "Insider trading in a continuous time Market model", *International Journal of Theoretical and Applied Finance*, vol. 1, no. 3, pp. 331–347, 1998.

[GRO 00] GRORUD A., "Asymmetric information in a financial market with jumps", *International Journal of Theoretical and Applied Finance*, vol. 3, no. 4, pp. 641–659, 2000.

[GRO 06] GRORUD A., PONTIER M., "Financial market model with influential insider investors", *International Journal of Theoretical and Applied Finance*, vol. 8, pp. 693–716, 2006.

[HIL 05] HILLAIRET C., "Comparison of insiders' optimal strategies depending on the type of side-information", *Stochastic Processes and their Applications*, vol. 115, no. 10, pp. 1603–1627, 2005.

[HIL 11] HILLAIRET C., JIAO Y., "Information asymmetry in pricing of credit derivatives", *International Journal of Theoretical and Applied Finance*, vol. 14, no. 5, pp. 611–633, 2011.

[HOW 60] HOWARD R.A., *Dynamic Programming and Markov Processes*, MIT Press, 1960.

[HU 05] HU Y., IMKELLER P., MÜLLER M., "Utility maximization in incomplete markets", *The Annals of Applied Probability*, vol. 15, no. 3, pp. 1691–1712, 2005.

[IMK 02] IMKELLER P., "Random times at which insiders can have free lunches", *Stochastics and Stochastics Reports*, vol. 74, no. 1–2, pp. 465–487, 2002.

[IMK 03] IMKELLER P., "Malliavin's calculus in insider models: additional utility and free lunches", *Mathematical Finance. An International Journal of Mathematics, Statistics and Financial Economics*, vol. 13, no. 1, pp. 153–169, 2003.

[JAC 79] JACOD J., *Calcul stochastique et problèmes de martingales*, Springer, Berlin, 1979.

[JAC 85] JACOD J., "Grossissement Initial, Hypothèse (H') et Théorème de Girsanov", in *Grossissements de filtrations: exemples et applications*, Springer, Berlin, 1985.

[JAC 03] JACOD J., SHIRYAEV A.N., *Limit Theorems for Stochastic Processes*, of *Grundlehren der Mathematischen Wissenschaften*, 2nd edition, Springer, Berlin, 2003.

[JAR 01] JARROW R., YU F., "Counterparty risk and the pricing of defaultable securities", *The Journal of Finance*, vol. 56, no. 5, pp. 1765–1799, 2001.

[JEA 90] JEANBLANC-PICQUÉ M., PONTIER M., "Optimal portfolio for a small investor in a market model with discontinuous prices", *Applied Mathematics and Optimization. An International Journal with Applications to Stochastics*, vol. 22, no. 3, pp. 287–310, 1990.

[JEA 00] JEANBLANC M., RUTKOWSKI M., "Modelling of default risk: an overview", in *Mathematical Finance – Theory and Practice*, Higher Education Press, Beijing, 2000.

[JEA 15] JEANBLANC M., MASTROLIA T., POSSAMAÏ D. *et al.*, "Utility maximization with random horizon: a BSDE approach", *International Journal of Theoretical and Applied Finance*, vol. 18, no. 7, pp. 1550045, 2015.

[JEU 78] JEULIN T., YOR M., "Grossissement d'une filtration et semi-martingales: formules explicites", in *Séminaire de Probabilités, XII (Univ. Strasbourg, Strasbourg, 1976/1977)*, Springer, Berlin, 1978.

[JEU 80] JEULIN T., *Semi-martingales et grossissement d'une filtration*, Springer, Berlin, 1980.

[JEU 85] JEULIN T., YOR M., (eds.), *Grossissements de filtrations: exemples et applications*, Springer, Berlin, 1985.

[JIA 11] JIAO Y., PHAM H., "Optimal investment with counterparty risk: a default-density model approach", *Finance and Stochastics*, vol. 15, no. 4, pp. 725–753, 2011.

[JIA 13] JIAO Y., KHARROUBI I., PHAM H., "Optimal investment under multiple defaults risk: a BSDE-decomposition approach", *The Annals of Applied Probability*, vol. 23, no. 2, pp. 455–491, 2013.

[JIA 15] JIAO Y., LI S., "The generalized density approach in progressive enlargement of filtrations", *Electronic Journal of Probability*, vol. 20, no. 85, pp. 1–21, 2015.

[KAL 02] KALLENBERG O., *Foundations of Modern Probability, Probability and its Applications*, 2nd edition, Springer, New York, 2002.

[KAR 87] KARATZAS I., LEHOCZKY J.P., SHREVE S.E., "Optimal portfolio and consumption decisions for a small investor on a finite horizon", *SIAM Journal on Control and Optimization*, vol. 25, no. 6, pp. 1557–1586, 1987.

[KAR 91a] KARATZAS I., LEHOCZKY J.P., SHREVE S.E. *et al.*, "Martingale and duality methods for utility maximization in an incomplete market", *SIAM Journal on Control and Optimization*, vol. 29, no. 3, pp. 702–730, 1991.

[KAR 91b] KARATZAS I., SHREVE S.E., *Brownian Motion and Stochastic Calculus*, of *Graduate Texts in Mathematics*, 2nd edition, Springer, New York, 1991.

[KAR 98] KARATZAS I., SHREVE S.E., *Methods of Mathematical Finance*, of *Applications of Mathematics*, Springer, New York, 1998.

[KAR 00] KARATZAS I., WANG H., "Utility maximization with discretionary stopping", *SIAM Journal on Control and Optimization*, vol. 39, no. 1, pp. 306–329 (electronic), 2000.

[KCH 13] KCHIA Y., LARSSON M., PROTTER P., "Linking progressive and initial filtration expansions", in *Malliavin Calculus and Stochastic Analysis*, Springer, pp. 469–487, 2013.

[KCH 15] KCHIA Y., PROTTER P., "Progressive filtration expansions via a process, with applications to insider trading", *International Journal of Theoretical and Applied Finance*, vol. 18, no. 4, pp. 1550027, 2015.

[KHA 13] KHARROUBI I., LIM T., NGOUPEYOU A., "Mean-variance hedging on uncertain time horizon in a market with a jump", *Applied Mathematics and Optimization. An International Journal with Applications to Stochastics*, vol. 68, no. 3, pp. 413–444, 2013.

[KHA 14] KHARROUBI I., LIM T., "Progressive enlargement of filtrations and backward stochastic differential equations with jumps", *Journal of Theoretical Probability*, vol. 27, no. 3, pp. 683–724, 2014.

[KOH 06] KOHATSU-HIGA A., SULEM A., "Utility maximization in an insider influenced market", *Mathematical Finance. An International Journal of Mathematics, Statistics and Financial Economics*, vol. 16, no. 1, pp. 153–179, 2006.

[KOH 08] KOHATSU-HIGA A., YAMAZATO M., "Enlargement of filtrations with random times for processes with jumps", *Stochastic Processes and their Applications*, vol. 118, no. 7, pp. 1136–1158, 2008.

[KRA 99] KRAMKOV D., SCHACHERMAYER W., "The asymptotic elasticity of utility functions and optimal investment in incomplete markets", *The Annals of Applied Probability*, vol. 9, no. 3, pp. 904–950, 1999.

[LAK 95] LAKNER P., "Utility maximization with partial information", *Stochastic Processes and their Applications*, vol. 56, no. 2, pp. 247–273, 1995.

[LAK 98] LAKNER P., "Optimal trading strategy for an investor: the case of partial information", *Stochastic Processes and their Applications*, vol. 76, no. 1, pp. 77–97, 1998.

[LÉP 78] LÉPINGLE D., MÉMIN J., "Intégrabilité uniforme et dans L^r des martingales exponentielles", in *Publications mathématiques et informatiques de Rennes*, University of Rennes, 1978.

[LIM 11] LIM T., QUENEZ M.-C., "Exponential utility maximization in an incomplete market with defaults", *Electronic Journal of Probability*, vol. 16, no. 53, pp. 1434–1464, 2011.

[LIM 15] LIM T., QUENEZ M.-C., "Portfolio optimization in a default model under full/partial information", *Probability in the Engineering and Informational Sciences*, vol. 29, no. 4, pp. 565–587, 2015.

[MAN 06] MANSUY R., YOR M., *Random Times and Enlargements of Filtrations in a Brownian Setting*, Springer, Berlin, 2006.

[MER 71] MERTON R.-C., "Optimum consumption and portfolio rules in a continuous-time model", *Journal of Economic Theory*, vol. 3, no. 4, p. 373–413, 1971.

[MEY 79] MEYER P.-A., "Une remarque sur le calcul stochastique dépendant d'un paramètre', *Séminaire de Probabilités* (Strasbourg), vol. 13, pp. 199–203, 1979.

[MOR 09] MORLAIS M.-A., "Utility maximization in a jump market model", *Stochastics. An International Journal of Probability and Stochastic Processes*, vol. 81, no. 1, pp. 1–27, 2009.

[MUS 10a] MUSIELA M., ZARIPHOPOULOU T., "Portfolio choice under space-time monotone performance criteria", *SIAM Journal on Financial Mathematics*, vol. 1, no. 1, pp. 326–365, 2010.

[MUS 10b] MUSIELA M., ZARIPHOPOULOU T., "Stochastic partial differential equations in portfolio choice", in CHIARELLA C., NOVIKOV A., (eds.), *Contemporary Quantitative Finance: Essays in Honour of Eckhard Platen*, Springer Science & Business Media, 2010.

[NIK 06] NIKEGHBALI A., "An essay on the general theory of stochastic processes", *Probability Surveys*, vol. 3, pp. 345–412, 2006.

[NIK 13] NIKEGHBALI A., PLATEN E., "A reading guide for last passage times with financial applications in view", *Finance and Stochastics*, vol. 17, no. 3, pp. 615–640, 2013.

[ØKS 05] ØKSENDAL B., SULEM A., *Applied Stochastic Control of Jump Diffusions*, Springer-Verlag, Berlin, 2005.

[PHA 01] PHAM H., QUENEZ M.-C., "Optimal portfolio in partially observed stochastic volatility models", *Annals of Applied Probability*, vol. 11, no. 1, pp. 210–238, 2001.

[PHA 09] PHAM H., *Continuous-Time Stochastic Control and Optimization with Financial Applications*, Springer, Berlin, 2009.

[PHA 10] PHAM H., "Stochastic control under progressive enlargement of filtrations and applications to multiple defaults risk management", *Stochastic Processes and their Applications*, vol. 120, no. 9, pp. 1795–1820, 2010.

[PIK 96] PIKOVSKY I., KARATZAS I., "Anticipative portfolio optimization", *Advances in Applied Probability*, vol. 28, no. 4, pp. 1095–1122, 1996.

[PRO 05] PROTTER P.E., *Stochastic Integration and Differential Equations*, Springer, Berlin, 2005.

[REV 91] REVUZ D., YOR M., *Continuous Martingales and Brownian Motion*, Springer, Berlin, 1991.

[ROU 00] ROUGE R., EL KAROUI N., "Pricing via utility maximization and entropy", *Mathematical Finance. An International Journal of Mathematics, Statistics and Financial Economics*, vol. 10, no. 2, pp. 259–276, 2000.

[RUN 91] RUNGGALDIER W.J., STETTNER ., "On the construction of nearly optimal strategies for a general problem of control of partially observed diffusions", *Stochastics Stochastics Reports*, vol. 37, no. 1–2, pp. 15–47, 1991.

[SON 87] SONG S., Grossissement de filtrations et problèmes connexes, PhD Thesis, University Paris VII, 1987.

[SON 13] SONG S., "Local solution method for the problem of enlargement of filtration", preprint arXiv :1510.05212, 2013.

[SON 14] SONG S., "Optional splitting formula in a progressively enlarged filtration", *ESAIM. Probability and Statistics*, vol. 18, pp. 829–853, 2014.

[TAK 14] TAKAOKA K., SCHWEIZER M., "A note on the condition of no unbounded profit with bounded risk", *Finance and Stochastics*, vol. 18, no. 2, pp. 393–405, 2014.

[WAG 80] WAGNER D.H., "Survey of measurable selection theorems: an update", in *Proceedings in Measure Theory*, Oberwolfach 1979, Springer, Berlin-New York, 1980.

[ZWI 07] ZWIERZ J., "On existence of local martingale measures for insiders who can stop at honest times", *Bulletin of the Polish Academy of Sciences and Mathematics*, vol. 55, no. 2, pp. 183–192, 2007.

Index